DARE TO SUCCEED

THE WORLD'S LEADING EXPERTS REVEAL THEIR

SECRETS TO SUCCESS

IN BUSINESS AND IN LIFE & **DARE YOU TO SUCCEED!**

Published by CelebrityPress®, Orlando, FL

CelebrityPress® is a registered trademark

Printed in the United States of America.

ISBN: 978-0-9886418-9-1
LCCN: 2013939392

This publication is designed to provide accurate and authoritative information with regard to the subject matter covered. It is sold with the understanding that the publisher is not engaged in rendering legal, accounting, or other professional advice. If legal advice or other expert assistance is required, the services of a competent professional should be sought. The opinions expressed by the authors in this book are not endorsed by CelebrityPress® and are the sole responsibility of the author rendering the opinion.

Most CelebrityPress® titles are available at special quantity discounts for bulk purchases for sales promotions, premiums, fundraising, and educational use. Special versions or book excerpts can also be created to fit specific needs.

For more information, please write:
CelebrityPress®
520 N. Orlando Ave, #2
Winter Park, FL 32789
or call 1.877.261.4930

Visit us online at: www.CelebrityPressPublishing.com

THE WORLD'S LEADING EXPERTS REVEAL THEIR
SECRETS TO SUCCESS
IN BUSINESS AND IN LIFE & **DARE YOU TO SUCCEED!**

CELEBRITY PRESS
Winter Park, Florida

CONTENTS

CHAPTER 1

DARE TO ASK!

BY JACK CANFIELD

If there is something to gain and nothing to
lose by asking, by all means ask!
— W. Clement Stone,
Author of *The Success System That Never Fails*

My first mentor was a multimillionaire insurance mogul, publisher, and author by the name of W. Clement Stone. When I was in my early 20s, he took me under his wing and taught me a series of success principles that still form the core of my work today. He taught me to take 100 percent responsibility for everything in your life, to totally give up blaming others, complaining about things, and making excuses for myself. He taught me to only think positive thoughts and to always focus on what I wanted, not what I didn't want. He taught me how to set specific and measurable goals and why it was so important. He taught me to visualize and affirm all of my goals as already complete, and to act as if they were all a done deal. He also taught me to take action as soon as I had an inspiration, what he referred to as "always do it now!"

Mr. Stone also taught me to limit the amount of time I spent watching television, which he referred to as "the income reduction box." He constantly reminded me that eliminating one hour of television a day would add up to 365 extra hours a year (that's a little over nine 40-hour workweeks, or two months) of extra time to devote to being productive. He also chided me to become what he called an "inverse paranoid"— someone who believes the world is plotting to do him good instead of harm.

But most important, Mr. Stone taught me the importance of asking. He would repeatedly remind me, "If there is something to gain by asking and nothing to lose by asking, by all means ask." This one principle has reaped great rewards in my life, and it can do the same for you.

Unfortunately, many of us are not great at asking. For any number of reasons stemming from childhood conditioning to traumatic rejections later in life, we have become afraid of the word "no." To be successful, you have to be willing to ask! ask! ask! and keep asking until you get a yes. No's are just part of the journey to finally getting to a yes. And it only takes one yes to radically change your life forever.

YOU HAVE TO REJECT REJECTION

When Mark Victor Hansen and I finished the first *Chicken Soup for the Soul* book, we flew to New York with our literary agent Jeff Herman. We met with about 20 publishers over the course of three days, and none of them were interested in publishing our book. "Collections of short stories don't sell," we were told. "The title doesn't work." "The stories are to Pollyanna—too nicey-nice." Later we submitted the manuscript by mail to 20 more publishers. They also said no! At that point, our agent gave us the book back and said he couldn't sell it.

Of course we were disappointed, but we never got discouraged. When the world said "no," we said "next!" We continued to reach out to publishers on our own. We also asked every member of our speaking and training audiences to fill out a "Commitment to Buy" form we created, indicating how many copies they would commit to buy when the book was finally published. We eventually had promises to buy more than 20,000 books!

Armed with copies of these forms and a backpack full of spiral-bound copies of our best 30 stories, we headed off to the American Booksellers Convention in Anaheim, California, where we walked the floor of the exhibit hall for two days talking to one publisher after another about publishing our book. But again we heard no, no, no! And hour after hour, booth after endless booth, we said next! next! next!

At the end of the second very long day, Peter Vegso and Gary Seidler, the co-presidents of Health Communications Inc., a small publisher from Deerfield Beach, Florida, agreed to read the manuscript when they got back home. Later that week Gary Seidler took the manuscript to the beach and read it. He loved it, and he and Peter decided to publish it. After more than 140 rejections, the book was finally published and went on to sell more than 10 million copies in 47 languages, launched a series of more than 200 books that has gone on to sell more than 500 million books worldwide, and created a brand now worth more than $100 million! Those hundreds of nexts have really paid off!

> *This manuscript of yours that has just come back from another editor is a precious package. Don't consider it rejected. Consider that you've just addressed it "to the editor who can appreciate my work" and it has just come back stamped "not at this address." Just keep looking for the right address.*
> — Barbara Kingsolver,
> Author of *The Poisonwood Bible*

In order to be successful, you have to reject rejection. Rejection doesn't mean no! It simply means not yet. It took us almost two years to get our book published and another 14 months before it got on the *New York Times* bestseller list. But once it did, it stayed in the number-one position for more than three years!

Don't get discouraged when you get a no. Just keep asking! You have to accept that you may get a lot of no's on the way to a yes.

JUST SAY "NEXT!"

Have you ever gone to a KFC restaurant? When Colonel Harlan Sanders left his home armed only with a pressure cooker and his special recipe for cooking Southern fried chicken he received more than 300 rejections, but he eventually found someone who believed in his dream. Today, because of his unwillingness to let the no's discourage him, there are now 5,200 KFC restaurants in the United States and more than 15,000 worldwide!

Remember, if one person tells you no, ask someone else. Remember this phrase:

SWSWSWSW

It stands for Some will. Some won't. So what! Someone's waiting! Some people are out there waiting to be asked—waiting to say yes. Along the way you'll definitely get some no's. So what—just keep taking action and making requests.

WHAT IF THEY SAY NO?

I once was hired to speak at an annual sales meeting for a company that produces about half the world's eyeglass lenses. They are that big. Interestingly, I was the first outside speaker they had ever hired. I arrived there early and met with some of the salespeople earlier in the day. During the conversation, I asked them if they knew who the top producers in the company were. They all said the same three names. Everyone knew who the top salespeople were: Mary, Robert and Martin. These three were selling 200 percent or 400 percent more than anyone else in the company. That night I asked the audience of 300 salespeople to raise their hands if they thought they knew who were the top three producers in the company. Almost everybody raised their hands.

I then asked them to keep their hand up if they had ever gone up to any of those three people and asked them what their secrets of success were. What were they doing that made them so much more successful? Not one hand remained in the air. Whoa! What a revelation! I have spent my whole life seeking out the peak performers that had the answers, that knew more than I did, that were getting faster and better results than I was. "Teach me," I would say. "I want to learn." And yet not one person in this organization had reached out for the information that was readily available to them.

I then asked them why they hadn't asked these top producers for their success secrets, and the answers came fast and were almost unanimous. "Fear of rejection." "Why would they want to tell me? I have nothing to offer them." "I didn't want to risk them rejecting me." "I didn't want to look foolish or look like I didn't already know." In essence—I didn't want to risk rejection. I'd rather look good than do good.

Nobody makes it to the top without support from people who are ahead of them on the path—athletes need coaches and managers; businesspeople need coaches, mentors and consultants; artists need teachers, agents and gallery owners; entertainers need managers and agents; politicians need mentors and campaign managers. We all need to look to those who have gone before us, who know more than us, and use their experience, wisdom and knowledge.

ASK FOR GUIDANCE

A few years ago I was in the dressing room of a television station in Dallas, getting ready to appear on a morning news show to promote my book, *The Success Principles: How to Get From Where You Are to Where You Want to Be.* As I often do, I asked the woman who was putting on my makeup if she had a dream—some ultimate goal. She answered that she wanted to own her own salon someday. I said, "That's great. What are you doing to make that happen?"

"Nothing," she replied.

"That's a bad strategy," I said. Why aren't you doing anything to make your dream come true?"

"I don't know what you have to do to own your own salon," she answered.

"Well, I have a radical idea," I said. "Why don't you go find someone who owns a salon and ask them how they did it?"

I was stunned when she said, "Wow, that's a great idea." I am always a bit taken aback when people don't see what is so obvious to me. But then most of us are not taught to ask others to help us. In fact, many of us get programmed by our parents to not ask, to not be a bother, to not impose ourselves on others.

MOST PEOPLE ARE WILLING TO HELP
IF THEY ARE ASKED

The truth that I have discovered is that most successful people are willing to share what they have learned with others who are sincere in their intention to succeed. It is a human trait to want to pass on what wisdom one has learned. Not everyone will take the time to mentor you, but most will—if they are asked! So you simply need to make a list of the people you would like ask for advice or to mentor you and ask them to devote a few minutes a month to you.

BE CREATIVE IN YOUR ASKING

Early in my career I had a very strong dream and desire to be an international peak performance trainer, impacting the lives of millions of people around the world. One of the people who was already doing that was Lou Tice, the co-founder and chairman of the Pacific Institute, whose work had positively affected tens of millions of people in more than 50 countries. Thinking that I could learn a lot from him, I called his office to ask if he would briefly mentor me. I was told that he was way too busy to do any individual mentoring. Undaunted, I sent him a personal letter suggesting that the next time he visited Los Angeles on business, instead of hiring a limousine service to transport him to his hotel and to his meetings, he permit me to pick him up and drive him to and from his various destinations in exchange for allowing me to ask him some questions.

Several weeks later I received a reply agreeing to my proposal. Not too long after that I picked him up at the Los Angeles airport, drove him to his hotel, and later to and from his speech. The whole time we were together I asked him question after question, which he graciously answered. In those few short hours, I learned a ton of valuable business lessons. Ironically, about a year later, both my company and his submitted proposals for a $750,000 training contract with the Los Angeles County Office of Education. Out of all the contenders, it finally came down to two proposals—The Pacific Institutes' and mine—and after two more days of interviews with the County Office, we won the contract. After Lou found out, he graciously called me, commented on what a fast learner I was, and congratulated me. My out-of-the-box creative ask had ultimately added $750,000 to our year's income!

ANOTHER CREATIVE ASK

Tim Ferriss, who later penned the bestseller *The 4-Hour Workweek*, also used a creative approach to get me to mentor him. At the time, Tim was about 26 years old and had not yet written his book. He knew he wanted to write a book and he knew he wanted me as one of his publishing mentors. He also knew I was very busy and most likely would say no. What he did was brilliant.

Tim joined a group called the Silicon Valley Association of Startup Entrepreneurs and volunteered to be their next program chair. He then called me and said he wanted me to speak there, and while they couldn't pay me anything, he would introduce me to some of the most powerful people in Silicon Valley who might be able to hire me as a consultant. Since the flight from Santa Barbara to Santa Jose is less than an hour, I agreed to come speak. Tim's real agenda, it turned out, was to get to know me, which was accomplished when we went out for food and drinks after the meeting. Tim is one of the most interesting and engaging people I have ever met, and we quickly became friends. Months later, when he asked me to be his mentor, it was a slam-dunk yes!

ASK AND YOU JUST MIGHT GET IT

Several years ago, Sylvia Collins flew all the way from Australia to Santa Barbara, California, to take one of my weeklong "Breakthrough to Success" seminars, where she learned about the power of asking. A year later, I received this letter from her:

I have taken a detour in my career path, and I'm now selling new developments on the Gold Coast with a company called Gold Coast Property. I work with a team of guys mostly in their 20s. The skills I have acquired through your seminars have helped me to perform and be an active part of a winning team! I must tell you how having self-esteem and not being afraid to ask has impacted this office!

At a recent staff meeting, we were asked what we would like to do for our once-a-month team-building day. I asked Michael, the managing director, "What target would we have to reach for you to take us to an island for a week?"

Everyone around the table just went silent and looked at me; obviously it was out of everyone's comfort zone to ask such a thing. Michael looked around and then looked at me and said, "Well, if you reach...(and then he set a financial target), I'll take the whole team (10 of us) to the Great Barrier Reef!"

Well, the next month we reached the target and off we went to Lady Elliott Island for four days—airfares, accommodations, food and activities all paid for by the company. We had the most amazing four days—we snorkeled together, had bonfires on the beach, played tricks on each other, and had so much fun!

Afterwards, Michael gave us another target and said he would take us to Fiji if we reached it, and we reached that target in December! Even though the company is paying for these trips, Michael is miles ahead from the enormous level of increased sales!

As Sylvia's letter so clearly illustrates, sometimes all you have to do is break out of your comfort zone and ask.

About Jack

As the beloved originator of the *Chicken Soup for the Soul*® series, Jack Canfield fostered the emergence of inspirational anthologies as a genre—and watched it grow to a billion-dollar market. As the driving force behind the development and delivery of over 500 million books sold through the *Chicken Soup for the Soul*® franchise, Jack Canfield is uniquely qualified to talk about success.

Jack is a Harvard graduate with a master's degree in psychological education and is one of the earliest champions of peak performance. He has developed the specific methodology and results-oriented activities to help people take on greater challenges and produce breakthrough results.

His proven formula for success reached global acclaim with his recent international bestseller, *The Success Principles™: How to Get From Where You Are to Where You Want to Be.* This book contains 64 proven principles for success used by top achievers from all walks of life. *The Success Principles*—and the entire empire of "Principles" books, audio and video programs, training and coaching programs—is Jack's most recent offering to the more than 500 million readers, students and clients he reaches worldwide.

Jack has had 47 books on *The New York Times* bestseller list. His other best-selling books—*The Power of Focus, The Aladdin Factor, Dare to Win, You've Got to Read This Book! and The Key to Living the Law of Attraction*—have generated millions of bookstore and internet sales, and have launched complementary products such as audio programs, video programs, corporate training programs, and syndicated columns to enthusiastic individuals and corporate buyers. His audio program, *Maximum Confidence*, has sold more than 350,000 copies through Nightingale-Conant alone. Jack's latest publication, *Tapping Into Ultimate Success: How to Overcome Any Obstacle and Skyrocket Your Results*, features a revolutionary cutting-edge technique to make achieving success easier than ever before. It is a must-read for those who are seeking to transform their lives and take action today!

For additional details on how to bring Jack to your next meeting, please call:
Teresa Collett
(805) 937-1199 (direct)
Email at Teresa@jackcanfield.com

For information on Jack's Breakthrough to Success training, coaching program, newsletter, books and other resources, visit his website at www.jackcanfield.com.

CHAPTER 2

NIGHTMARES NEVER LAST, GREAT DREAMS DO

BY COLLEEN HAWTHORNE, MD

I am a mental health physician. In other words, I'm a medical doctor who specializes in the treatment of the brain, mind and emotions, otherwise known as a psychiatrist. Whether providing medical treatment to inmates or the homeless, the chronically mentally ill or the worried well, or our most noted leaders and celebrated elite, helping people to live their most optimal lives is my life passion and mission. In my mind, every life is precious. Regardless of predicament, persuasion or position, my charge is to help people to create and celebrate holistically healthy, full and vibrant lives.

From the coveted vantage point of a mental health physician, I hear people's real stories. The unpretentious, uncut, unmasked and unadulterated details of people's lives—the good, the bad and the ugly. So I can tell you firsthand that, in most cases, the stars that shine most brightly today have seen some of their darkest yesterdays. When onlookers see successful people, often, they see their glory, but they don't know their real behind-the-scenes stories. The reality is that most highly successful people reached some crossroad in their life that caused them to make a decision to change their life in a significant way. Whether their decision to change came by way of mishap, tragedy or inner conviction, something caused them to realize that they desired more, needed more and deserved more out of life. They reached a turning point where they decided they could no longer settle for less or keep sleeping on their dreams. They decided to stop hitting the snooze button of life and wake-up!

ANSWERING LIFE'S 911 WAKE-UP CALL

I feel qualified to talk to you about how to get back up when you find yourself slumbering through life. Not so much because of my professional expertise, but because I've really been there. I've had a 911 wake-up call or two in my own life.

A few years ago, I found myself facing surmounting health challenges. For some time, conventional physicians like myself could not uncover exactly what was going on. I went from specialist to specialist and had test after test. As test results continued to come back negative, doctors became more perplexed, and I became more uncertain about my future. Being sick and tired became more than just a poetic metaphor and cliché. At times, I could barely find enough strength to get through each day. One day, I decided that I had to make up my mind whether I was going to give in to the circumstances or forge the fight of my life. I reminded myself that I had worked too hard, sacrificed too much, and had too many unfulfilled dreams and aspirations to give up. I decided to fight, and I developed a relentless fighting spirit.

Over time, through much determination, some desperation at times, and a great deal of prayer—my own prayers as well as those of many loved ones, answers started to emerge. I was referred to an amazing naturopathic doctor who put the pieces of the medical mystery together. He uncovered that I had developed severe adrenal fatigue and that multiple undiagnosed allergies put my body in a hyper-allergic state. Finally, an appropriate treatment plan could be put in place to restore my health.

The knowledge and lessons I continue to gain as a result of my experiences have served not only to enhance my life but the lives of many who are seeking ways to live more healthily, fully and vibrantly.

AWAKENING THE SLEEPING GIANT IN YOU

My healing journey became a time not only of physical recovery but also of profound personal discovery. It became a time of honest evaluation and introspection. An opportunity to look at what I needed to change to become healthier, more whole and more fulfilled. And a time to answer the clarion call that reawakened the creative artist in me. What seemed at first to be a never-ending, frightening nightmare was a gift that changed the trajectory of my life.

I started moving into new dimensions of my life purpose and gave myself permission to freely express my creativity and uniqueness. I decided that I could no longer try to fit into the prefabricated, predetermined, and often restricted mold of what has, unfortunately, become managed-care medicine. I freed myself to practice psychiatric medicine with my natural, therapeutically creative style, and I decided to serve only in environments that value the importance of doing what is necessary to ensure that patients receive the best possible health care. Also, I decided to expand my professional repertoire, and I now enjoy reaching people on a broader scale, as an author, speaker, life coach, consultant, and media medical expert.

GET BACK UP

We're all human. On our life journeys, we are sure to have triumphs, but challenges and setbacks are also inevitable. Even the most highly accomplished and greatest gurus go through tough times. The real question is, when life knocks you down and you feel like you're slumbering through life, how do you get back up? How do you confront your challenges, face your fears, gather your strength, emerge from whatever proverbial security blanket you started hiding under, and get back up?

For a while, as I struggled to deal with my health challenges, I found myself sleep walking through life. But, deep down I knew I was filled with dreams on the inside. Eventually, I had to face the sleeping giant within me. This meant I had to learn some new ways of doing things and let go of some old habits that were not serving me well. In essence, I had to reinvent my life. I knew if it was going to work, this time it could not feel like all work.

In the upcoming section, I share five key principles and strategies that helped me to become more holistically healthy, happy and fulfilled. In teaching others how to use these keys, it is amazing to hear their remarkable stories about the powerful positive shifts they have made in their living. It is my hope that this information can help you too.

5 KEYS TO AWAKEN THE SLEEPING GIANT IN YOU

1. Know What You Really Want

Most people don't have clarity about their life purpose and true desires until they become intentional about defining and clarifying them. Becoming your strongest self starts with knowing what you really want and what you were created to do. In order to be successful in accomplishing your authentic life goals and dreams, they need to be in alignment with your purpose and core values.

For me, it had long been my heart's desire to reach broader audiences in new and exciting ways. But until I dared to take an honest look at what I wanted at this season of my life, I remained stuck. Once I clarified and defined my purpose, and acknowledged my true desires, my enthusiasm came back. That gave me the momentum to move forward.

Throughout your life, ask yourself if you are you doing is what you really want in life. Make sure that your vision for your life is not becoming diminished or distorted by the desires and expectations of others. You cannot allow people or life circumstances to continually shift your focus and direction. This will naturally happen at times, but it's important to always get back on your destiny path as quickly as possible.

Not being clear about what you want and making the expectations of others a priority over your own is a habit. It's a habit that can, and must, be broken. Before you make any decision, stop and ask yourself these questions:

- Is this something I want or want to do, or what is expected of me?

- Would I ask this of myself?

- Is this in alignment with my purpose and core values?

Studies show that people who know what they want and are living a life that is aligned with their core values and life purpose are happier, healthier and more productive.

2. Let Your Difference Make the Difference

Never be afraid to be the real you. Living in sync with who you really are liberates you to experience your most optimal life. When you stay in tune with who you really are, your creativity comes alive. When you try to be somebody else, you get out of sync, off beat, and thrown off course. Learn to be comfortable with who you truly are. Embrace the value of your own unique brand, and do so unapologetically. Like the saying goes, "You were born an original; don't die a copy."

As a physician, I have spent much of my creative energy scripting not onto parchment or canvas but onto the bleeding hearts, minds and souls of hurting people in the typical doctor-patient role. More recently, I came to realize that underneath the sterile uniforms and conformity of conventional medicine, the artist within me was vying to have her say. Sometimes colorful, therapeutically unorthodox, and a bit edgy, I am commonly told, "You don't look and act like a typical doctor. You're so real. You really listen. I feel comfortable with you." I no longer try to hide this side of myself, or try to fit into an expected mold. Today, I embrace and understand the importance of expressing my unique presence, creative style and passion for excellence. Over the years, my patients have taught me that within these qualities flows life and healing.

People who are going places in life believe in doing ordinary things in extraordinary ways and will do what it takes to move away from things that are stagnant, mediocre, or mundane, because this interrupts and retards their creative rhythm and flow. Your authentic difference can make a real difference in the world. Extraordinary generates change and progress.

As the Irish author, playwright and poet Oscar Wilde wrote, *Be yourself; everybody else is already taken.*

3. Practice Positivity

To have healthy success, adapting a lifestyle of positivity is a must. Positivity is not simply being optimistic or thinking positively. Positivity is not defined by a big yellow smiley face or the slogan, "Don't worry, be happy." It's not found in clichés or catchy sayings like, "Just do it" or "Fake it till you make it." Although commonly used, these approaches may allow you to feel better for a little while, but they do not yield authentic or lasting results.

Positivity is a mind-set and an attitude of certainty, affirmation, assurance and confidence. It must be developed, cultivated and practiced in order to become your lifestyle. It's a powerful life transformation tool, that when used even in small measure, yields huge results. Positivity requires changing patterns of negative emotions and behaviors into positive emotions and actions. The more positive experiences you have, the more positivity you get, and the healthier and more effective your life becomes. Positivity has a cumulative effect.

Positivity brings your body, mind and spirit into healthy alignment. We perform best when we are strong physically, mentally, emotionally and spiritually. Proper nutrition, regular exercise, adequate rest and positive belief are prerequisites for peak performance and lasting success. Even small changes in these areas will make a big difference in the way you feel and perform.

The brain loves positivity. When we encounter positive experiences and engage in healthy, novel activities, and physical exercise, the endorphin dopamine is released into the body. Dopamine boosts your energy, stamina, alertness, creativity, and sense of happiness and well-being.

4. Stay Around the Right People, Places and Spaces
The company you keep has everything to do with being successful in life. The person you become is determined by the sum total of the people you surround yourself with. The right company brings the right results, while the wrong company depletes and leads to poor outcomes.

Growing and nurturing healthy relationships is not an option but a necessity for achieving success. Scientific studies show that our brains are wired to be relational and that people are more generative, productive, healthy and happy when they have strong social relationships and good partnerships.

When like-minded and like-spirited people get around each other, they ignite each other's creative energy. You know that incredible feeling you get when you're around someone who just gets you? You feel like you're on the same page, speaking the same language, and humming the same tune. Things seem to click almost effortlessly. Feeling understood, genuinely accepted, and valued allows you to feel emotionally safe, which liberates you to be more open, receptive, and genuinely expressive.

5. Flow With the Rhythm of Life

The art of living a balanced life is living life with purpose, flow, rhythm and harmony. Along with loving relationships, life balance ranks at the top of the list of the necessary ingredients for optimal life success. Maintaining life balance comes naturally to some but for most; it is a skill that has to be learned and cultivated.

To increase life balance, invite more life into your life. Keep things lively, fresh and alive. Like adding the right spices to a recipe to create an enticing meal, adding spice to your life makes for more zestful living. Don't let your home life become bland by adding the same old, same old. When you're at home, get off of the sofa, put the remote down, and step away from the television and computer sometimes. Keep the environment in your home cheerful and alive. Add a little extra to the ordinary, and create some extraordinary memories with your family and friends.

Practice these principles at work too. Find unique ways to make work more of an adventure. Take a different route to work. Go for a walk during your break. Eat different foods for lunch. Wear clothes that make you feel radiant, not drab and uncomfortable. You will feel more energized, and your workday will feel more pleasant and go more smoothly.

Everyone knows that to achieve success in life you have to work hard. But studies have found that play is also essential for success. In fact, some studies suggest that playing is even more important for achieving healthy success. The value of play was unrecognized or underemphasized in the early lives of many, especially some high achievers. Instead, intellectual achievement was the focus, and playtime was considered a luxury to be indulged in from time to time or only after all the work was done. Recently, research has proved that there is a strong, positive correlation between regular play, good success and good health.

Rest and relaxation are essential. You have to take time out to prevent burnout. Getting proper rest allows you to be more physically efficient and intellectually and mentally proficient. You don't lose time by resting; in the long run, you are saving time because you become more productive. When you feel tired and drained, often, the simple restorative antidote you need is time to do "nothing on purpose."

In closing, I applaud you on your efforts to improve your life. Continue to exercise your faith, maintain your focus, and remain open to making changes when necessary. Keep investing in your learning as you are doing by reading this book. Knowledge is power, and having good information helps you to live your most optimal life.

Your next big win is in front of you. Keep moving forward. Here's to your success!

About Dr. Hawthorne

Colleen Nadine Hawthorne, MD, is a mental health physician, writer, speaker, life coach, and health and wellness consultant. She is the founder of A Renewed Mind Behavioral Health, LLC, and Colleen Hawthorne Coaching and Consulting Services.

Dr. Hawthorne has practiced psychiatric medicine for over 20 years, providing services to patients from all walks of life, from people in the most deprived inner-city communities to renowned leaders and celebrated elite. As a coach and consultant, her passion and focus is providing services to health professionals, executives, and religious leaders and their families. She has a heart for serving people whose lives involve leading and helping others. Dr. Hawthorne is often sought out by leaders, due to her keen understanding and sensitivity to leaders' needs, recognizing that leaders sometimes need a safe, emotional space where they too can to be heard, affirmed and supported.

In addition to providing services through her private business entities, Dr. Hawthorne provides psychiatric services in community mental health centers in the Washington, DC, metropolitan area. Recently, as an attending psychiatrist and team leader in the Department of Psychiatry at the Walter Reed Army Medical Center, in Washington, DC, she proudly served our military troops and their families and trained military-enlisted psychiatric residents and medical students.

Dr. Hawthorne helped to pilot the Mental Health Court Urgent Care Clinic at the District of Columbia Superior Court,while serving as Medical Director. She has also served as Regional Lead Psychiatrist for the Maryland Department of Corrections.

Dr. Hawthorne formerly served on the faculty of the Emory University School of Medicine, where she was an Assistant Professor of Psychiatry and Attending Physician at the Emory University Hospital and Clinic. She was an elected Health Professions Advisor for prospective medical students, for the coveted Harvard University Health Professions Program.

Dr. Hawthorne has held numerous leadership positions and medical directorships, in inpatient and outpatient psychiatric settings, in Texas, Georgia, Maryland, and Washington, DC.

Dr. Hawthorne completed her undergraduate studies in biology at Howard University, in Washington, DC, where she graduated magna cum laude. She received her doctor of medicine degree from the Tulane University School of Medicine in New Orleans,

Louisiana. Dr. Hawthorne continued her medical training at the Baylor College of Medicine in Houston, where she completed her internship in internal medicine, neurology and psychiatry. At Baylor, she also completed her residency in general psychiatry and fellowship in psychosomatic medicine and consultation-liaison psychiatry.

Affectionately dubbed "Dr. C" by her patient's and colleagues, Dr. Hawthorne has been a featured guest on various radio and television programs, providing expertise in the area of psychiatric medicine, mental and emotional health and wellness, and mental health and spirituality.

In her forthcoming book, Dr. Hawthorne challenges people to "stop hitting the snooze button of life" and charges them to move forward on their success journeys, even in the midst of life challenges.

To learn more about Dr. Hawthorne, please visit: www.DrColleen.com or www. DrColleenHawthorne.com.

CHAPTER 3

MORTON'S OR MCDONALD'S: HOW I LEARNED TO TAKE THE LEAP OF FAITH AND CREATE THE LIFE OF MY DREAMS

BY TIMOTHY BILECKI, ESQ.

Struggling for the vast majority of my thirty-something years, I was one of those guys who had no choice but to pay for a value meal at McDonald's on the credit card and hope it went through. So imagine how exciting it was to make breakthroughs in my personal and business lives that gave me the ability to routinely take a group of colleagues to Morton's Steakhouse, order the best steak on the menu, a few bottles of Heitz Cellar Martha's Vineyard cabernet and pick up the tab without hesitating or stressing. There is a certain power in doing that and it's not to show off to friends, colleagues or clients that you now have the ability to pay for a several thousand dollar dinner. It's in the perception of others and the belief in yourself and your worth. In business, if you want to succeed and attract the clients you want and not the clients you need, it is critical that your business—and perhaps the rest of your life— be Morton's and not McDonald's.

FROM JAG TO RICHES—IT'S ALL ABOUT TAKING RISKS

Today, I live in Hawaii and run an incredibly successful law practice with a unique specialty that enables me to travel around Asia and the rest of the world defending U.S. military personnel who have been accused of serious crimes at court-martial. Each day I am working and getting closer to realizing my personal goals: freedom of time, freedom of money and freedom of location. It's the job of my dreams. But as you might guess, it didn't happen by chance. It's something I created for myself after taking many wild risks. The unknown can be scary, but we all have the potential to succeed if we take the leap of faith.

Life was a lot different three years ago before I started my practice. I was a 32-year-old Captain serving in the U.S. Army Judge Advocate General's (JAG) Corps as a criminal defense attorney in the "Senior Defense Counsel" position. I was responsible for the provision and oversight of all criminal defense services for the Army in Asia. I was stationed in Korea and coming to the end of my Army contract. After initially signing up for a three-year obligation, I was stationed at Fort Hood, Texas, and then extended in my second year to do a three-year tour in Hawaii. I fell in love with Hawaii, its people and all it offered. I dreamed of living there the rest of my life. But that's not the way a military guy is supposed to think. You go where they send you—and you dream on your own time. The "needs of the Army" called, and I was yanked out of my island paradise in Hawaii and sent to Korea.

Jumping in with both feet, I did the best work of my Army career while in Korea and zealously defended dozens upon dozens of Army soldiers stationed throughout Asia facing court-martial charges. I gained a reputation as one of the best defense attorneys in the Army. I enjoyed the Army and was passionate about the defending those accused of crimes. My two years in Korea came to an end in the blink of an eye, and after seven years in the JAG Corps, my obligation of service was about to expire. Talk about a crossroads. The options were clear. I could continue with my JAG Corps career or resign my Army commission, venture into the abyss and start my own law practice. As they often say, with risk comes reward. The tough part is staring the risk in the eye and taking it!

SEEING AN OPPORTUNITY—AND FINDING YOUR NICHE

As I sit now, writing this from a beautiful resort on the beach in Thailand, the decision I made seems like a no brainer. But at the time, it felt like straying from the herd and going against the grain. I was dealing with a lot of personal issues that I could have used as excuses to stay in the safety zone. I had suffered a huge financial loss with the "housing bubble" condo I had bought in Hawaii. I had practiced law for eight years but was essentially broke. I had little to nothing in the bank, no assets, and my minimal retirement account was wiped out. And I still had over $100,000 in student loans from my days at Boston College and the University of Miami School of Law. I wasn't in any position to move back to Hawaii, one of the most expensive places to live in the United States, and start a law practice. Then again, when passion takes you over and an opportunity presents itself, you have to take it. The timing is never perfect. If you wait for perfect timing, your time will expire.

The Army offered me a pretty sweet deal to stay, including a $60,000 bonus, a secure salary of over $100,000 a year, guaranteed free health care and another step toward military retirement at 20 years. Nearly everyone I knew told me that I would be crazy to walk away from that. Looking back these were people who had not yet taken off the blinders. I have learned that many people envy the reward but few will take the risk. Still, part of me bought into what they were saying. The prospect of getting out of the military and starting my own law firm was daunting. I had a young son to father and to take care of. Where would I live, how would I pay the rent, how would I set up a law firm with little to no money and how would I keep the practice afloat?

So where was my light of opportunity in all this crazy darkness and confusion? Asia. While practicing law there the previous two years, I had discovered an untapped market. I could do exactly what I was doing in the Army (defending service members stationed in the Pacific), only I could do it better as a civilian without the constraints of the military. The clients, not the government, would be paying me. It would be no different than a person accused of a crime hiring a criminal defense attorney instead of going with the public defender. There was already a niche market for this type of legal service and maybe a dozen or so people in the country who were known to be the best in the business.

Few, however, would fly from the East Coast or anywhere in the United States to defend a soldier in Asia accused of a crime.

But seeing the niche market and capitalizing on it are two different things. I remember reading Donald Trump's book *The Art of the Deal* when I was in junior high. He preached the idea that luck is when opportunity meets preparation. I always remembered those words, which originally came from Seneca, a first-century Roman philosopher. My "luck" while I was making my decision on whether to stay in the Army or not was when one of the top civilian lawyers in the industry I was trying to enter (privately defending soldiers around the world) was retained on a high-profile case in Korea. My opportunity was the chance to work with him and learn how to emulate his success. The preparedness came from ensuring that I would be the military lawyer who was working as co-counsel on the case with him and giving that case everything I had. The "luck" of working with one of the best in my industry while making this critical decision helped change everything for me.

WINNING THE CASE—AND SETTING LOFTY, CONCRETE GOALS

We won the case, and while the details of it are not important, my key takeaway was that the blinders were off. I realized I could do what this other lawyer did, add my personal experiences, my own flavor, and make it work for me—despite the inherent risks.

After working that case together, he became my mentor in all things business, and years later I am happy to call him a close, personal friend. He also gave me a book that helped change my way of thinking completely: *The 4-Hour Work Week* by Timothy Ferriss, which encourages a paradigm shift in thinking from working for someone else the rest of your life with the hope of a retirement at the end and instead taking the bull by the horns and designing your own lifestyle that gives you the elusive freedom of time, money and location. I read the book twice in one month. That, combined with seeing someone else succeed at what I envisioned myself doing ignited my passion. I looked at where my life could be in 10 years after traveling either the road of safety or the road of the unknown, and I dared myself to succeed and make it on my own. Within two weeks, I submitted my paperwork to resign my commission. In less than six months, I would make it or break it on my own. The proverbial bridge was burned.

Unfortunately, a dream, a vision and a spirited discussion over a beer does not pay the bills and with my resignation submitted, I was staring down the barrel of reality. If I was taking all the risk, I wanted all the reward. To that end, I set a goal to not just establish a law firm that defended military clients in the Pacific; I set a goal to be the best at what I did. I didn't want to simply be the premier attorney in this market; I wanted to take over and dominate it.

If you are going to set goals in life, set them high so that you will not be disappointed after you achieve them—no matter how lofty they seem. And be prepared for the crunch of hard work and long hours. I researched and studied all the other attorneys and law firms who took military cases in Hawaii, Korea, Guam and Japan, and tried to figure out their individual strengths and weaknesses, to learn who the dominant players were, and to do what may have seemed like a hostile takeover. I sought out and formed a strategic alliance with my then mentor and now close friend, and we essentially pied off the globe and determined that each of us would take cases in certain regions. Mine was the Pacific. I remember discussing this with him over a drink after we finished trying the case together. I told him that if our industry was the soda industry, he could be Coke and I wanted to be Pepsi. All others could be RC Cola, Shasta and the like. The problem then was he was already Coke, and I was still an Army Captain with nothing more than a resignation and a dream. Perhaps struck by my tenacity or my will to think big, we agreed to the strategic alliance, and I set out on a course for Pacific market dominance.

After setting up and establishing a website, I ate, slept and breathed Search Engine Optimization (SEO), and did the vast majority of it myself because I had a nonexistent budget. By my last day in the Army—with the help of my mentor—my site was on the top of the Google organic searches for my keywords. I had an outsourced answering service in place, my trusty MacBook computer, and hopefully, an empty chair at a Starbucks in Honolulu to work from. My firm, The Bilecki Law Group, LLLC was born.

MORTON'S OR MCDONALD'S—
MY FOUNDING PHILOSOPHY

Now it was up to me to create a mission statement to bring clients in the door and work my way to the top. I have always known that pricing and perception are the keys to any successful business. Charge a premium price and deliver an ultra-premium service; don't swim with the bottom feeders. Because my website was doing well in Google and my reputation as a tenacious litigator in Korea had spread, my phone started to ring with potential clients needing representation. After I listened to their needs, understood the scope of the representation, and made a decision that I wanted to take on their case, I had to do a fee quote. I desperately needed the money and felt a tremendous pressure to lowball the price so I would get the client. For just a moment before I spit out the fee quote, I thought about my pricing philosophy, my Morton's or McDonald's mantra, and went for it.

Let's assume that based on my research (these numbers will be fictitious to illustrate the point) the local lawyer on the island who accepted military cases would quote $15,000 and one of the big-name lawyers from the mainland would quote $30,000 for the same case. I paused momentarily and then, without hesitating, quoted the client $37,500. I remember the phone call to this day. After quoting a fee significantly higher than anyone else, even those with more "brand recognition" and experience, the potential client was taken aback and asked why I was so much more expensive than everyone else he talked to. With complete confidence I told him, because I am Tim Bilecki and in this business, as in life, you get what you pay for. The conversation did not last that much longer, and the client hired me. Shortly thereafter, I had another phone call from another potential client, and I made a similar pricing decision and was hired again. In less than one week after arriving in Hawaii, and out of my small Waikiki hotel room, I had made more money in one week than I would have made in six months in the Army. I delivered the goods and won both those cases. The $60,000 bonus the Army dangled in front of me now looked like peanuts, and I never looked back.

SIMPLE RULES TO GUIDE YOUR PATH

It's been an incredible three-year whirlwind for me, and I have never been happier and more fulfilled in my life. My practice has grown beyond my wildest dreams; I have an amazing family and the goals I set just three years ago have all been attained. My goals are now bigger, and my sights set higher. If you want to be a winner, you must have a relentless desire to push, do more and to succeed. This is all possible for anyone at the crossroads in life. Each day, I remember my business philosophy and use principals to guide my personal and business decisions. They are simple but powerful, and I pass them along to you.

- *Be a risk taker.* Many envy the reward, but few take the risk.

- *Set high goals.* If you set your goals low and achieve them, prepare for disappointment.

- *Charge a premium price.* Let the suckers discount; raise your prices.

- *Deliver the goods.* Charge a premium price and deliver an ultra-premium service.

- *Success by association.* You are the average of the five people you associate with most.

- *Don't forget your roots.* If you forget where you started, you will never realize where you have gone.

About Timothy

Timothy Bilecki is a Honolulu, Hawaii-based defense attorney who defends U.S. Military service members facing criminal charges in military courts. While Timothy travels worldwide to defend clients, his primary focus is on cases in the Pacific, including Hawaii, Guam, Mainland Japan, Okinawa and Korea. He specializes in defending sex crimes, war crimes, fraud, international drug trafficking or other violent offenses.

He is the managing attorney of his own practice, The Bilecki Law Group, LLLC and has been recognized as one of the Top 40 Trial Lawyers in the Country Under 40 Years Old by the National Trial Lawyers Association. He is also an "A group" graduate of the prestigious National Criminal Defense College; a member of the National Association of Criminal Defense Lawyers; co-founder and co-host of the Military Law News Network; and his cases has been featured on various national and international media outlets, including CNN, Fox News and *USA Today*.

Timothy works with a dynamic team of experienced investigators on each of his cases to ensure that they are thoroughly investigated, that no stone is left unturned, and that he knows more about the case than the government. His investigations prior to trial are both local and international. Some have led him to far-flung places across the globe, including the barangays of Manila, the streets of Cambodia and the villes of Korea. His mantra is premium pricing for premium representation, and he has a passion for winning. Timothy has the distinction of having taken over 100 cases to trial in military courts, with unparalleled results.

Prior to starting his own practice, he was a member of the U.S. Army JAG Corps and lauded as one of the best trial attorneys in the Army. Timothy's first duty assignment in the military was at Fort Hood, Texas, where he served as a military defense counsel. He was then stationed in Honolulu and served as a Special Assistant U.S. Attorney and later as an International Law Attorney focusing on the Asia-Pacific Theater. Finally, he concluded his military career with a two-year tour in Seoul, Korea, as the Senior Defense Counsel for the Army in Asia.

Timothy is married with one son, and in his spare time, enjoys international travel, auto racing and spending time with his family. To learn more about Timothy and his practice, visit www.bileckilawgroup.com or call (808) 275-4620.

CHAPTER 4

AN AMERICAN DREAM

BY DR. LEONID YELIZAROV

THE BEGINNING

My American peers are baby boomers… but I do not really consider myself one. Although my father found himself outnumbered by women 2 to 1 after the conquering of Berlin—what may sound like a reward to a young man—he left his youth behind with his dead brothers on the eastern front. The cheers and trumpets of the victory parades caused nothing more than a painful ringing in his ears when he came back to a silent home to serve as the man of the house at age 11. No one could escape the loss, grief, and hunger plaguing nearly every family in every neighborhood of the USSR.

I was born and raised in a region not far from the Caucasus Mountains bordering the Caspian Sea—the unlikely melting pot of the USSR. Father's title earned our family a two-bedroom apartment in a housing project built for families of Air Force members. A two-bedroom flat for a single family was a "luxury," but life was far from luxurious.

My father told me stories of a generation that had survived the Russian Revolution, world wars and famine. Stories of how, back on the German front, soldiers like his brothers would forgo using their rations of soap for weeks at time just to send the soap back home where it would serve as currency. Money was worthless when there was no food to purchase. A dozen bars of soap were gold, however, when traded for a few loaves of bread to feed his parents and sisters.

The health effects of war and famine led to my father's early passing. Mother was left to raise my brother and me with the support of our extended family. Growing up, I noticed that the other kids in my neighborhood weren't as close with their extended family. "Why is that?" I once asked my mother. My mother's reply taught me a lesson I would hold for the rest of my life. "Son, when your father and his brothers were fighting in the war, all of our distant relatives had to come together to survive the tough times back home. The families that came together and supported each other survived, while many other families perished." From that day forward, I developed a respect for family unity that I would hold and preach almost daily to my children.

Eventually, I became a dentist and married. What was once a relatively spacious three-room flat was now the burgeoning home to my mother, my wife and our two children. We enjoyed it and were doing well financially, even as times in our country got worse. The Cold War (coupled with the pitfalls of communism) drove the Soviet Union to the brink of collapse, and many of its republics began to revolt for their independence. On top of difficulties associated with communist rule, such as a lack of amenities and long lines for necessities, city streets became venues of corruption with violent protests, black markets and evictions of families who did not belong due to their ethnicity. The melting pot I once enjoyed—Baku—was drying up quickly and pogroms weren't far enough in the past. I had to act quickly to protect my family.

In the end, the lack of humanity around us, not a poor financial situation, prompted our decision to leave the USSR. Where to start over—Moscow, Israel or the United States—became the question. At the time, there was a big push for Jewish refugees like me to move to Israel, but that would not resolve my fears for my family's safety. I wanted to move to America, the land of democracy and freedom, but communist propaganda had me fearing the guns, violence and kidnapping associated with this "land of freedom." Moving to Moscow would have only delayed an inevitable, subsequent immigration away from our impoverished, corrupt, communist nation. Ultimately, I moved my family to America and began one of the most difficult journeys of my life in pursuit of the American dream.

THE JOURNEY

The first step was to persuade my large extended family—and it was not easy. Though everyone agreed that we needed to make a move, not everyone agreed where to go. After difficult and relation-straining deliberation, I managed to convince my family to apply for a visa to the United States. We applied at the U.S. Embassy in Moscow.

Fortunate to have a few relatives who had immigrated to Los Angeles, we had a little idea of what America would be like. We knew little more than America was a land of opportunity. After selling most of our personal items for pennies on the dollar and paying about $700 per person to apply for our visas and citizenship, we packed what little we were able to bring in the allotted one suitcase per person and immigrated to a country we had not seen, half a world away.

America granted visas to my mother, wife, and children first. We packed lightly, hid the little money we had in the children's shoes, bid farewell to our friends, and began the journey. "At least I know someone will be living like a human," one of my closest friends told me as we hugged each other goodbye.

THE DREAM

We arrived in Detroit, Michigan, not speaking a word of English. There was no time for sightseeing, nor was there any money for food. My education, license, and dental practice in the USSR were far from honored here in the United States, so my brother-in-law (who sponsored our visas) helped my wife and I find work as dishwashers and bussing tables in a restaurant. We saved up to purchase an old car and rented out a small apartment. I used the car to get a second job delivering pizzas.

My mother stayed in our apartment with the kids while my wife and I worked day and night. We were thankful that she was around and that she raised our children mindful of their Russian heritage. Eventually, however, she had to work as a nanny to help make ends meet. This meant that our young children would no longer have supervision, since we couldn't afford day care for them either. We asked a kind neighbor to watch over our youngest, while we enlisted another neighbor to help us get our oldest (only 4) to be accepted into kindergarten. He was too young to attend, but the school district allowed it, seeing as we had little other choice.

During the hours when we weren't working or tending to our children, my wife and I would flip through the pages of an English-Russian dictionary to learn a few words here and there. We knew that without learning the language, we would be bound to our vigorous lifestyle in poverty, and I wasn't ready to settle down being a dishwasher and delivery boy just yet. By chance, I learned that there was an opportunity to attend a dental school in Boston. Without hesitation, in the spirit of a pioneer immigrant, we packed our belongings yet again and moved to Boston.

My wife and mother worked while I was a dental student all over again. I would leave early in the morning and come home late at night. Though I knew the material, I did not know the language. It isn't an exaggeration to say that going through dental school for the second time was more like going through English school for the first time. Life wasn't easy for my family and I throughout this process, but I began to get a sense of what America represented.

By the time I earned my dental degree, I had decided that I wanted to start my own practice. I did a good bit of market research and found that Atlanta was a growing city and a good place to set up shop. For another time, we packed our belongings and headed south. In fact, from the time of immigration to the time my family settled down in Atlanta, we had changed nine addresses in eight years. My wife and I were determined to do everything it took to provide our family with a better life than the one we had known back in the USSR.

Before I could open my own practice, I worked for a few clinics around town. When the timing was right, I set up a small practice in what was then a small town, Alpharetta, Georgia. Since then, the town has grown, and so has my practice. In a matter of 10 years, my family went from poverty to leading comfortable lifestyles.

My life experiences have made me a proud American. Unlike many Americans, I know what it is like to live a life without freedom and self-determination. I know what it's like to live in a country full of obstacles and barriers. Despite the politics and philosophical disagreements many have regarding the path and direction of our nation, America will always be a welcoming home for those who are determined to lead a life of their dreams. The American dream is far from impossible or unattainable.

In fact, the only thing in this nation that prevents the realization of the American dream is the belief that the dream is no longer reachable, or a belief that you are entitled to have your dream realized for you. I have lived in a dictatorship that proactively suppresses dreams—and our great nation is far from that.

THE LEGACY

In America, even an immigrant, without knowledge of the language or money to support his family, can realize the dream with little more than hard work and determination. As an American living the American dream, my legacy must be to encourage others to seek the American dream.

From my beginnings in the USSR, to my journey half way around the world, to my dream of not only becoming a dentist again but building an even bigger life and practice than I could have realized in the USSR, I have made some observations about the excuses some will use to avoid pursuing the American dream.

The American Dream Is No Longer Attainable
False. Turn on the news or read a magazine and you are likely to see a story about someone who made it big doing something. Regardless of what that something is, that person is proof that the American dream is still attainable. I have lived under a dictatorship where corrupt "wolves" prowled the streets and sabotaged businesses to keep people oppressed. We Americans have no such excuse.

No one will hand you your dream on a silver platter, however, so be prepared to work for it. Determination is the key. I have never seen anyone who tried hard to do something, who failed completely. I have seen people give up when they get to a rough patch. Why should anyone feel entitled to succeed immediately? Yes, you might have to go without some comforts for a while if you are investing your pennies in a new business or in an education, but when you succeed, the success will be much sweeter for having had those bitter moments.

Jump Into the Pool With Childlike Enthusiasm
We have all been to a pool or the beach and tested the waters with a toe, only to find that the water is too cold for comfort. Adults will sometimes try to ease themselves into the water, and then they become stuck halfway in. They don't feel the discomfort of the cold on the bottom

half anymore, but they know that going in the rest of the way will be displeasurable for a moment. Often they return to shore and report that they just cannot handle the water that cold. Children, and the wisest of the adults, jump right into the cold water. They inherently know that the momentary discomfort of something new should not keep them from the excitement.

Approach the pursuit of the American dream with that same childlike enthusiasm and belief that once you get through the momentary discomfort and insecurity, the swimming will be easy. I had little knowledge of the United States when I arrived here. I learned the language, albeit slowly, and rebuilt my career.

There will always be challenges as you pursue your dream. The only person who can stop you from pursuing it, however, is you. You control whether or not you climb out of the pool when you are already halfway in. If you started a business and operating it proves to be more difficult than you planned, you have options. You can hire a consultant to assist you or take additional classes to hone your business skills.

Sometimes You Have to Depend on Others

My extended family living and working together taught me the importance of occasionally relying on others while pursuing the dream. Create a support network of friends, neighbors and family on whom you can depend. There is no shame in asking a neighbor to watch your children once a week so that you can attend a class or two. When you have free time, offer some of it to the others around you as well, so that they can pursue their American dream.

You can trade what you have for what you need to get to the next step of your journey. Just as I had traded in my previous life to start a new one in a better land, and just as my relatives traded soap for bread, you can barter for education, goods or services to help you reach your goals.

Be Willing to Follow Your Dream

If you dream of a better life for your children, is there any sacrifice too great to attain that goal? What is to stop you from moving across the country to take a better-paying job? If your answer is that you don't know anyone there, I can tell you from experience, you will soon make friends. If you know the language where you are going, then you are still steps ahead of where myself and many other Americans like me began.

Know that sometimes there will be enormous stress. Even in a dental office, there are the challenges and struggles of staffing and managing the business side of the practice while still seeing patients. For your dream to materialize, family members might have to take on extra responsibilities or an extra job in order to make ends meet for a while. None of this is insurmountable.

The American dream is not dead. Each day in America, we awake with the opportunity to pursue whatever dreams we have, unfettered by the constraints of communism or racial unrest or violence in the streets or lack of simple necessities. Each person who has achieved his American dream—whether on his own or with the assistance of a friend or two—has the obligation to assist someone else in pursuit of his or her dream. This is the beauty of America. Even if you grew up in poverty, or without a parent, or have had to begin again due to the loss of a job or other circumstances, you still have a choice. Your choice is to pursue a new dream or stay where you are and remain stagnant. In America, no one will do it for you, but no one will stop you either.

About Dr. Leo

Dr. Leo Yelisarov is one of the world's leading experts in cosmetic and implant dentistry, is a member of the Academy of General Dentistry, the Dental Organization of Conscience Sedation (DOCS), the Academy of Cosmetic and Implant Dentistry, and the Alpha Omega Fraternity. He is also the honored recipient of Diplomate Status, the highest status of Dental Implantology within the International Congress of Oral Implantologists. His passion for cosmetic and implant dentistry have allowed him to give people beautiful smiles and restore function in missing teeth, which translates into his nonprofit work with the Annual Free Dentistry Day Event, where he gives back to the community that helped him prosper.

Dr. Leo was born in August 1958 in Baku city, the former USSR. He graduated from high school in 1975. Dr. Leo continued his education at Azerbaijan State University for medical/ dental training from 1975 to 1980. He did his residency in periodontal and prosthodontic dentistry in the USSR and practiced as a general dentist from 1980 to 1990.

After 10 years of practicing in the USSR, he and his family moved to the United States. In August 1992, he was accepted to Tufts University School of Dentistry in Boston for advanced dental study. He completed the four-year program in two years and graduated in November 1994. Dr. Leo started his practice in 1996 and has gone from 0 to 10,000-plus patients in a span of 15 years.

In 1988, Dr. Leo penned a chapter in the *Book of Periodontics* regarding pre- and post-periodontal surgery with a unique red laser hand piece. He has also written numerous articles from 1985 to 2008 on oral health for various newsletters.

In 2007, Dr. Leo became one of 14 dentists in Georgia and one of only 450 dentists nationwide to receive this Diplomate Status. Candidates are chosen from among those who have most significantly contributed to the art and science of oral implantology. Dr. Leo was awarded Diplomate status a second time by the board of directors of the American Dental Implant Association on September 2011 in Miami.

Dr. Leo and his family reside in Alpharetta, Georgia. His wife, Diana, holds a MBA and masters degree in economics in the petroleum and oil industry. She also has a minor in computer programming. He has two children, Yuri and Kamilla. Yuri graduated from the Georgia Institute of Technology with a BS in electrical engineering. He is now a certified patent attorney after completing law school at Georgia State University. Dr. Leo's daughter, Kamilla, graduated from Georgia State University with a bachelor of arts in design.

CHAPTER 5

IS YOUR SUCCESS PERMISSION SLIP SIGNED?

BY ALONZO M. KELLY

Some of my earliest memories about kindergarten and grade school are not actually related to class. They are related to the field trips we took. I believe I remember them so easily because first and foremost the trips were cool! I also remember that they didn't happen very often so missing one would have been devastating to me as a child. Whether it was going to the zoo, spending an afternoon roller skating, or visiting the local museum, going on field trips were the best days of school. Of course, the only thing standing between me and this amazing journey was turning in a signed permission slip.

As a child, everyone knew when the trip was scheduled, what was in store for the day, how much it would cost, and the itinerary for a day sure to please and amaze. As kids, we would talk about the upcoming trip among ourselves, where we were going, and who we would hang out with. We even had a seat-assignment drawing for the bus that highlighted who we should sit next to on the journey. The trip, however, never seemed to be as real as the day our teacher handed out the permission slip for us to take home, have our mom or dad read carefully, sign, and turn back in to the teacher. As children, this seemed like the simplest of tasks. Or was it?

UPON FURTHER INSPECTION

First, let us examine the components of a permission slip a bit closer. The traditional permission slip contains language informing you that arrangements have been made for you to enjoy an amazing day with a host organization. What you will be doing on the trip and how you are going to be protected (or supervised) are also spelled out. Terms about when the bus will leave and when it will return are clearly defined. Finally, space is available for parents to communicate any allergies or health issues that may prevent you from participating on the trip. So in a nutshell, this little piece of paper is your golden ticket to participate in the amazing experience.

If all it takes is a simple slide of the pen from a parent, why did some us have such great anxiety when the teacher handed us the form to take home? It could be for any number of reasons. Perhaps we recently did something wrong and feared that our parents would not allow us to go. Perhaps we had convinced ourselves that our past grades and performance would prohibit us from be able to participate. Or maybe the reason we stressed about asking for permission was because we did not feel we deserved to go. I actually remember a friend telling me once in class that he did not think he would be able to go because it was only for the good kids.

PERMISSION TO SUCCEED

What do the memories of childhood field trips and permission slips have to with success? Only EVERYTHING! As adults, we are in complete role reversal when it comes to opportunities to be successful and giving ourselves permission to do so. Many years ago I started a practice of asking two simple questions before I began a speech. The first question is, Do I have your permission to present to you as though we are family? The second question I ask is, have you given yourself permission to be amazing yet? It is interesting how many people say they have given themselves permission to be amazing, but their behavior leads me to believe otherwise. This is no different than my classmates talking about how much fun the trip would be but hadn't yet asked their parents to sign the permission slip.

As a working professional, my anxieties of seeking permission seemed to be greater than those I held as a child. Let us assume for a moment that the field trip we have been invited to attend is a place called Amazing. Let us also assume that we are all invited to attend and that space on the bus will not be limited. The only thing required of you is to review the language contained in the form and, of course, sign it. You will learn that Amazing is a place that impacts your mental, spiritual, and emotional well-being. There is a fee for entrance, but the cost of staying home would be far greater. As you read the slip, you can picture people in your life who have visited this place not once but seemingly at least once a week! Now, all you have to do is sign the permission slip and you're in.

WHO'S IN CHARGE?

Who is responsible for signing your permission slip as an adult? I have clients who seek such permission from their children, spouses, co-workers, friends, and some adults are still seeking permission from their parents. Remember, we are not talking about a trip to the zoo or a day at the roller skating rink. We are talking about a trip to Amazing where success is on full display. My question for you at this point is simple and powerful; why would you ask someone else for permission to be amazing and successful? This is the secret that successful people have figured out. Successful people give *themselves* permission to be successful. They sign their own slips and get on the bus.

Successful people are not driven by pride but success. How we feel about ourselves and the values associated with that are pride. Pride is a very powerful trait to have but can also be the very reason that we never give ourselves permission to be successful. Pride protects us from putting ourselves in a position to be judged, ridiculed, critiqued, or laughed at. Pride serves as inspiration to want to be successful but holds us back from the actions of becoming successful. Pride can be the very reason that we do not ask for help (because we believe we should know the answer) or consider taking the bus ride to Amazing (because we believe we do not deserve to go).

When I reflect on this issue, it becomes blatantly obvious to me that more often than not, we get in our own way of success. We are accustomed to seeking the approval of others. As babies, we look for approval from our parents. As children, we seek approval from our friends. As young adults, we seek approval from the community. As working professionals, we seek approval from our bosses, co-workers, customers and clients. When do we break the cycle of needing others to validate our self-worth? When do we stop seeking the approval of others to be who makes us happy? I submit to you the time is now.

YOU DESERVE IT!

I cannot think of a single person in history, recent or otherwise, that achieved success without first believing that they deserved it. Notice I said achieved success and not assumed success. People who achieve success realize that no one is going to hand it to them. Being born into wealth does not make you successful; it makes you wealthy. Winning the lottery does not make you successful; it makes you rich. From senior leaders in Fortune 500 companies to the local entrepreneur doing big things in the community, everyone who has ever made a difference first started with the belief that they deserved to be successful and signed their permission slip to take action.

You will not ever be able to please everyone since there are far too many people with unique likes, tastes and opinions. Successful people realize at some point that while they are waiting for the approval of others, life would be busy passing them by. They choose to get on the bus and enjoy the ride rather than remaining at home and playing it safe.

THERE'S NO COMPARISON

I am successful and the hurdles I have faced in the process make it even more incredible. It does not require me to compare my success with anyone else's success, however. Pride would dictate that I compare my life to someone who society has deemed to be successful and use it as a benchmark for how far I have to go. The permission slip in grade school did not contain a sliding scale of how much fun I should expect. It simply said I should go. Similarly, my permission slip for success contains language that says what I should experience and that this experience would be my own.

Case in point is when my friends are critically judging the person on a professional sports team who never seems to enter the game. While they are criticizing the player as not being good enough, they seem to ignore the obvious: The person they are criticizing is a professional athlete, likely a millionaire, and one of only a few who are good enough to be invited to join the team. It proves that people will judge you no matter what, criticize you no matter what, and judge whether or not you deserve to be where you are. Success is absolutely attained, and there are no scenarios that leave you free from the opinion of others. From inventions that create conveniences in our lives, to fights for justice that ensure our rights and freedoms, we would be lost if the people who lead the way had not first given themselves permission to be amazing.

7 SUCCESSFUL MIND-SET TIPS

Here are my tips to ensure a successful mind-set, which ultimately leads to success in life:

1. *Know that success is not an exclusive destination that is only open to the privileged few.* All are welcome to attend provided they have received the necessary permissions.

2. *You, and no one else, should be responsible for giving you permission to be successful.* It does not eliminate your need to partner with others for space, resources or information. Realizing you need help from others is part of the journey to success.

3. *Let go of the need to satisfy everyone at all times.* Giving yourself permission to be successful relieves you of the responsibility to make sure that your happiness comes second to the happiness of others.

4. *You deserve to be successful.* Remind yourself of this fact as often as you possibly can. There will absolutely be challenges along the way. My mentor likes to remind me that sometimes you have to swim upstream in order to achieve success. Similarly, as children we recognized quickly that being on the bus to the field trip was much better than being left behind because we wanted to avoid the inconvenience of traffic.

5. *Giving yourself permission to be successful is not the same as being arrogant or conceited.* When you give yourself permission, what you have declared is that you are going to go for it. You are mindful of the experiences of others, both good and bad, but the excitement of finding out for yourself is worth the potential road blocks along the way.

6. *Focus on your mind-set and what you believe will make you happy rather than comparing yourself to others.* There will always be someone who has more and someone who has less. It is a waste of time to worry about what others have.

7. *Present yourself as a success.* You may not be where you ultimately want to be, but leave no doubt that you are on your way. This includes your attitude, language, attire, and even the company you keep.

Let me be the first to congratulate you on taking the first and most important step to becoming successful: giving yourself permission to be amazing! You absolutely deserve it.

About Alonzo

Giving full credit to his faith and his grandmother, Alonzo is the ultimate success story. A dynamic executive coach, best-selling author, and radio host, he is quickly gaining international and global attention as a premier consultant, strategist and groomer of talent. Alonzo is recognized as one of the nation's leading experts on leadership development, strategic planning and professional goal achievement. His most recent work includes co-authoring a best-selling book with legendary leadership expert Brian Tracy. In addition, Alonzo was selected to be interviewed on the television show America's PremierExperts, which airs on major networks across the country, including NBC, ABC, CBS and FOX.

As the founder, president and CEO of Kelly Leadership Group LLC, Alonzo continues to build the brand of what leadership development is all about. Since forming the organization in 2009, KLG has served thousands of individuals through personal and professional development, delivered training to a plethora of Fortune 500 companies and nonprofit organizations, and is consistently retained to be the keynote speaker at large and small events across the country. Alonzo is the host of the live internet radio show "Leadership: The Way I See It" and owns the unique empowerment clothing line, My Own Truth.

Alonzo holds a bachelor's degree in accounting, a master's degree in public administration, a master's degree in human resources and labor relations, and an MBA. He is a member of Alpha Phi Alpha Fraternity Incorporated and has received countless awards for his leadership and service. Visit www.kellyleadershipgroup.com to learn more about how KLG is building stronger leaders who produce amazing results.

CHAPTER 6

DARE TO SUCCEED WITH STORYSELLING: PUTTING YOUR STORY INTO ACTION!

BY NICK NANTON, ESQ., AND JW DICKS, ESQ.

In the middle of 1999, the entrepreneur had just cashed out of one internet start-up and was thinking about what his next venture would be when a friend left a message asking him if he was interested in investing in an online business that would sell shoes. Even though the dotcom bubble was at its peak, he was inclined to delete the voicemail and move on. It sounded like, as he put it later, "the poster child of bad internet ideas."

But when he was confronted with the fact that footwear was a $40 billion-a-year business and that mail order sales already accounted for 5 percent of those sales, he rethought the offer and decided to make the investment after all.

The dotcom bubble popped big-time the very next year, but the shoe company was still standing. It brought in over a million in sales in 2000 and quadrupled that amount in 2001. The entrepreneur began to see that this could work and decided to become more involved as co-CEO. He began to develop both a vision and a goal for the company.

The goal? To achieve $1 billion in annual sales by the year 2010—and to make *Fortune* magazine's "100 Best Companies to Work For" List. The vision? They would no longer be a company that just sold shoes; they would be a company that provided the best possible customer service—that just *happened* to sell shoes.

They retrained their customer service agents out of any bad habits they may have picked up at other companies, such as keeping calls as short as possible to make as many sales as possible. Instead, agents were directed to give customers lengthy advice, even to the point of sending them to competitors' websites if they couldn't meet their needs. The company also put new hires through a four-week "customer loyalty" training program—and then, after that program was completed, they made those new hires an incredible offer.

The company would pay them $2,000 to *quit*.

Why? Well, if the new employee didn't really care about what company they worked at, they would take the money and run. However, if they responded to the company culture, if they felt like this was the place for them, they would stay and be dedicated to the company's vision.

Over 97 percent turned down the two grand.

By the year 2008, the entrepreneur met one of his goals two years early—the company hit $1 billion in annual sales. And the next year, he met part two of his goal, as the company made the *Fortune* list of the 100 best companies to work for.

Tony Hsieh, the entrepreneur, had built Zappos into an incredible inspiration to the business world with its unique customer service ethos. And in November 2009, Amazon bought the company for close to $1.2 billion total with the understanding that it would still operate independently with its vision left intact.

STORYSELLING'S UNIQUE POWER

StorySelling is when you create a narrative for yourself or your company that's designed to hit your customers where they live. Our agency is a complete believer in this branding strategy, because we've seen the awesome results it brings to our clients. When you put StorySelling into action in your day-to-day internal and external business activity, you really do "Dare to Succeed"—and this chapter will tell you how to do just that, using Tony Hsieh and Zappos as a prime example.

Nick interviewed Tony a couple of years ago, and we will be sharing excerpts of that talk throughout this chapter. This exchange perfectly captures the necessity for StorySelling:

Nick: I've heard a quote from you about Zappos being a service company that just happens to sell shoes. Most people think, "If I'm a widget maker, I make widgets, and that's what I do."

Tony: Well, my advice for any business or entrepreneur is whatever you're doing, just think bigger. Take the railroads, for example, they were a great business at one point, and then cars came along, airplanes came along, and now they're not such a great business. They thought of themselves as being in the train business, but if they thought of themselves as being in the transportation business, then they would have been much better off. We thought, if we build the Zappos brand around the very best customer service, then we're not limiting ourselves to just shoes.

Zappos' logline became, "We may sell shoes, but we're really about providing the most amazing customer service on the planet." Their narrative became, "We don't care what it costs us in extra employee costs, training, time and even sales, we are going to break the 'normal' business sales mold and do whatever it takes to meet our customers' needs." Or, in the words of Tony:

Tony: We actually take most of the money that we would've spent on paid marketing or paid advertising and put it into the customer experience. We really think of those as our marketing dollars and let our customers basically do the marketing for us through word of mouth and their loyalty.

Now, let's drill deeper into how they brought that story to life—and how you can do the same with yours.

THE INSIDE JOB

If you want your StorySelling to be as powerful as possible, you must work from "the inside out." If anyone else who represents your organization doesn't believe in your narrative, you may be talking the talk, but you're definitely not walking the walk—and, sooner or later, your customers are going to know it. That means you have to hire people who fit into the culture you want to create—and properly train them in that culture. Here's more from Tony on that subject:

Tony: We actually do two sets of interviews for everyone we hire to work at our headquarters here in Las Vegas. The hiring manager and his/her team interview for the standard experience, technical ability and so on. But then our HR department does a separate set of interviews purely for a cultural fit. So we've actually passed on a lot of really smart, talented people.

Here are four big action steps to take in order to ensure you and your employees are creating the story you want to tell within your company:

Action Step #1: Clearly Articulate Your Core Values
This is the big one. Your core values should become the bedrock of your StorySelling. We help clients create and implement them in such a way that they become essential components of their narrative.

Of course, we're sure you've seen big corporations paste giant meaningless blocks of copy on their websites and call them core values, and we all immediately recognize that some copywriter has been hired to make up some nice-sounding words that actually have little to do with how they do business. Unfortunately, cynicism is the instant reaction to that kind of verbiage.

That's why it's crucial that you create core values that are *understandable, relatable and actionable*.

For example, below you'll find the 10 core values that Zappos promotes. You'll see the language is very natural and the messages are very clear:

1. Deliver WOW Through Service

2. Embrace and Drive Change

3. Create Fun and a Little Weirdness

4. Be Adventurous, Creative, and Open-Minded

5. Pursue Growth and Learning

6. Build Open and Honest Relationships With Communication

7. Build a Positive Team and Family Spirit

8. Do More With Less

9. Be Passionate and Determined

10. Be Humble

Consider this approach when breaking down your narrative into bullet points for those inside your operation to take on board (and for those *outside* your operation to read and admire).

Action Step #2: Make the Abstract Actionable

It's one thing to say "Deliver WOW Through Service"—it's another to make it happen. Whatever your core values happen to be, you need to put in place concrete methods to transform those values into real habitual business behavior, both by employees and yourself.

For example, here's how Tony made sure that customer service representatives had genuine interactions with customers.

Tony: Our approach is no scripts and not to measure efficiency in terms of the call times, which is how most call centers are run. Instead, we focus on the culture and make sure everyone in the company understands our long-term vision about building a Zappos brand to be about the very best customer service. They know the goal when a customer hangs up is for the customer to walk away thinking, "Wow, that was the best customer service I've ever had."

Action Step #3: Hold Everyone Accountable to Your Narrative (Most of All, Yourself!)

As we noted, the usual statement of corporate values isn't taken seriously by employees or even management; it's usually more of a public relations ploy rather than any substantial initiative. When it comes to StorySelling, however, your narrative must be taken seriously by all concerned. There should be incentives for masterfully following through on that narrative—and consequences for violating it.

Action Step #4: Keep Your Narrative Alive Internally on an Ongoing Basis

You know the old saw about sharks: They have to keep moving forward or they die. Your StorySelling narrative is no different—which is why it's important to find ways to keep it a living, breathing animal through constant attention.

For instance, Zappos publishes a yearly "Culture Book" that runs up to 480 pages long and continues to reinvigorate their StorySelling. Here's Tony on this ingenious innovation:

Tony: *It's a book we put out once a year. We ask all our employees to write a few paragraphs about what the Zappos culture means to them, and, except for typos, it's unedited. So you get to read both the good and bad. You know how on websites there are customer reviews? These are basically kind of like employee reviews of the company. And we give it to prospective job candidates and even customers, vendors and business partners, just so people can get a pretty good sense of what our culture is like.*

The above four action steps create the kind of culture that supports your narrative, rather than subverts it. And that's to your benefit: The secret here is that StorySelling doesn't just grow your business on the customer side—it also strengthens it internally. If you implement it effectively, you'll find your employees will feel as if they're part of something bigger than just another business. In turn, they'll be more motivated to fulfill your narrative, they'll work together more efficiently, and you'll find yourself with a happier and more productive operation.

TAKING IT TO THE STREETS

If you have your internal StorySelling tactics in place, then it's time to deliver your narrative to the outside world in a unified and consistent way. Every time you interact with the public is in reality an opportunity to solidify your StorySelling and cement your logline with customers and clients.

Apple, of course, is a textbook example of how to make this happen. Through every aspect of its external operation—from their stores to their marketing to their actual products—the elements of coolness and innovation are on full display.

Obviously, you want all aspects of your business to work as well as possible, but you want to make doubly sure that you excel to the full extent of whatever aspect your StorySelling emphasizes.

Here are a few *external* areas where it's essential that your narrative takes center stage:

Your Marketing and Advertising

Make sure none of your marketing efforts contradicts your overall StorySelling strategy. An ad agency may have the most brilliant idea for a TV commercial in the world, but if that commercial directly conflicts with the storyline people have already accepted about you, you're in trouble: The public will reject the message and possibly even get angry at you.

For example, KFC actually tried a campaign in 2003 that advertised how *healthy* their food was. Nobody believed their claims and an *Advertising Age* writer called it "desperate and sleazy." The reason the fast-food chain finally pulled the ad? "Brand protection." [1]

Your Corporate Communications

How you interact with the public as a company is also vitally important to your StorySelling efforts. For example, if you're positioning yourself as a slightly secretive and mysterious organization in order to hype whatever your next new product or service is, you might want to limit any exposure to the absolute minimum. For example, the Segway, the motorized upright two-wheeled device for pedestrians, is frequently the butt of jokes these days; however, before it was released, its development was very top-secret—and, to facilitate some high-profile leaks that would create a lot of excited anticipation, it was only shown to such luminaries as Steve Jobs (who said it was "as big a deal as the internet") and billionaire John Doerr (who said it was more important than the internet!). The pre-release hype and mystery was so huge that the irreverent Comedy Central series *South Park* did a whole episode about it.

In contrast, Zappos, of course, took a completely different approach to its corporate communications, based on its StorySelling narrative—by enthusiastically embracing transparency:

Tony: *One of our core values is about being as open and honest and as transparent as possible. So we do that with our employees. We share lots of data with our vendors, and we have tours that come through every*

---

1 Kate MacArthur, "KFC Pulls Controversial Health-Claim Chicken Ads," *Advertising Age,* November 18, 2003

day. They spend a full day or sometimes two days with us, and they're listening on calls and see how we score them, or spend a few hours with our recruiting team and we share the actual interview questions we ask and so on.

Your Content

Another very effective way to convey your story is to create content that explains and promotes your StorySelling narrative; this content can come in the form of books, articles, blogs, videos, speaking engagements and one-on-one interviews. Content like this positions you as more of a thought leader rather than just another business person out for free publicity—and, just as important, your vision is seen as the innovative business strategy that it is rather than a marketing gimmick.

We are big believers in this concept—and we work hard to place our clients in such major media outlets as CNN, CNBC, FOX News, the major network affiliates (NBC, CBS, ABC and FOX), and in such national publications as *USA Today, Inc.* magazine, *Forbes, The New York Times* and others. These aren't ads we're talking about—this is substantive content that showcases these entrepreneurs and their visions. This exposure is, of course, important to increasing their visibility, but from a bottom-line profit point of view, it's more important as a demonstration to their current and potential customers of their prestige and recognition in the world at large.

The real takeaway we want you to have from this chapter is you should never look at StorySelling as a kind of coat you can just put on and take off when convenient; instead, it has to be seen as an integral part of both your internal and external business image. While some lapses in your StorySelling narrative are inevitable, they should be minimal and quickly corrected.

When you tell a story with integrity and consistency, the public believes in that story and in you. That's how you establish that all-important element of trust—and that's how you ultimately dare to succeed!

About Nick

An Emmy-winning director and producer, Nick Nanton, Esq., is known as the top agent to celebrity experts around the world for his role in developing and marketing business and professional experts through personal branding, media, marketing and PR to help them gain credibility and recognition for their accomplishments. Nick is recognized as the nation's leading expert on personal branding as *Fast Company* magazine's expert blogger on the subject and lectures regularly on the topic at major universities around the world. His book *Celebrity Branding You®* has also been used as the textbook on personal branding for university students.

The CEO of The Dicks + Nanton Celebrity Branding Agency, an international agency with more than 1000 clients in 26 countries, Nick is an award-winning director, producer and songwriter who has worked on everything from large-scale events to television shows with Bill Cosby, President George H.W. Bush, Brian Tracy, Michael Gerber and many more.

Nick is recognized as one of the top thought leaders in the business world and has co-authored 16 best-selling books alongside Brian Tracy, Jack Canfield (creator of the "Chicken Soup for the Soul" series), Dan Kennedy, Robert Allen, Dr. Ivan Misner (founder of BNI), Jay Conrad Levinson (author of the "Guerilla Marketing" series), Leigh Steinberg and many others, including the breakthrough hit *Celebrity Branding You!*

Nick has led the marketing and PR campaigns that have driven more than 600 authors to best-seller status. Nick has been seen in *USA Today,* the *Wall Street Journal, Newsweek, Inc., The New York Times, Entrepreneur* magazine and FastCompany.com and has appeared on ABC, NBC, CBS, and FOX television affiliates around the country, as well as on FOX News, CNN, CNBC and MSNBC, speaking on subjects ranging from branding, marketing and law to "American Idol."

Nick is a member of the Florida Bar and holds a J.D. from the University of Florida Levin College of Law, as well as a B.S./B.A. in Finance from the University of Florida's Warrington College of Business Administration. Nick is a voting member of The National Academy of Recording Arts & Sciences (NARAS, home to the Grammys), a member of The National Academy of Television Arts & Sciences (home to the Emmy Awards), co-founder of the National Academy of Best-Selling Authors®, and an 11-time Telly Award winner. He spends his spare time working with Young Life and Downtown Credo Orlando and rooting for the Florida Gators with his wife Kristina and their three children, Brock, Bowen and Addison.

About JW

JW Dicks, Esq., is America's foremost authority on using personal branding for business development. He has created some of the most successful brand and marketing campaigns for business and professional clients to make them the credible celebrity experts in their field and build multi-million dollar businesses using their recognized status.

JW Dicks has started, bought, built, and sold a large number of businesses over his 39-year career and developed a loyal international following as a business attorney, author, speaker, consultant, and business experts' coach. He not only practices what he preaches by using his strategies to build his own businesses, he also applies those same concepts to help clients grow their business or professional practice the ways he does.

JW has been extensively quoted in such national media as *USA Today,* the *Wall Street Journal, Newsweek, Inc.*, Forbes.com, CNBC.com, and *Fortune Small Business*. His television appearances include ABC, NBC, CBS and FOX affiliate stations around the country. He is the resident branding expert for *Fast Company's* internationally syndicated blog and is the publisher of *Celebrity Expert Insider*, a monthly newsletter targeting business and brand building strategies.

JW has written over 22 books, including numerous best-sellers, and has been inducted into the National Academy of Best-Selling Authors. JW is married to Linda, his wife of 39 years, and they have two daughters, two granddaughters and two Yorkies. JW is a 6th generation Floridian and splits his time between his home in Orlando and beach house on the Florida west coast.

CHAPTER 7

HOW TO LIVE A LIFE WITH NO LIMITS

BY DENNIS M. POSTEMA

"If you think you can or think you can't, you're right."
— Henry Ford

Recently, I met with my team to go over some ideas about an upcoming project. As we discussed the goals of the project, the hopeful outcome, and how to incorporate my new ideas into the plan, one of the team members asked me what kind of limitations I wanted to place on the project. Kidding around with him, I said that I had no limits. None—and neither should the team.

Later that evening, I was thinking about the conversation, and I realized that when it comes to the work I do and what I feel my capabilities are, I'm actually not kidding when I say that there are no limits. I truly feel that I have no limitations hanging over me, restricting the reach of my utmost potential—no limits on what I am capable of and none on what I can accomplish.

LIMITS? WHO NEEDS 'EM?

Who's to say I should have limits? When Napoleon Hill wrote, "Whatever the mind can conceive and believe, it can achieve," in his famous book, *Think and Grow Rich*, he gave the world a concise version of the secret to success. By sharing it in a book, he was making sure it no longer stayed a secret but an accessible strategy for everyone.

Yet still, with such a simple blueprint for success readily available, each day people limit themselves—their lives, their passions and their work. Rather than conceiving, believing and achieving, they take the wind out of the sails of their own dreams. They truncate their potential before setting off on that initial exploration to discover its true borders.

The truth is, no matter what your burning desire is—whether it's to be a great entrepreneur or invent something amazing—you can do it. You can, but only if you allow yourself to live without limiting your own potential.

FEAR AND THE DESIRE TO CONTAIN IT

We learn about limits at a very young age. As babies, gates prevent our access to stairs and rooms with sharp objects and chemicals. For many of us, the word no is our first, because we hear it so often as our parents try to control our actions and environment. While this kind of limitation is normal and healthy for defenseless children, it creates a strong sense of fear and trepidation in us that can keep us from exploring concepts and activities outside the invisible box of "safety" that our collection of life experiences builds around us.

One exercise that can help you bust through this invisible barrier is to understand the obstacle for what it is—a manifestation of your fears. What fears? Heck, all of them. Fear of failure making you feel bad, fear of success making you feel alienated, fear of looking silly or getting hurt, and fear of disappointment. Fear is a natural and healthy part of life, but many of our fears are based not on self-preservation so much as on limiting our emotional pain. This can be to our detriment, especially when we are overprotective of our psyche, which is not as delicate as you might think. Limitless thinking does not involve an absence of fear; it involves the courage and conviction to move past it and not allow it to control your destiny. If you visualize limitations simply as fears, you have a much better chance of busting through them and conquering life.

It seems like a difficult prospect, but really it's more frightening than it is hard. It's like that first time you rode your bicycle without the training wheels, or the first time you drove a vehicle without a parent or other adult sitting in the passenger seat. If you'd told yourself you couldn't do it, you'd still be driving back and forth to work with one of your parents today—and wouldn't that put a major kink in your life? As an adult,

you now know exactly how dangerc
in that car every day and navigate t
weather with barely a thought of what
trained driver to mentor you. You work
process is routine—even though the sa

IMAGINATION: THE ULTIMATE

What is your reality? What do you want
age we're taught that the imagination is a
it's not useful in "real life." Any kid who's
to be a rock star, actor or dancer knows that   ѵ.ɪᴇn see
those fanciful dreams as dangerous. We are ___ ᴜᴜr dreams are reckless
and might possibly pave the road to failure and disappointment while
real opportunities, those practical, rote things that everyone chases, are
squandered. But this knowledge, put there by social conditioning and
loving parents and partners who fear for our futures, is false. It's the
dying carcass of a defeatist lifestyle—and if you allow it to bind you,
you'll never know what you could be missing.

Let me explain: Whatever you can imagine in your mind, no matter
what it may be, that imagined vision represents the reality of what your
limits are. Just as a painter would have a difficult time creating a work
of art that he couldn't imagine and see in his mind's eye, so, too, will
you have a difficult time having a future that you don't allow yourself
the freedom to imagine.

I think it's important to note that I don't say these things as one of those
fortune-favored people who've never had to deal with adversity. The
year I turned 20 was one of the most difficult and important periods of
my life. This was the year I was laid off for the first time, and I learned
about sorrow when I lost my 24-year-old brother in a car accident.
Threaded among the tragedy of this life-changing year were some
triumphs. I landed the job of my dreams and, less than a year later,
was promoted to a trainer, then manager. I might have thought that feat
impossible, but it wasn't, which was how I realized the only limits my
life had were those I imposed upon myself.

When I was 23, I lost my dream job, just after a tragic fire in my parents'
barn took the lives of eight horses that had been in our family for years.
But it was the same year that I started my first company—a risky move

nes and friends did not support. I didn't allow
o my life, though, and neither should you.

and 2009, I had some of my greatest business successes
personal health problems. Despite being diagnosed with
e colitis and enduring three surgeries that included having my
removed, wearing a colostomy bag, and eventually having my
olon reconstructed, I started a second company as an extension of
the first—but this one I took national. I also graduated college—yes, I
graduated college after starting two successful businesses, and in spite
of my hospitalizations, surgeries and health problems. How? How could
I not when I didn't place limits on what I thought I could achieve?

The truth is, there will always be obstacles on your path to success.
Some of these obstacles will be in the form of other people who shun or
make fun of your dreams and goals. Some of them will be in the form
of personal life events far beyond your control. But these events—no
matter how tragic or seemingly insurmountable—can only get in the
way of what you achieve if you grant them the power to do so.

BOUNDARIES VS. LIMITS

While limits are not helpful when trying to reach your ultimate life
dreams, boundaries can be. We've all heard stories of individuals
and businesses that went too far trying to live a dream that they were
unsuited for or that they were, for some reason, unable to realize at
the time. Without setting boundaries that clearly spelled out the risks
these individuals or business were willing and able to accept, they lost
everything and were forced to start over. For some, this kind of hiccup
becomes just another ingredient in their recipe for success. For others, it
carves a deep gash in their lives and leaves them with a major financial
injury, a living wound that never heals.

By establishing boundaries that determine what you're willing to risk
or lose and what situations—whether personal or financial—indicate a
need to reassess your journey to a limitless future, you can ensure that
you still have solid ground beneath you at every part of your journey.
It's important, however, to understand that meeting a boundary and
having to readjust does not mean that your dream is unattainable or
should be abandoned. It simply means that you've reached a personally
established roadblock—you need some time to take stock of what you

did right and wrong in order to create a new plan for going after it again.

Limitless thinking is not about quick fixes and overnight success. It is a long-term process that ensures you eventually reach your full potential. Keep this in mind as you readjust your pathway when certain boundaries are reached. Otherwise, a sense of urgency might overtake you and lead to irrational thinking and actions, which are limiting in themselves.

PERMISSION AND APPROVAL

No matter what is happening around you, you have complete control over your future. I would need dozens of hands in order to count how many times I've had business ideas that have been laughed at and ridiculed. Truth is, there's not a millionaire or billionaire who hasn't been laughed at one time or another if they shared their ideas with the wrong people.

No matter how carefully you select your confidants, there's still a chance they may not be able to support your vision and believe in your goals. Not everyone can understand the concept of no-limits thinking and in many cases, it's not their fault. Brian Tracy, author of *Eat That Frog!* tells us that only 1 percent of the population can take the risks and think like an entrepreneur. Those you love and respect in your life may not be part of that extremely thin 1 percent, so whether it's your spouse, friends or parents, you have to take their input and negativity with a grain of salt. You can listen to them and evaluate the truth, significance and potential of what they're saying, and draw conclusions about how it will affect you if they are right, without allowing it to put a limit on your thinking.

When the naysayer is your spouse, it can be more difficult. Marriage is a partnership, so limitless thinkers with spouses who don't share their mind-set must find a way to balance the psychological comfort of a spouse with their own need for limitless thinking. One great way to do this is to discuss with your spouse the boundaries you plan to set. For example, let's say you want to attempt a certain path toward your goal, but you want to limit the amount of money you spend on the way. By allowing your spouse to help you set that boundary, you can ensure that his or her priorities are observed and respected while you're still allowed the opportunity to take risks.

There are times when you have to ask your significant other to trust that you have a dream or a plan and hope that they do. One of the biggest upsets I've seen in my years of training agents is when a spouse doesn't understand the agent's dreams or goals. Often, the spouse's limits and fears ruin the agent's confidence and stunts his or her goals and future potential.

While support from those you love is wonderful, you must not look to others for approval or permission to embrace the idea of no-limits thinking. One of the toughest mistakes many potentially great leaders and entrepreneurs make is waiting for approval. You have to be the guardian of your own life and future. If you rely on the opinions of people who don't understand your dreams or who are limited by their own fears and disappointments, you end up living someone else's life rather than your own. If you've examined your dreams critically by exploring the drawbacks and risks you might encounter on your way to achieving them and it still feels right to go for it, you need to unleash the power within and remove the shackles of limitations. Go forth with confidence, imagination, hope and positivity.

FIND SUPPORT

While your spouse, family, friends, co-workers and others may not understand your desire to live without limits, some may find a way to support you. Don't be afraid to rely on them when the road gets bumpy. This is one of the reasons I'm very blessed. My wife supports me in whatever crazy ideas I have. She may not understand them, but she knows with my passion and hard work, if there is even a remote chance of success, I will make it happen. Recently, we hit a huge snag with the release of my updated and expanded book that didn't allow it to be released on time. We had thousands of dollars into a marketing campaign and all sorts of people in the industry sticking their necks out for us. I was devastated but determined to make it right, and my wife had my back. She brought my spirits up each day—and she wasn't alone. Those people who were sticking their necks out not only said they understood but shared that snags like this happened to them too over the years. They offered tons of great advice that really helped me get the situation back on track.

Surround yourself with successful, positive people and, in your mind, appoint them as your unofficial board of directors. Stay away from the naysayers who don't have the aspirations you do. After the book release snag, my book hit number one on Amazon in two categories. My wife woke me up for work the next day and said, "Time to get up, you number-one best-selling author, you." Now those are the kind of people you need on your team.

At the end of the day, the ultimate message is that we each need to take possession of our thinking and take the limits off our future, just as our parents took the training wheels off our bicycles. The only things you have complete control over are your thoughts. Don't relinquish control of them to outside forces or allow them to determine your limitations.

About Dennis

Dennis M. Postema is a successful entrepreneur, best-selling author, speaker, and registered financial consultant. His dedication to his agents and clients has helped his business flourish and made him a 2012 recipient of the 10 Under 40 Award given by the Defiance Chamber of Commerce.

As a teen, Dennis got a taste of the true challenge of entrepreneurship by working side by side with his dad, part owner of a machine, tool and die shop. Dennis started out in his freshman year of high school and worked his way up from cleaning toilets to driving a truck and, eventually, operating the machines. Through this experience, Dennis was able to watch his father manage the shop and eventually buy it. For Dennis, this laid the foundation for the idea that he could live his life his way—without taking on the limits to success that can stop a promising career in its tracks. He says, "It was a great experience to learn and grow from. Having a mentor like my father in business at a young age left me with a lot of insight and helped me fall in love with the idea of being my own boss."

Dennis has committed his career to solving the insurance and retirement issues faced by his clients. After working as a captive agent for a large insurance carrier, he realized he could offer his clients more options, better products and a more secure future if he went independent—so at age 23, he did.

Today, Postema Insurance & Investments (PI&I) works with over 90 carriers to ensure that all clients are served by the most highly rated, competitive insurers, and given access to the best products in the industry. PI&I has over two dozen agents and offices in five locations throughout Ohio, Indiana and Kentucky. Dennis's focus on helping clients, rather than simply selling them products, landed him on the cover of *Agents Sales Journal* (Senior Market Edition) in 2011.

Not content to focus exclusively on PI&I, Dennis launched Postema Marketing Group (PMG) LLC in 2009. His objective was to help independent agents across the country achieve their goals and see their agencies thrive while expanding their focus on client needs and product offerings. With PMG, Dennis combines the same "help rather than sell" approach with one of the broadest product lines in the business.

In 2012, Dennis released his first book, *Retirement You Can't Outlive*. The expanded version, released in 2013, quickly became a number-one bestseller on Amazon. Written in an easy-to-understand format, this essential guide to a worry-free retirement is turning countless long-standing investment perceptions upside down—and putting readers' retirement plans right side up. On April 22, 2013, Dennis released his second book, *Avoiding a Legacy Nightmare*, and it also quickly became a number-one best-seller on Amazon. *Avoiding a Legacy Nightmare* is a practical and legacy-changing guide to the hidden consequences of selecting the wrong beneficiaries for insurance policies, annuities and retirement accounts.

Dennis has many exciting book releases slated for 2013 and 2014. Each has been designed to offer helpful tips and guidance for amateurs and experts alike. The next book, *Financing Your Life*, is a comprehensive guide to every aspect of personal financial planning that a family can face. In addition to the above accolades, Dennis also received the 2013 Distinguished Alumni Award from his alma mater, Northwest State Community College, for his success in the industry and community.

Visit: www.daretosucceed.net or www.motivationandsuccess.com to learn more.

CHAPTER 8

BECOME EMPOWERED:
OVERCOME THE WONDER WOMAN EFFECT

BY JENNIFER CALANDRA

Every woman has a story...

Life, for some, has been filled with incredible opportunities that have led them in unexpected directions. Others have spent their lives on a never-ending roller coaster of life's uncertainties, pain and strife. Some have stayed single by choice. Some entered marriages never expecting them to end in divorce. Others have spent a lifetime with their husband, never once thinking that there would be a day that he would be gone and she would be alone. Regardless of what we have faced, we are by what we have experienced.

I spent almost a decade of my life in an extremely volatile marriage full of violence and abuse—physical, mental and emotional—at the hands of someone who promised to love, cherish and care for me. In those moments, I never realized how affected I was or how it would affect my future. At the time, I had no idea that I was losing who I was, my identity, my zest for life, my spirit, my hopes and dreams. There were very few good days; most were spent in the fear of what was about to happen. I got to the point of functioning in "survival mode" and did whatever I had to do to make it through another day.

My divorce ultimately saved my life. Although I was "free," I was in a fog trying to gain my footing. I fluctuated between periods of depression, denial and blatant anger. I found myself questioning God and seeking answers. Why did this happen to me? How was I going to move past this? I spent many months soul-searching in counseling, coming to grips with what had become of my life. I felt incredible guilt for hiding the abuse from my family and friends. I felt overwhelming shame for allowing this to happen to me. I felt a deep sense of helplessness. I did not know who to turn to for guidance as I picked up the pieces of my life.

Then my reality sunk in. I was on my own. My ex-husband was in prison for the abusive things he did to me, and I now had the sole responsibility to provide for myself and my young sons. The chapter of my life being a victim was over. I had no choice but to move forward, find myself again and live as a survivor.

My life had been such a whirlwind; slowly I realized how profoundly my past had affected me. My past defined who I had become as a person. As I started to heal, I slowly, but surely, began to rediscover bits and pieces of who I had been. I was determined to teach my sons that regardless of what you are handed in life; it's your choice to make it better. We are responsible for our own decisions, and those decisions define our destiny in life.

As I began to gain confidence, little by little things got easier. There were days I celebrated small victories. Other days I would put my children to bed and sob myself to sleep. I worked multiple jobs to provide for my sons and had to learn how to be very frugal, budget and save money. Every penny mattered and was accounted for. I enjoyed the opportunities I had every day to share life with my children and watch them thrive in an environment not tainted by negativity, abuse and chaos.

Over time, as I rediscovered myself, I was drawn back to the very faith that I once questioned. Being the daughter of a pastor, I became very involved in the church my father led and realized the strength I gained. My past had developed muscles, not wounds. Although my experiences left me full of questions, it also equipped me. I noticed a new, very deep level of compassion and empathy for others. People were drawn to me. They wanted to share their stories with me, and I became a wonderful listener. I found a sense of purpose in helping others; I felt as if I was finally reclaiming my life. I learned the vital importance of forgiveness and how it is a stepping stone to true healing.

In 2005, I was extremely blessed to meet the Love of my life, who then became my husband. A man who saw my heart and helped me realize that I had so much to give. A man who saw value in me, who appreciated, respected and grew to love a very broken woman. That man is my best friend, my confidante, my business partner and husband, Phil.

My husband and I co-founded a thriving and well-respected financial planning and wealth management firm. As I continued on my journey to heal and seek my purpose in life, I felt God leading me in a direction to help other women; a way to "make my mess my message." As God continued to refine me, I learned that I, too, was duped by the "Wonder Woman Effect." I made a conscious effort to help prevent other women from doing the same thing.

I decided to establish a division of our firm that would provide financial education, guidance and empowerment to women. I'd become an advocate to help them make sense of things in their own financial lives, to take control. I also wanted to provide a safe place where women could come to share their concerns and fears, and their questions about money and investments. This would be a warm, comfortable environment to receive the guidance that they may not have sought elsewhere.

I have been blessed to have had conversations with hundreds of amazing women, hearing their stories, laughing with them, crying with them, and helping them define their new lives. Regardless of what life event gives me the opportunity to meet with a woman—divorce, loss of their spouse, a health issue, loss of a job, or an event that has drastically affected their lives—many are in a fog. They try to make sense of what just happened. They ask themselves: How does this affect me? Where do I go from here? And for some women, the thought of doing *anything* is overwhelming, so they allow themselves to stay stuck and choose to do nothing. *Our decisions define our lives. Choosing to do nothing IS a decision.*

As a Registered Financial Consultant (RFC), I empower women to take control of all aspects of their lives, starting with their finances. Being truly wealthy encompasses far more than merely money. However, having a strong financial cornerstone is imperative. Money affects every area of our lives: our relationships with friends and family, our sense of purpose, our physical as well as mental well being. I have firsthand knowledge and experience in learning to build true wealth for myself. Is it frightening? *Yes!* But moving forward starts with one small step. You need to become the captain of your financial ship and take control!

HOW TO AVOID 5 COMMON TRAPS WOMEN FALL INTO

There are five common traps women fall into that you should be aware of:

1. My Hairdresser Told Me...

Women seek other women as a support network...for everything from what outfit to wear, to child-rearing advice, to career choices, to money decisions. Women not only listen to one another, but they feel they are heard and understood by one another. While it's perfectly fine to seek and receive advice from friends, neighbors, your hairdresser, or your friend from church, do not act on financial advice from people who are not qualified to give it. Just because a particular stock, mutual fund, or investment property is right for your friend, does not mean it is right for you. We are all individuals with different needs and goals. It's important to make sure that your financial plan is custom tailored to your circumstances, needs and goals.

2. Playing the Peacemaker

Many women try to maintain the peace in every relationship. We don't like to hurt people's feelings, and we certainly don't want anyone to ever be upset with us. This could devastate your financial life. I have met widows and divorcees who are so afraid to move from their current financial advisor because they are a peacemaker. Their husband built a relationship with a particular advisor or advisory firm, and women feel guilty about leaving. They fear hurting their feelings or not fulfilling the working relationship their husband established. Over 70 percent of women will change their financial advisor after divorce or the loss of their spouse, but it takes them a very long time to move. This applies to women who are single as well. Do not allow a relationship with an unproductive advisor outweigh planning your retirement based on your goals and needs. If you do not hear from your advisor, or if you have a gut feeling that something is not right with your investments, fire them and move on.

3. I Own What!?!

Get involved! Just like an ostrich buries its head in the sand to hide, many women are completely unaware of their current financial situation. It is important to know what you own, why you own it, and how it fits into your overall financial plan. I spend a great deal of time meeting with women, helping them discover what and why they are doing what they are doing. I also spend time helping them open statements that have been sitting in a drawer, unopened. It is also vital to understand that your investments need to correspond with your financial stage in life. There are certain strategies that may have worked perfectly when you were working and accumulating your nest egg, but those same strategies may not work as you move into retirement. Ask the questions, make the necessary changes, and gain a very clear understanding on how—and if—your money is working for you.

4. A Man Is *Not* a Financial Plan!

Regardless of your marital status, you need to have an understanding and knowledge of your finances; not only what you have but why you have it. Some women have known from childhood that they wanted to be a wife and a stay-at-home mom. Being a mom is the hardest job in the world, with the lowest amount of pay. Others chose a career and a family; they contribute financially to the household but do not directly manage the household budget. Men, instinctually, are hunters, gatherers and providers. In many relationships, the man is the head of the household; he pays the bills, maintains the finances, and selects the investments. In turn, he assures the wife that it is all handled, in case he passes away first. While this is a very loving idea and seemingly provides a sense of security, it could be doing more harm than good. Women are outliving men by 10-12 years. In many cases, they are left with a financial mess, and as they try to make sense of things, it is very easy to become overwhelmed with their new role. Couples need to have the "money talk" often, as we are not promised tomorrow. Having a hands-on approach with your finances is vital and may prevent a lot of headaches as well as heartache, should you be faced with a similar situation.

5. The Wonder Woman Effect

As students of life we, as women, are doctors, nurses, counselors, confidants, friends and nurturers. God wired us this way. We have the babies, we take care of the home, and in most cases, we are the caregivers as life goes on. We put everyone and everything in the forefront and worry about ourselves last. In all of our closets, we have a cape that we tie on and fly out the door in every time anyone needs us. Regardless of what we have going on in our own lives or if we even really want to, we stop what we are doing and run to the aid of someone in need. I do the same exact thing. I am a wife, a mother, a daughter, a friend and a business owner. My life is very hectic, and there are never enough hours in the day. Regardless of anything, if I received a call from my husband, sons or someone else I love, I would absolutely race to be there to help them.

While being selfless is a noble character trait, it inevitably catches up with us. Some of the "Wonder Women" I have met focus their attention on everything and anything except themselves. One day they wake up, they are 60 years old and realize how quickly time sped by. It dawns on them that by not paying attention to their own financial life, they are nowhere near where they thought they would be by this stage in life! In some cases, it may be too late to live the life they dreamed of in retirement. It took a while for me to realize I had fallen victim to this as well. During life, I worried about my family finding out about the abuse…I worried about my kids having what they needed…I worried about the people I was helping at church who had come to depend on me…I worried about *me* last. It's important to hang up the cape every once in a while, and check in to make sure you are on the right track financially, spiritually and physically. If you aren't, ask the questions and make the changes necessary. Put *yourself* on your to-do list!

After many years of counseling and healing, I have learned some very important lessons. It is extremely easy to blame others, whether it is our ex-husband, the government, our boss, etc. The sooner we take the responsibility for the choices we make and have the strength to ask for help, the better our lives will be. We are 100 percent responsible for what we do, what we *don't* do, and how we *respond* to what happens to us. We control whether or not we stay bitter for what has happened to us or make our lives *better.*

Our firm has helped hundreds of people take control of their financial life, prepare for their Golden Years, and enjoy the retirement they always dreamed of. I often wonder why my path in life went off course, why I experienced all that I did. I absolutely believe it was to prepare me for what I do now every single day of my life. It is a blessing to have the opportunity to share my story with others so they can learn from it, and it gives me the opportunity to accompany them on their new journey in life.

About Jennifer

Jennifer Calandra has established a nationwide reputation in the financial services community for her experience and compassion in working exclusively with women and their finances. She is a Registered Financial Consultant (RFC) and is a member of the International Association of Registered Financial Consultants.

Jennifer is the Cofounder and COO of Calandra Financial Group LLC. Clients of Jennifer enjoy her caring spirit and attention to their individual needs. She is the President and Creator of W.O.W. (Women of Wealth), a division of Calandra Financial Group that focuses on education and financial guidance for women. She is a member of the National Association of Professional Women (NAPW), in addition to Women in Financial Services (WIFS), and she has received the highest award the state of Kentucky can bestow, The Kentucky Colonel for civic leadership.

A native of the Philadelphia area, Jennifer currently resides in Kennesaw, Georgia, with her husband and business partner, Phil, and their four sons. Jennifer is an active member of Burnt Hickory Baptist Church and enjoys spending time with her family (which includes their dogs, Max and Harley), cooking, and riding with Phil on their Harley-Davidson motorcycle.

CHAPTER 9

HOW TO GET ANYTHING YOU WANT...SERIOUSLY, NO B.S.

BY NATHAN JUREWICZ

You've heard it before by some annoyingly positive self-help guru or "motivational" speaker who's been taking way too many happy pills: "You just gotta speak your goals into existence by declaring them to your friends and family members. You gotta declare what you really want!" Yeah, right. Most people tell me, "Easier said than done."

Not everyone, just 99 percent of the population. They go on to tell me about their situation as if it's so different than anyone else's on the face of the planet. I often hear things like: "You haven't met my spouse, Nathan. They will leave me if I try that because I got bills to pay." "I get what you're saying, but if I try this and fail my friends/spouse/co-workers will say they told me so." "That law of attraction stuff is B.S. That crap doesn't work. I live in the real world." There are more excuses (I'm sorry, I meant to type "responses") than I'm even listing here, but trust me, I've heard just about all of them.

The truth is by telling your friends/family/co-workers what you intend to accomplish it holds you accountable and puts so much fear in you that it forces you to take action and actually do it. Most people would rather channel their fear into being more afraid of what will happen if they fail (meaning, they will get the "I told you so" speech). In a minute, I'll get to the "happy-medium solution" that will make everything make sense, so just keep reading. I'm not here to tell you how much of a loser you are for not having the balls to declare your goals because, at your core, nobody is a loser. Just keep reading.

The difference between the 1 percent and the 99 percent is that they are more afraid of what will happen if they don't even try than they are if they try and fail. And if they fail and don't get what they want after they publicly embarrassed themselves, you know what happens? It normally leads to something else that was better than the original goal that they were thinking about the first place.

Read that last sentence again. It's a big one. How do we declare our goals to our friends or family and believe in unicorns without them thinking that we are crazy? You have to make two sets of goals:

1. Public Declaration Goals: These are the goals that are only a few levels above what any normal person would think is achievable. Goals that you know for a fact that you can do.

2. Unicorn Goals: These are the goals that are so crazy that if you went public with them, your friends would tell you that you're crazy and you may actually get locked up in the psych ward. "That can't happen, Nathan. It's impossible and doesn't exist."

Yeah, I know it doesn't exist. But neither do unicorns. With unicorn goals, you have to stay silent about them until the time is right. Here is an example: A homeless guys declares to all his homeless friends that he's going to be a professional Nascar driver. On top of this, he is going to win the Daytona 500. For sure, that guy is getting ignored or locked up in the psych ward. On the other hand, let's say a guy has a real band that is playing music at local bars and is building a following of local fans. He tells people that he's going to get a record deal. He could even say, "I want to be the next Justin Bieber" before he even has one fan. People may still think he's crazy, but he won't get locked up.

One of my students, James Alexander, did exactly this. He started playing the bass guitar in high school and got really good. He joined a band and then revealed his unicorn goal of opening for the Dave Matthews band. All of his 99 percenter friends told him he was crazy and that it couldn't happen. Twelve months later, you know what happened? You guessed it, he opened for the Dave Matthews band and proved all his friends wrong! Think about how satisfying that must have felt! (In case you don't know… it felt awesome!).

The steps necessary to actually achieve that goal will be released in the book I'm writing, *Get Anything You Want, No B.S.* So stay tuned. Here's an excerpt from *Get Anything You Want, No B.S.*:

"But wait Nathan! What about my spouse?" This one is more sensitive and I don't want to be single-handedly responsible for breaking up any marriages, so read carefully and tread lightly. You have to set a "frame" for your spouse to live up to when declaring your goals. This is called *Frame Control* and we will be going into extreme depth on this subject in the book. I'll give you an example: Jay is married to Sue. Jay did everything he was supposed to do in life according to what society told him to do.

- Went to college

- Got the degree

- Got the $100,000 per year job

- Invested in his 401(k)

- Lost most of his 401(k)

He's now 42 years and won't be able to retire comfortably at the rate he's going unless he hits the lottery. He has two options:

Option 1: Stay comfortable and "safe" and just work his job until he withers away and dies or somehow gets fired through no fault of his own. Then possibly go protest on Wall Street and judge the big, evil corporations for not giving him his fair share. (I'm not saying that the big corporations are or are not evil. All I'm saying is let's call a spade a spade.)

Option 2: Do something about it: Get a higher paying job or go start his own business and change his life.

Since my background is in "make money in real estate by flipping houses" and "make money online by teaching people a specific skill," we will use real estate as an example. I'm going to assume he wants to do real estate. You are going to observe what I'm doing to see how I'm teaching people how to get anything they want on the internet and just copy me without giving me any money (unless, of course, you want to). Fair enough?

Here is what Jay should *not* do when explaining to his wife what he wants to do to accomplish his goals: "Honey I want to go to this seminar on how to flip houses because, financially, we're not going to be able retire at the rate we are currently going at now. It all seems legit, and this one dude was just like me and is now making a boatload of cash flipping houses. The seminar is only $97 to attend."

That is a *bad* idea. Because what could happen at the seminar is that people are going to use all kinds of Jedi mind trickery to get you buy a $10,000 coaching program that you can't even really afford. Some of the less ethical organizations in this industry will tell everyone at the beginning of the seminar that if you want to make money in real estate you have to go into debt. Then they will instruct you to call your credit card companies to increase your credit limit during the seminar. At the end of the seminar they will tell you, "You actually can make money in real estate with no money and no credit but only if you have the secret, magic method. We teach you how to do it in our coaching program, which is $10,000." You reply, "I can't afford that, and my wife will kill me." They then respond by telling you, "But you just told me that you were able to increase your credit limit by at least $15,000, didn't you? It only makes sense to spend it on coaching so you don't need money for real estate right?"

Jay is now stuck. He has no way to get out of this sale because he got duped by the super-persuasive con man. His choice is either to put it on his credit card and then explain to his wife what happened or to walk out and tell them, "No, this isn't for me." (Which is what he should do.)

Disclaimer: I'm not saying there is anything wrong with selling coaching or consulting services for a profit. I'm a capitalist. All I'm saying is it's a disgusting habit if you're doing it in such a way that preys on selling services to people that they can't really afford. I myself sell consulting services that cost an exorbitant amount of money, but I only offer my services to people who can easily afford it. Make sense?

Here is what Jay *should* have done: He should first set an example for his spouse by doing something small and spending as little money as they can comfortably afford. If he can't afford anything, then spend nothing. Then he should set a "Frame" that his wife has to live up to. *(I'm going to give an example of this in just a sec, so just chill. I can't explain the secrets to life in one paragraph. But you're smart and you already knew that. Not everyone does. This paragraph is meant for the idiots that need instant gratification, not you. If you have a spouse that 100 percent completely supports you no matter what, then count your blessings because you're extremely lucky. If you have a history of buying into opportunities and doing nothing with them, can you really blame he/she for not supporting you? Don't blame them. Place the blame on you because if that's what your track record is, then it is your fault. Just accept it, and don't do it again, deal?)*

So, anyway, Jay needs to set a frame that his wife has to live up to, but he has a track record of buying into opportunities/seminars/whatever and doing nothing with them. The following paragraph is how he should approach it. I'm going to bold all the text where it specifically states the frame that his spouse has to live up to.

"Honey, I just want to let you know that **I appreciate you standing by my side even when I spent money on some so-called "business opportunities" in the past.** The truth is, those opportunities were actually really good, but I didn't take the action necessary to make them happen. I'm working on it. I realize it may not be wise to go and blow money that we don't have on another opportunity, but at the same time, I don't want to stay where we are financially and I don't see an "out" with the current job I have. I'm going to try it again and hold myself accountable by blogging about my journey to close my first real estate deal within the next 90 days. I understand that I could completely fail, but if I put it out there publicly, it will force me to take action, and who knows, the exposure from Facebook might even open some doors and get "in" with certain real estate people that I normally wouldn't have. **I can definitely see that you've been making some changes in the past few months, and I know that it has been difficult for you to tolerate me.** All I'm asking is for you to believe in me while I'm on this journey. I'm not going to spend any more money on seminars or coaching until the real estate business can actually pay for that. **I appreciate everything that you've done for me.**"

If you come from a completely humble and sincere point of view, they almost can't not support you. Yet, when I explain this concept, I've had people tell me, "Yeah, but Nathan my spouse hasn't supported me. They haven't been making any changes, so screw them!" It doesn't matter. If you really love your spouse, you will lead by example, even if they are not in a "loving you back kind of mood" (that's called unconditional love, btw. Neat concept—you should try it).

Don't lie, though. Meaning, don't tell them you've noticed that they are doing something if they aren't really doing it. Instead, word it like, "I can tell that deep down you want to support me, but haven't because of my 'shiny object' syndrome," or something more like that. Deep down that is true, even if you think it's not. People are inherently good. It's the influence around them and the actions you may have taken that may have caused them to shut down and become "bitter."

Every situation is different, and you need to try to avoid worrying about an exact script. Trying to copy my script exactly is a bad idea because it probably won't come out of your mouth correctly, and even worse, may even come across as insincere. Instead, focus on getting better at learning Frame Control. In the book, I will break down this concept in even more detail, so if you're not confident enough to declare your goal to your friends, then don't worry about it yet.

So you're homework assignment is to declare your goals to your friends, on Facebook, and on a blog (you can get one made on Fiverr.com for five bucks), if you feel comfortable. I always follow my own advice so here are my three declarations (the non-Unicorn ones):

1. I hereby declare that I'm going to write a *New York Times* #1 best-selling book that teaches people how to get anything they want (no b.s.) by using the exact same strategies taught in the book to launch the book.

2. I'm also going to become a scratch golfer by the end of the year using the strategies taught in the book. (Yes, it applies to athletes also). I'm currently about a 20 handicap and on any given day and will shoot anywhere between an 85 to a 95 for a regular 6,300 yard course.

3. I'm going to have my own TV show on a regular network. (This is already in the works but hasn't gotten sold to a network with real sponsors yet.)

Now, for my Unicorn Goals:

I can't tell you. It's a secret!

I'm using all the strategies that I teach to get what I want, and you're going to get to see it unfold on www.leopardpill.com. You can root me, on or just watch me fail miserably. I'm cool either way. I'm not afraid to fail.

Be Bold. Make Things Happen.

About Nathan

Who is Nathan Jurewicz?

He has leopard-print hair, he intentionally underdresses at private events, and he uses these things to fuel his insecurities to keep himself single.

But let's back up.

After being secretly bullied through the eighth grade, his parents further bulldozed his social skills by pulling him out of public school and home schooling him. (In all honestly, he does have amazing parents, and you're about to see why.)

After making no money as a street juggler, he stumbled into retail sales, which is just as glamorous as it sounds. Eventually, he became an entrepreneur and excelled in stuff like real estate and internet marketing.

Despite these things, he's made a habit of stumbling into opportunity after opportunity. By accident…sort of (not really). I don't understand it either.

He teaches actionable, step-by-step methods for getting anything you want. (Unless you're trying to start a meth lab. Knock that shit off and get your ass to church.)

His heroes are Tiger Woods, Tim Ferris, Tony Stark, Dudley DoRight, Jesus, and that dude from the viral Dollar Shave Club YouTube video (Google it).

His favorite thing to do is inspiring others to achieve their goals (no matter how big or small that goal may be) in a completely unconventional way. This isn't the "Ra-Ra" feel good stuff either.

And he's about to teach you how to get anything you want.

Seriously…No B.S.

CHAPTER 10

INTERNET MARKETING FOR LAWYERS 101

BY MICHAEL WADDINGTON, ESQ.

If your goal for your business is to be like everyone else in your industry: moderately successful, average and predictable, then skip to the next chapter. In the hyper-competitive world of running a small business, being average or predictable will guarantee that your small business will fail.

After receiving my Juris Doctor from Temple Law School, I served in the U.S. Army as a criminal lawyer. Upon completing my service in the Army, at the age of 32, my wife and I opened our own law firm following conventional wisdom passed down from generations of seasoned attorneys; we were nearly broke within six months. Our overhead was too high, our marketing was ineffective, we were charging too little, and we were working long hours with little to show for it.

We had followed the advice and guidance of many local lawyers; how could we be failing? After analyzing our situation, we realized that the lawyers that were giving us advice were average. They made a decent living, but they were not extremely successful, nor were they viewed as the top lawyers in our city. They spent their time fighting over scraps, struggling to make a living. We did not want an average law practice; we wanted an outstanding law practice. Therefore, we had to model our business on outstanding lawyers, not just in our city, but also from across the U.S.

My goal was to become a nationally respected lawyer with a successful law practice by age 40. Instead of learning from average lawyers, I studied the best, the top 1 percent of solo practitioners. I attended expensive legal conferences where top lawyers hung out and shared advice. I talked to top lawyers and learned their secrets. I read their books and learned about their failures and successes. Like a dry sponge, I soaked up their wisdom and I was on the path to success. I then improved on their techniques by leveraging the power of the internet and technology. By applying technology to the techniques used by top lawyers, I was able to grow my business exponentially.

By the age of 34, ahead of schedule, I was an internationally known lawyer with a lucrative law practice. I regularly had cases covered by CNN and *The New York Times* and every major newspaper. Business was booming, and we dominated our competitors using the internet and technology. In 2009, I started helping other lawyers implement my techniques to build profitable law firms. To date, I have helped hundreds of lawyers build and market their law firms. While the principles I learned from the top lawyers still apply, they must be combined with cutting-edge technology to gain a vital edge over your competition.

FIVE PILLARS OF LEGAL MARKETING SUCCESS

1. Define Ultra-Specific Marketing Goals and Timelines

While basic, you must define ultra-specific marketing goals and corresponding timelines. Write down who the perfect client for your firm is and what their typical fee would be. Then calculate how much money you want to earn monthly and annually. Next, figure out how many of your ideal clients you would need to reach your goals. Shape your marketing strategy around targeting these clients and reaching your set goals.

Many lawyers never determine what their marketing goals are. Everything you do to market your law firm must contribute to your reaching your specific goals. Logically, any law firm's objective should be to obtain more clients and generate more revenue for their business. Where most lawyers fail is that they do not set specific marketing goals and build a strategy around reaching those specific goals.

Many lawyers haphazardly waste time and money on internet marketing campaigns not specifically tailored to help them reach their set goals.

For example, lawyers often want to spend money on social media campaigns using Facebook and Twitter. Social media tools are useful for some businesses but are a waste of time and money for others. Before you spend money on any marketing, including social media, you should specifically articulate, in writing:

- How will this marketing help me reach my goals?
- How does this type of marketing fall into my overall marketing strategy?
- What will my return on investment be?
- How will this marketing attract our ideal client?

If this type of marketing will not help you reach your goals and does not play an important role in your overall marketing strategy, then don't do it. Don't waste the time and money.

Across the United States, many criminal defense lawyers spend thousands of dollars building their Facebook pages. I have never had a single criminal attorney tell me that they got a client from their Facebook page. Therefore, a criminal defense lawyer is probably better off spending time and money on another more profitable marketing technique.

If you handle high-asset divorces, then you should focus on targeting people with money. Thus, putting law firm ads on bus stop benches would likely not help you attract wealthy divorce clients. This sounds like common sense, but lawyers across the United States spend years and waste tens of thousands of dollars on advertising that does not target the clients they want and need to reach their goals.

2. Be Respected and Visible in the Local Community

Your goal as a lawyer and businessperson is to become a credible authority with expertise sought by the community. You want the people with whom you live and work to recognize you in the community, but you must be present and active in the community for this to happen.

Being present means participating in the community while going about the business of living your life. Many lawyers think that they are too busy to volunteer. Naturally, their work and family take up the bulk of their time, so family time and free time are precious commodities. One way to get involved in the community and spend time with family is to choose an activity that involves both. If your child plays soccer, coach the soccer team. People will always ask what you do for a living, which creates an opportunity to hand them a business card without having to spend any of your marketing budget to prompt them to ask for one. People tend to hire people that they know and like. Getting involved and respected by the community is vital to building your reputation and business.

3. Be Seen as "The" Expert

To be viewed as "the" top lawyer in your field, you must build your reputation and gain social acceptance and recognition as an expert. The easiest way to accomplish this is to gain positive media exposure. Any time you or your firm are written up in the local paper, a community newsletter or have a case mentioned on television, this adds to your credibility and establishes you as a trusted authority and sets yourself apart from your competitors. Get as much exposure as possible; volunteer to teach at local high schools or sponsor law clubs. Get endorsements from other attorneys or include testimonials from happy clients.

Credibility cannot be invented. You have to do the work to build yourself up. You must take on challenging cases and go above and beyond what the average lawyer does. For example, to become a famous criminal lawyer, you must take on and win high-profile cases. Books and movies are made about brave trial lawyers that fight cases despite the overwhelming odds. Nobody admires a lazy attorney who spends his days pleading all of his clients guilty or handling super cheap divorces, and few people want to hire such an attorney.

If you want to become a top lawyer, you must become an expert and be perceived as an expert by the community.

4. Price Your Services Properly

One of the quickest ways to position yourself as an established, successful attorney is to bump your rate up above many of your competitors. People do associate price with excellence. People will complain—in a bragging way—about their successful and *expensive* attorney. It is human nature. If you under-quote your fees, you are often perceived as cheap and less experienced and not as good as a more expensive lawyer, whether it is true of not. By charging more, you will be able to spend more time on your cases and be more readily available to your clients, which is worth the premium price.

5. Never Do Anything Worthless

Many lawyers waste hours every day on frivolous matters. They do the same when it comes to marketing their business. They waste time and thousands of dollars on marketing that does not bring in clients. For example, when was the last time you reached for the phone book to find a product or service? Do you even know where your phone book is? Unbelievably, the phone book is where the many lawyers continue to spend the bulk of their marketing dollars. It sounds unbelievable, but it is true. Check the phone book website in your city and you will see that the majority of lawyers still pay for banner ads and enhanced listings. In my experience not many people go to the phone book or the phone book website to look for a lawyer—they go to Google.

Still others, thinking bigger must be better and lured by empty promises from the big marketing companies, find themselves locked into costly long-term contracts with poor results. Bigger may not be better, but it is more expensive. The simple fact is that if your practice is not on the first page of search engine results, your online presence is worthless. Whether your budget is $1,000 a month or $10,000 a month, make sure every dollar is well spent. Most of all, do not throw money away on a website that you are too busy or too unable to maintain. With every marketing endeavor, you should make sure that you are targeting your ideal client. Otherwise, you are losing time, money, and moneymaking opportunities.

HIRE A MARKETING EXPERT AND
LET THEM DO THEIR JOB

As a lawyer and SEO consultant with 15 years of experience, it is frustrating to talk to lawyers who believe they know everything there is to know about internet marketing. Nobody knows everything about SEO. I don't know everything. I am constantly learning and keeping up with SEO trends, which are constantly changing.

Many lawyers know enough about SEO to make them dangerous. I have had these "know-it-all lawyers" call me for a consultation and then repeatedly interrupt me mid-sentence and say things like, "I already know about Google+, but I want a Twitter account. . ." (when they have not even claimed their Google+ profile), or "I already know about link building, but I want to dominate the New York City area for criminal defense, and I don't want to spend more than $1,000... and I want to be No. 1 by next month."

Worst of all, the know-it-alls call for a consultation and then waste 45 minutes of my time arguing with me about why I am wrong, bashing their previous five SEO companies, and trying to prove that they know it all about SEO. It reminds me of law school, where first-year students think they know more than everyone else, including the law professor. Know-it-all lawyers are obnoxious and often have trouble becoming top lawyers. Their personality gets in the way. Just because someone has a law license does not mean that they are smarter than everyone else, including their SEO consultant.

Bottom line: Don't be that know-it-all when it comes to SEO. Listening to a 45-minute talk about SEO during a bar luncheon does not qualify you to tell your SEO specialist what to do. Lawyers should leave SEO to a SEO professional. Find a qualified expert, take their advice, and be patient.

IS YOUR INTERNET MARKETING CAMPAIGN ON THE RIGHT TRACK?

Does your internet marketing campaign reach and convert your ideal client? To determine if your internet marketing campaign is on track, you need to be able to answer the following questions:

- **What keywords am I targeting? (i.e., "Miami Bankruptcy Lawyer")?** Know what keywords to target to reach your chosen audience. Use the wrong keywords, and you will be wasting time and money attracting cases that you do not want.

- **Where does my site currently rank in Google and Google+ for these keywords? (You must check this monthly)?** Tracking your website rank is one way to determine if your internet marketing campaign is on track. You should expect to see positive upward movement in your website's rank. If not, then you must analyze your strategy and tweak it as necessary.

- **How long are visitors staying on my site, what are they viewing on my site, and are they sharing information from my site?** Studying the interaction and behavior of people visiting your website is crucial to understanding whether your site is helpful and useful to your visitors. You must strive to make your site as beneficial to your visitors as possible so that they see you as a thought leader in your area of expertise. If most visitors are leaving your website after 10 seconds, then you need to improve the quality of our content.

- **Is my site 100 percent optimized for these keywords?** If not, what needs to be fixed? An SEO professional can determine if your website is under- or over-optimized for your keywords and adjust it accordingly. If your website is overly optimized, then search engines may penalize it. If your website is under optimized, then it will not rank for competitive internet searches. Finding the right balance is key.

- **Is my website properly designed for Google?** What can be improved? Your website's code must be as modern as possible, load quickly, and be easily readable by Google search engine spiders.

- **Is my site properly designed for my customers? How can I improve their experience?** Your customers want information. Give them what they want. Videos—in which you discuss your area of expertise, the law—give potential clients far more insight into your firm than does your resume or your law school awards. Videos show your credibility or they don't. Speak about something you know well. Speak with conviction and don't try to wing it on something you don't know much about. You should be able to talk about the top 10 questions asked of you most frequently. Create a list of those top 10 questions potential clients ask when you have an initial consultation and then use them to film 10, 1 minute videos for your website.

- **Does my site give five reasons a client should hire me?** This is basic, but most lawyer websites do not convey to the visitor why they should hire that lawyer. Listing your resume and the history of your firm is not enough. Your site should state the top reasons why you are an expert and the best qualified lawyer for the job.

- **Is my Google+ Listing claimed?** Claiming your Google+ business listing is easy and free, yet many businesses have not properly claimed their listing. If your listing is not claimed, then you will not rank in the local search results. You must claim your listing, or you will not get local clients online.

- **Is my Google+ listing optimized? What needs to be done?** Your Google+ listing must be completely filled out and optimized. Properly optimizing your listing is crucial if you want to appear in the top seven in Google Local search results.

- **Is my site consistent with Google algorithm updates?** Be prepared to make changes when the algorithms change. If Google changes the way it ranks websites, you need to be ready to counter it. Otherwise, you are running the same tired play when the game has changed. You don't keep using your running game when your players are being sacked right and left.

ESTABLISH AN ADVERTISING BUDGET

One way to determine your budget is to begin by determining how much you want to make. If you want to bring in half a million dollars, you aren't going to get there by spending $1,000 a month on marketing. A good rule of thumb is to spend about 10 percent of your goal on marketing to bring in that $500,000. Most people want to spend as little as possible and make as much money as possible, an unrealistic expectation.

MODIFY YOUR MARKETING PLAN ANNUALLY

Don't be afraid to cut marketing expenses that don't net you revenue. Reallocate those resources into something that is working or a marketing tactic you haven't tried before. Many law firm marketing plans fail because the attorneys aren't willing to try something new or because they don't know what isn't working because they aren't tracking their results. Aggressively spending to wisely market and track your campaigns will yield you more in the end. Spreading your advertising dollars too thin can result in ineffectiveness on all fronts.

TRACK YOUR MARKETING RESULTS

If you do not take the time to track your marketing, you will waste valuable resources and will not see a return on investment. You can track via telephone numbers by designating which numbers are used in which marketing avenues. You can use Google Analytics and Google Webmaster Tools, free, to track the success of your website marketing campaign.

One final thought: Always properly vet and research the people you hire to do your marketing. I would venture to say that at least 50 percent of law firms use a marketing company who *also* represents their competition. As a lawyer, you cannot ethically represent conflicting parties. Why would you expect your marketing company to be able to market for you and your competitors as well? Ask about their experience, and make sure that the person you are hiring is going to be accountable for getting the job done. Many company's sales representatives sell you with big promises and then pass you off to someone else to do the work, never to be heard from again.

About Michael

Michael S. Waddington, Esq., started building and marketing websites in 1997, when he was a first-year law student at Temple University School of Law. He is now one of the most recognized experts in the field of internet marketing for lawyers and online video marketing.

He is the founder and president of Legal Niche Pros LLC, a boutique internet marketing firm that manages high-level marketing campaigns for law firms across the United States.

Legal Niche Pros excels at video production and marketing, SEO, website design, social media, and strategic planning for law firm marketing campaigns.

Michael is also a noted commentator, writer, and lecturer on internet marketing and the ethics of lawyer marketing. His Lawyer Marketing YouTube channel has over 2,500 subscribers and 365,000 unique views.

Michael was a former Army JAG lawyer and is recognized as a national authority on military law as well as a noted media consultant. Michael has tried over 150 contested criminal jury cases worldwide (in the United States, Europe and Asia).

Michael has been reported on and quoted by hundreds of major media sources worldwide as well as provided consultation services to "60 Minutes," "ABC Nightline," CNN, CBS, the 2010-12 Golden Globe-winning TV series "The Good Wife," CNN Investigative Reports, Katie Couric, the BBC, German Public Television and others.

In 2009, he appeared in the CNN Documentary, the "Killings at the Canal." Some of his cases have been the subject of books and movies, including "Taxi to the Dark Side," a 2007 Academy Award Winner, and Brian De Palma's "Redacted." DePalma also directed "Scarface" and "Carlito's Way."

Michael was born in New Castle, Pennsylvania. He graduated Magna Cum Laude from Duquesne University in Pittsburgh, with a BA degree. He earned his law degree from Temple University School of Law in Philadelphia. At Temple, he successfully completed, with honors, Temple's Nationally No. 1 Ranked Trial Lawyer Training Program.

He is a licensed attorney and a member of good standing in the following State Bar Associations: Pennsylvania, Georgia, New Jersey and South Carolina.

LinkedIn profile: www.linkedin.com/in/michaelwaddingtonlawyer
Legal Niche Pros website: www.legalnichepros.com

CHAPTER 11

WHEN LIFE HITS A WALL... BOUNCE BACK TO GIVE BACK

BY LIANA LEORDEANU

Ten years ago and just out of college, I was riding high. I had a prestigious job with a global health-care company. Within two years, I was managing a sales force of 1,500 people and launching pharmaceutical drugs as a National Product Launch Manager. I was making a fantastic six-figure income, being able to buy anything I wanted, go anywhere I wanted, and having dinner with some of the finest people in business. Although I worked nonstop, I loved it, and I felt I was living my ideal life. I was well on my way to rising to the top…and then something happened that changed my life forever…

FACING MYSELF

It was three months later when I awoke from the coma. My parents heard this terrible scream coming from the hospital room where they thought I was unconscious. They rushed in to find me unhooked from all the IVs and medical devices, standing terrified in front of the mirror, examining my disfigured face. I thought I was in a nightmare seeing myself so horribly disfigured. I had little ability to comprehend if it was reality or a bad dream. I was truly blessed to wake from the coma… and in time I also had to awaken to the realization that my previous life—the one I used to define as an "ideal life," with all the trappings of success—was over.

TRAGEDY, RECOVERY, NEW LIFE MEANING

Driving home one evening, I had a terrible car accident, caused by an unknown driver. As I turned sharply to avoid the oncoming vehicle, I hit a black ice patch and lost control of my car, hitting a rock wall on the side of the road at 50 miles per hour, and the air bag did not deploy. The accident was so horrific that my head and my face were completely disfigured with almost every bone in my face and skull fractured or missing. The dashboard went all the way to my brain, crushing my forehead, my nose and the sinuses. The top of the car crushed through my temple, fracturing most of my skull bones, the cheek bones, destroying my left eye, and my jaw. I was left unconscious in a severe coma at the site of the accident. I was unrecognizable.

Arriving at the emergency room, the surgeons diagnosed me with Severe Traumatic Brain Injury (TBI), giving me a slim chance of survival of 24 hours and very little chance of awakening from my coma. If I miraculously did, I would likely be permanently disabled, in a near-vegetative state for the rest of my life with memory deficits, motor skill problems, speech impairments, and very little cognitive ability.

It has taken 33 reconstructive surgeries to piece me back together, but I feel blessed for beating the odds and for being given a second chance. The person I am today has been 10 years in the making, and I don't take a day of life for granted. In spite of my surgeons' initial predictions, I recovered fully and have regained all my damaged abilities to the fullest. Doctors today consider me a medical miracle from a recovery standpoint since tests show almost no signs that I've had severe TBI. It truly WAS a miracle! I am eternally grateful for the enormous dedication I received from the numerous surgeons, family and friends who devoted their time and attention to me so I could recover as well as I did. I am most grateful to God since I now realize He has a great plan for my life.

My road to recovery has been long and painful and full of challenges. In addition to the physical trauma, there have been financial troubles caused by the inability to work for a few years after the accident while simultaneously having to pay for expensive surgeries. Health problems, lack of career, financial hardship, and deformed facial features all resulted in feeling excluded from my extensive social network, as if I no longer belonged. I was also affected from a pride standpoint. My looks and success status were things I had been proud of, and they had been severely altered. Getting back to "normal," let alone "successful" seemed impossible.

Throughout my ordeal, there were times when I thought I was going to die. Giving up would have been so much easier, and sometimes, it was tempting. For a while I asked, "Why me, God? Why would you let this happen?" I didn't get any answers to my question, just pain. One day, I started thinking that maybe there was a reason I survived. Instead of in a sense blaming Him for my problem, I changed the question, and instead I asked "Why did I survive?" "What is your plan for me now?" As a result, I started to reflect on what I took for granted prior to this accident. I found that what I once thought was my "ideal life" may not have been so ideal after all, and I started to see things differently. I decided to trust that God had a different plan for me now; a better plan, and in order for me to live that plan, I had to "Bounce Back to Give Back"! This time God answered my question. Bouncing back from this has healed me and made me passionate about living a life that gives back to others. This is how I discovered fulfillment.

SHIFT YOUR THINKING, CHANGE YOUR LIFE

Surviving and overcoming this terrible tragedy required I navigate through incredible challenges. One magnificent truth about humans is that we have the power to change our lives based on the smallest realizations. One of the ways to do that is to shift our thinking and our focus. Throughout my journey, I've uncovered some important tips to achieving fulfillment, happiness and success that I'd like to share with you.

Although miracles happen, a miracle by itself is not enough. What matters most is what you choose to do with your miracle, no matter how small or large it is. My survival and outstanding recovery is a miracle, and I am so grateful to my Lord, my father in Heaven, for giving me a second chance at life. But what matters most is what I choose to do with this gift, this second chance. It is your choices in life and beliefs that define your destiny and bring about results. No matter what happens, you always have a choice to decide how you feel and what you are going to do. You can choose to be exceptional, embrace life, and live it to the fullest … or you can choose to give up. The most difficult aspect of my trauma was regaining confidence and learning to accept my deformed face that suddenly replaced my previous lovely face. It took time for the physical and emotional reconstruction, but I can now say, "This is what I have been given in life. I can choose to be miserable and give up or I can embrace it and make it a success story." I chose to embrace life, and I haven't regretted my decision. I believe it was because of that decision that I figured out my life/career purpose and recently got engaged to the man of my dreams. Things will always happen in life. Tragedies and challenges do shape our lives, but they do not have to define who we are. You get to choose how you define it or if you are going to let those things define you.

Another big lesson I learned was that you can focus on the wrong things in life by placing too much emphasis on financial success. This can keep you from the deeper rewards of following your calling, your passions and dreams. The person I was 10 years ago, busy and motivated to get that next promotion was just a Little Liana. Today, I have decided to step into the BIG LIANA. Instead of looking through a small window of need and fear, she now has a very large window of opportunity, compassion and care for all people. Today, I realize that financial success and personal fulfillment are two separate things, which can exist side by side. Achieving true life fulfillment is more about experiencing the joy of giving rather than the happiness of receiving. The law of reciprocity and the law of attraction say that you can't expect to get back love if your love has a lock on it. We get back what we put out. We should love and care for as many people as possible and focus on those around us in order to receive with abundance. I urge you to step into your BIG SELF, whatever that means for you, and fulfillment in your life will follow.

Life has wonderful moments as well as struggles, adversities and sometimes heart wrenching moments. Our attitude toward adversities is the key ingredient that determines our ability to overcome them. How do you define life? Do you see it as a "contest" or a "trial" where you could either win or lose? Or maybe you see it as an "ocean" that can be can be calm or rough? Do you see it as a "gift" to be shared with dear ones? Regardless how you see life, you need to accept that life is unpredictable, and adversity most likely will happen. Prepare yourself today by **cultivating faith, courage,** and **perseverance** to overcome hardship and triumph. I spent several years after my accident feeling so much regret and loss over my previous life, getting **caught up in the** *self-pity* game, struggling to understand "why it happened to me?" I was living locked up in the prison of the past by projecting my 10 years of suffering into the present. Then I realized that dwelling on something I had no control over was fueling bitterness, resentment, causing me to act like a victim, and none of these feelings helped the healing process or overcoming any sort of obstacle. Just like a fighter whose been knocked down, I had to get up off the canvas of life and fight back since I decided I wasn't a victim and I didn't want to be acting like one. I figured bouncing back and healing would be the best way to live a fulfilling life, and in doing that, I could share my story with others. Once I changed my attitude toward the event and I stopped allowing the past to control my present, a world of wonderful opportunities opened up to me that I was previously denying myself. I became aware of the present moment, all around me, amazingly available and full of tremendous joy, life ready to embrace me in its veil of opportunities.

Each of us has been given specific gifts, talents and passions so that we can serve others. Too often, many of us live a scripted life or a life that may not even be intended or good for us. I realized that in order to change my life and go for my dreams, I also had to appreciate my blessings again and be grateful for the numerous gifts I have, despite this trauma and injury. Once I recognized and appreciated that, I was able to get a clear vision of how I could serve others and what I wanted my life to look like. You don't need a crisis like I had to shift your thinking and create that extraordinary life. Shift it now! Don't delay!

COURAGEOUSLY FOLLOW YOUR DREAMS, WITHOUT DELAY AND WITHOUT EXCUSES

Pursuing your dreams requires courage, so decide now to be courageous! The trauma that I endured helped me discover my true calling in life, empowered me to follow my dream and to not give up, despite the terrible obstacles. I could have chosen failure or mediocrity, but instead I chose success and to inspire others to achieve their dreams and life goals. This choice required COURAGE. Because of what happened to me, I would love to be a role model for others to not delay pursuing their dreams and goals, and to start doing things they have a passion for. There's always going to be a reason for not doing what you want, but when you start pursuing your dream, that dream takes on a life of its own, and gives you positive energy and inspiration. After I realized I was kept alive for a purpose, I dreamed of inspiring people to believe they can accomplish whatever will create happiness and success in their lives so they live an extraordinary life that is full of joy and passion. I didn't have this dream originally when I was climbing the corporate ladder. This dream has been unveiled after the accident. Sometimes you have to re-evaluate what's going to make you fulfilled. I've been waiting for 10 years to muster up the courage to go for my dream! If you have a dream, wondering if you should go for it, don't wait; do it now! I'm doing it, so you have no excuses. I have learned that courage is not absence of fear, but acting in the presence of fear, in spite of fear.

All my challenges did not take away my desire to go after my dreams and do what makes my life fulfilled. My Transformational Speaking and Life Mentoring business wouldn't exist if I had continued to look back and live in the past. Doing that would have prevented me from sharing my story with the world, which is how I want to give back by inspiring others. When it feels like something has been taken away from you, release it and keep moving forward. What's done is done, and there are plenty of new and wonderful things to be discovered if you look ahead and not behind.

We all experience traumas and obstacles in life, but these adversities can be the catalyst for living the life you were born to live. Don't take a single day for granted and don't give up. It's my hope that my story will encourage you to overcome whatever is holding you back in your life. I now teach my clients strategies to work through their fears, grief, withdrawals, resentments and shame so they can move around whatever they perceive to be an obstacle on their way to success and fulfillment in life. If you are still wondering if you can do what you really want to do, make the decision to take that step today and go for it! Don't wait. Do it now!!

Let me leave you with this: Whatever is holding you back, whether it's physical, or emotional, or financial—whatever it is, I want you to commit to bouncing back to give back. Bounce back to give back! Dare to dream, to make your vision your mission, and ACCEPT NO EXCUSES FOR YOURSELF!

About Liana

Liana Leordeanu, a highly respected speaker, life strategist and author is passionate about inspiring others to uncover their purpose, stretch beyond their self-imposed limits and experience the greatness that is within them.

Always a high achiever, Liana landed her first job at a global health-care company, quickly climbing the corporate ladder and being promoted through the ranks in seven short years. She rose to positions of prominence, including business development, corporate trainer, national product launch manager, and managed a 1,500 person sales staff. At the top of her career, her life changed permanently one night due to a tragic car accident. With extensive brain trauma and the near complete collapse of her facial bone structure, Liana had to endure a journey that would reshape her life. She miraculously survived through a coma and numerous reconstructive surgeries. She grieved for the person she once was, only to find there was more to herself than could have ever imagined. Only during her grieving process and throughout her long recovery did she realize she had been focusing on the wrong things: Believing that career success and financial prosperity were the most important factors in having a happy life, her profound shift from asking, "Why did this happen to me?" to "Why did I survive?" fundamentally changed the way she saw the world. She is now dedicated to spreading her message of hope and that it's never too late to define your destiny. Through Refacing Life, Liana empowers her audience and clients through her story and unique laser-beam perspective that helps others excel at being truly happy and to create life choices that reflect that desire, as well as helping people discover what's *really* important and how they should make life choices that reflect that.

Her success in the corporate world of sales and marketing, combined with her achievements as a business owner, have given Liana particular insight into how people relate to themselves and to each other and why those relationships are critical components of living a healthy and happy life. She believes and teaches the Law of Reciprocity. She shows others how by giving more, they will receive more, and when this happens, life is reshaped, and they can finally live in a way that directly reflects who they were born to be. Her clients say she is "inspiring, supportive and compassionate," as she teaches strategies that allow them to work through their fears, grief and obstacles that keep them blocked from success.

Liana knows from personal experience that life is infinitely precious. She knows that life can offer second chances and opportunities to commit to following your dreams. Liana encourages others to pursue what really moves them, as well as how to shift their thinking and focus in order to design and develop the extraordinary life of freedom and fulfillment they deserve. Merging biology, neuroscience, her experience in the medical field, as well as spirituality and business savvy, Liana powerfully motivates others to recondition their mind-set so they can overcome any adversity and use life-altering circumstances to create a life of purpose and passion.

Liana has earned the NLP/Life Coaching Practitioner Certification and is currently working on her Master NLP and Time Line Therapy Certifications as well as the EFT Certification.

As a member of the Giving Foundation of Wake Up Women, LLC, (a resource foundation with a mission to encourage women around the world to discover their passion and turn that passion into profit), Liana is a contributing author to a series of forthcoming books, including *Wake Up Women Be You: Spread Your Wings and Fly and Wake Up Women Pony X-Stress: A Better Way to Mane-tain,* dedicated to empower women worldwide to live the life of joy and prosperity they were meant to live. In addition, she is also the author of her own soon-to-be-published book, *In the Face of Change: Survivor Secrets to Design a Life of Purpose and Fulfillment.*

For more information on Liana, please contact her office at (772) 261-4377 or via email at Liana@RefacingSuccess.com. You can also learn more about her by visiting her company Facebook page at www.facebook.com/RefacingSuccess or her company website at www.LianaInc.com.

CHAPTER 12

SOCIAL MEDIA MYTHBUSTERS:
HOW TO "DARE TO SUCCEED" IN THE ONLINE REVOLUTION

BY LINDSAY DICKS

You know what they say...

"Always do what you've always done...
and you'll always get what you've always gotten."

Over the last two decades, the internet has revolutionized just about everything when it comes to business (not to mention our daily lives!). Instant communication. The ability to create all-powerful databases. The incredible speed, affordability and ease of marketing.

Not many so-called futurists foresaw this kind of technological game-changer back in 1950. They were too busy getting excited about the flying cars that were sure to come by the year 2000! (Well, we *do* have drones, but, unfortunately, we don't get to ride in them and zoom over rush-hour traffic.).

All the breakthroughs I've detailed above, however, were only the first steps in the online revolution. What's happening now was foreshadowed when the techies announced that "Web 2.0" was about to explode on the scene in 2002. Web 2.0 is basically what we have today—the ability to create regular, meaningful and impactful interaction on the web, and go far beyond the original static "brochure" pages that made up the first wave of business websites.

During the past decade, evolving internet technology has resulted in the creation of online powerhouses, such as YouTube, Facebook, Twitter, and the newest sensation, Pinterest—as well as a complete transformation of the internet marketing landscape. Smart, savvy businesses are leveraging these powerful new tools to the max in order to boost their visibility, create vibrant fan bases and, of course, drive new avenues of additional revenue.

The question is, are you reaching out to ride this new wave of online prosperity? Or are you still on the beach, waiting in vain for web surfers to come ashore to where you're sitting?

If so, you may have a long wait. That's why what you're about to read will hopefully motivate you to shake off the sand and get ready to dive in!

BREEDING A DYNAMIC DIGITAL DNA™

The most important thing we try to impress upon our clients is that the very first thing almost every prospective customer and client is going to do, when they decide whether or not they're going to go ahead and purchase from them, is Google their names.

Because the results of that search could mean the difference between whether a consumer chooses you or your competition, logic dictates this crucial conclusion:

> *Whoever best controls and maximizes their online presence,*
> *best creates the conditions for ongoing business success.*

Want proof? A recent survey by Dimensional Research says that an overwhelming 90 percent of consumers use online information to decide who they're going to buy from.

Gone are the days where you can just have a website. Yes, websites have moved way beyond those static brochure sites I mentioned earlier to engaging, interactive, multimedia websites packed with plenty of marketing firepower. But that's still not enough to effectively connect with your online audience. That's why every business needs a social media strategy.

The problem is that the rapid pace of growth in that world has created a bewildering and plentiful set of options from which to choose. Business owners not only don't have enough information to make the right social media choices, but the information they do have is often just plain wrong.

In this day and age, that kind of misinformation can be deadly to your business. Yes, you have your hands full just running your company or practice—and yes, it's understandable that you don't feel you have the time to become an expert at online marketing. But if you don't at least make the effort to go beyond a website-only mindset, you risk your competition making the crucial customer connections that you could be making instead.

In this chapter, I'm going to serve as your very own personal Social Media MythBuster—no extra charge!—and puncture the falsehoods that could lead you around in circles, rather than toward a powerful, integrated online strategy. So get off the beach and into a sea of opportunity—because, with what I'm about to tell you, you'll definitely begin to develop the skills to swim to social media success.

SOCIAL MEDIA MYTH #1:
"I DON'T HAVE TIME TO TWITTER!"

...or Facebook or post on Tumblr or YouTube or...well, whatever you're thinking about doing. Well, the truth is, social media doesn't demand a huge amount of time in order for you to have an effective presence on it. As a matter of fact, you could devote as little as 15 minutes a day—or even every other day—and make it work for you. The goal is to make it a regular habit, a fixed and scheduled task during your workweek, and you'll soon start to build a solid following, especially if you also take the time at the outset to decide on a defined strategy so that every day you have a specific checklist of social media tasks to accomplish.

SOCIAL MEDIA MYTH #2: "MY CUSTOMERS DON'T WANT FACE TIME WITH ME ON FACEBOOK!"

You may still be in the mind frame that only kids, teens and twenty-somethings are swarming social media these days. So NOT true. As a matter of fact, the fastest-growing demo in social media these days are seniors, even though, in fact, every conceivable age group is embracing social media sites (except maybe the under-3 set).

There are over a billion people worldwide using social media today—that's roughly the size of the audience for 10 Super Bowls! And you better believe many of your current and potential customers are a part of that crowd.

SOCIAL MEDIA MYTH #3: "BUT I ALREADY HAVE A WEBSITE!"

Well, congratulations on that! Of course, that's incredibly important—you want your customers and prospects to have a place to find out all they can about you, your products and your services.

BUT...

...when it comes to the internet, yours is only one of over a half-billion active websites out there, according to the latest statistics. Unless someone is specifically searching you out, it's highly unlikely you're going to get a lot of "walk-in" traffic.

That's the BIG advantage of social media—you don't have to worry about getting anyone to come there, because it's already where *everyone goes*. Millions of conversations are going on every day on these sites—and you should be a part of them, taking every opportunity to share your expertise. That visibility is an important factor in driving people back to your website to find out exactly what you have to offer.

SOCIAL MEDIA MYTH #4: "I NEED A MILLION FOLLOWERS AND/OR FRIENDS TO REALLY BE A SOCIAL MEDIA SUCCESS! THAT'S IMPOSSIBLE!"

Ashton Kutcher may have 14 million Twitter followers, but that doesn't mean you have to. As a matter of fact, you need to think more about quality rather than quantity when it comes to your social media contacts.

If you attract 50 people in your target market, that's a whole lot better than 500 who would never even think of buying from you! And with the right targeted social media strategy, you'll pick up the exact kind of leads you want—and build a fan base with real profit potential.

SOCIAL MEDIA MYTH #5: "THERE ARE TOO MANY SOCIAL MEDIA SITES TO DEAL WITH—I CAN'T DO THEM ALL!"

Facebook. LinkedIn. Pinterest. Twitter. YouTube. Google+. You're right—you probably *can't* do them all.

The thing is—you don't have to.

That's why I use the phrase *"targeted* social media strategy." I mean, how many avenues for advertising are there? Here are a few: direct mail, TV, radio, and billboards. Should you not advertise because there are too many of those venues to choose from?

Social media is no different. Some businesses are born to interact on LinkedIn, others are perfect for Pinterest. Your best bet is to consult with a social media expert and try to hone in on the site where you'll find the most potential customers and get started there!

Also keep in mind that there are applications that allow you to update your status across multiple social media sites. That makes social media multitasking much easier.

SOCIAL MEDIA MYTH #6: "LINKEDIN IS ALL BUSINESS, AND FACEBOOK IS FOR FRIENDS AND FAMILY."

That was the case in the beginning—and LinkedIn is still mostly just for business purposes—but increasingly, business owners, professionals and entrepreneurs are using Facebook and Twitter to connect with other businesses. So don't limit yourself to LinkedIn, as the other sites I just mentioned have much more robust interaction elements and enable productive connections to happen much more easily and frequently.

SOCIAL MEDIA MYTH #7: "I CAN'T SAY EVERYTHING I HAVE TO SAY IN 140 CHARACTERS OR LESS!"

Well, you just said that in only 63 characters!

But seriously, think of how many momentous thoughts were articulated in less than 140 characters: "We have anything to fear but fear itself." "That's one small step for man—one giant leap for mankind." "I have a dream."

The point is, you don't have to write a novel to capture the attention of your audience—just drop a handy hint or impactful thought that reflects your expertise and gives people something to think about. Also remember, your tweets can contain links that will take readers to more substantial content on your website, blog, or wherever.

SOCIAL MEDIA MYTH #8: "SOCIAL MEDIA IS THE MAGIC FIX MY BUSINESS HAS BEEN LOOKING FOR!"

I'm sorry to have to break the news, but, ever since they made the last *Harry Potter* movie, magic has seen a dramatic downturn in the marketplace!

I am, of course, a huge advocate of social media, but you can't expect miracles from it or any other marketing tool. It's all in how well you use it and how strong and consistent your strategy is.

Another cautionary note: Social media requires *time* to truly demonstrate its effectiveness. It's all about establishing relationships and building trust—and, as you know, that doesn't just happen overnight. People need to see, over the long run, that you're authentic, you know what you're talking about, and that you have something genuine to offer. The time you invest wisely in social media today leads to great results tomorrow.

SOCIAL MEDIA MYTH #9: "I CAN'T POSSIBLY CREATE ENOUGH CONTENT TO KEEP UP!"

There's no question that posting content, such as blogs, articles and videos, is crucial to creating a strong Digital DNA™. But that's a very separate issue from your social media usage. Remember, in many cases, we're only talking about writing something 140 characters long!

Social media is, again, simply about relationships—creating a daily status or two, sharing a quote you particularly admire, or commenting on someone's else's post where you feel you can add something to a conversation. "People buy people," as the old saying goes, so all you really have to do is be personable!

SOCIAL MEDIA MYTH #10: "I CAN'T KEEP MONITORING MY SOCIAL MEDIA 24/7!"

Some businesspeople stop themselves from social media because they think they would have to constantly keep an eye on their Facebook page or Twitter feed in case they need to respond to something immediately.

Nothing could be further from the truth.

As I mentioned earlier, you can simply schedule a few minutes each day to accomplish your ongoing social media goals. As a matter of fact, there are applications that allow you to "prepackage" your tweets and release them at designated times throughout the day—without you having to lift a finger! That way, you look like you're putting a lot more time into social media than you really are.

Your social media activities should be *consistent,* but not *constant*— otherwise, you start looking a little like a stalker! It's fine to take a look a few times a day at your social media activity when you have a moment and you feel like checking out what's going on, but more than that is really not necessary for social media success.

SOCIAL MEDIA MYTH #11: "HEY, WHO NEEDS ADVERTISING? I CAN JUST DO SOCIAL MEDIA FOR FREE!"

Earlier in this chapter, I compared social media to advertising, in the sense that there are many ways to do both effectively. What I did NOT mean to imply is that social media should somehow take the place of advertising.

Both are important, but both accomplish different goals. Social media, once again, is all about building personal relationships—connecting with your audience, letting them see who you are and facilitating trust and understanding. Advertising is, of course, more about blowing your own horn and directly telling people about what you're selling—obviously an important thing to do!

Advertising and social media definitely complement each other, but they do not resemble each other. When you market too obviously and too heavily with social media, people tune you out. That's why you should always offer something interesting, useful or humorous on social media—something that *adds* to the overall conversation, not distracts from it.

I hope this chapter has cleared up a few of the main misconceptions many people have about social media. Social media is now a fact of life, just like movies, TV, radio and other types of media became after they were introduced. That means it can be easy to take it for granted or ignore it altogether, because it's been around a few years.

That, to me and other marketing experts, is a big mistake. There is simply too much opportunity to develop real connections that pay off in ways that other marketing avenues can't deliver.

If you haven't already, make your move and join in the social media conversation. Sometimes talk can be cheap, but in this case, many businesses are finding it to be incredibly profitable!

About Lindsay

Lindsay Dicks helps her clients tell their stories in the online world. Being brought up around a family of marketers, but a product of Generation Y, Lindsay naturally gravitated to the new world of online marketing. Lindsay began freelance writing in 2000 and soon after launched her own PR firm that thrived by offering an in-your-face "Guaranteed PR" that was one of the first of its type in the nation.

Lindsay's new media career is centered on her philosophy that "people buy people." Her goal is to help her clients build a relationship with their prospects and customers. Once that relationship is built and they learn to trust them as the expert in their field, then they will do business with them. Lindsay also built a patent-pending process that utilizes social media marketing, content marketing and search engine optimization to create online "buzz" for her clients that helps them to convey their business and personal story. Lindsay's clientele span the entire business map and range from doctors and small business owners to Inc 500 CEOs.

Lindsay is a graduate of the University of Florida. She is the CEO of CelebritySites™, an online marketing company specializing in social media and online personal branding. Lindsay is also a multi-best-selling author including the best-selling book *Power Principles for Success* which she co-authored with Brian Tracy. She was also selected as one of America's PremierExperts™ and has been quoted in *Newsweek*, the *Wall Street Journal, USA Today, Inc.* magazine as well as featured on NBC, ABC, and CBS television affiliates speaking on social media, search engine optimization and making more money online. Lindsay was also recently brought on FOX 35 News as their Online Marketing Expert.

Lindsay, a national speaker, has shared the stage with some of the top speakers in the world such as Brian Tracy, Lee Milteer, Ron LeGrand, Arielle Ford, David Bullock, Brian Horn, Peter Shankman and many others. Lindsay was also a Producer on the Emmy-nominated film Jacob's Turn.

You can connect with Lindsay at:
Lindsay@CelebritySites.com
www.twitter.com/LindsayMDicks
www.facebook.com/LindsayDicks

CHAPTER 13

ACHIEVE YOUR DREAMS— BY FAITH, NOT BY SIGHT

BY BRANDON OSHODIN

I had one goal. I wanted to be the best trainer in the world. Problem was, I knew how to get myself in shape but not others.

I looked it up many times, and the average trainer made only $20K to $40K a year on the high end, and with my skills, I thought I was below average. All the trainers I knew had college degrees and knew more than me. Everybody was telling me to go to college and get a business degree or become a physical therapist, because it's like personal training, but you have a degree. That way, if it fails, you can get a job as long as you have that piece of paper.

I gave up on my dream. I got a job at a gym working in membership sales and went to school full time. I was a sales giant—top in the company actually. I was only 21, but I was hungry. I took the worst club in the company to the top earner in the company. As for school, I was getting A's on everything. It wasn't easy all the time, but you know I can't say it was difficult either; it just took effort.

Everybody was happy for me. My mom was proud of me…from the outside things looked great; on the inside, I was in hell. I saw the trainers in the gym doing what I wanted to be doing, making almost no money, but I wanted to do it. I saw how they didn't really live the healthy lifestyle they preached or cared for their clients, and I wanted to come in like a super trainer with a cape and actually be the go-to guy that gets results and that everybody would know was serious about fixing problems.

But I had bills, responsibility and class. I didn't want to let anyone down. Most of all I had looked at the personal training test, and it looked like another language. I was scared to fail, but my desire to train was on fire. Work and school started to slip. I was so miserable. I would wake up and just lay in bed and be lethargic, knowing that I would spend another day of my life going through the motions, doing something I hated and not even doing it well anymore. So I dropped out of school, and me and a couple of actual certified trainer friends started a boot camp.

I wanted it to be called Authentik Fitness because we offered true results, and we really cared about getting people results and meeting their needs on a physical, mental and spiritual level. I spelled it with a "k" not a "c." The business was authentik but not in the way people are used to seeing training. We did two or three boot camp classes and made, maybe, $30, then everybody quit.

For me, it was pure bliss. I had so much fun creating workouts and coaching people through them that I knew it was what I wanted to do forever. So I dropped to my knees and asked God to please make a way for me to become an elite trainer. I had all types of bills, but in my spirit, he spoke to me. He said have faith, so I did. I quit my job, and with no personal training certification, no gym, no money, no clients and no help, I went to a local park called Hoover Dam and sat in my car all day on Twitter marketing my services. I read hundreds of library books and magazines, learned everything there was to know about personal training, anatomy, nutrition, functions of the body, psychology, marketing and sales—you name it. I only had four clients, so I had plenty of time.

The whole time I was reading I had remembered something one of my high school teachers, Mr. Miller, had told me that really impacted and changed my life. He grabbed me one day after coming into school late, like I always did, looked me in my eyes, and said, "Brandon, think about your future family; you're not just doing this for yourself. Think about your mom…who's going to take care of her? Think about the people in your life who make sacrifices so you can be here, and think about the life you are in right now, creating for your future wife and kids. You're only doing what you know how to do, but I know there is more to you than you are showing. Whatever it is that you have to do to get your mind right, do it—be relentless. Always be relentless; make a goal and be relentless in achieving it. Wake up."

Ever since that day when things got rough I would always hear that speech in my head as clear as the moment he said it; funny how words can change your life. Then I thought I need to hear more encouragement through this bleak situation. Summer was ending, I still had only four clients at just $15 a session, and it was getting too cold and rainy to train at the park, so I started listening to the greats like Bob Proctor, Jack Canfield, Les Brown, Jim Rohn, Earl Nightingale, Zig Ziglar, Napoleon Hill, Og Mandino, and countless others. Since I had no money, I read books and I listened on YouTube and every other possible free way to get the information. I would listen to them and their story and get motivated for a few hours, but then later think this can't happen to me. Am I a fool for wasting time listening to this rah-rah feel-good crap. After all, I don't know anyone else who listens to this, and it's embarrassing when people find out that I do.

Every day I woke up, nothing changed. I was still broke and giving literally all I had to my craft, but I kept listening. Finally, it got too cold, and I had to get a job at a call center. I made more money than I did training, but I was so miserable. It was like being a dog tied to a short leash; I couldn't leave my desk or my phone. As a fitness trainer, the food that they had going around the office, in addition to the lack of movement, almost broke my sprit. But slowly I started to get comfortable in the job. I was still training a couple clients on the side but not promoting that much anymore, just telling the girls in my office I was a trainer and flexing my arm to show what used to be a muscle, but now turning into fat. Then one day I ran across a new book called, *Three Feet from Gold*, and it was like God was speaking to me. The book was about not stopping right before you hit your destiny and had hundreds of stories of successful people and how the only thing that made them successful was the fact that they didn't quit when things got hard. The day I finished that book I knew what I had to do. I went to a local gym to interview for a personal training job. Even though I had no certification, I did have experience because I was already training and got my few clients results. I pleaded my case and the manager took me on as a training salesman and told me when I got certified, I could switch to training.

My desire burned hot again. I never went back to the call center after that. My plan was to sell some training, make some money, take the training test, ace it, and live the life—simple. I worked that sales job for two and a half months and got only three sales and made about $200 during that whole time. Meanwhile my dog got me evicted from my apartment, and in the process of moving, I wrecked the U-Haul I rented by backing into a school bus and a fence, racking up thousands of dollars in damages. My mother was very ill in the hospital, and I still had bills coming in left and right. I worked from 5:30 am to 9 pm at the gym every day, except Sunday, for no pay, just to be around prospective clients and to perfect my craft—studying, reading and experimenting all day. Then from 9:30 pm to 2 am, I was bouncing at a Mexican nightclub for $50 a night, even though I don't speak any Spanish, breaking up fights and sometimes almost getting stabbed.

There came a point where I had to make a decision. I had been sleeping in my car for a little while, and I knew I had to either pay my car note or buy a personal training certification. I went all in and bought the certification, and stopped sleeping and bouncing so I could just study and read. I learned all the material in five days, took the test on the sixth day from when I purchased it, and got a 98 percent. I was pumped—I was finally certified.

I thought I was just going to start making money and live happily ever after in my dream job, but the switch from sales to training took almost a month. Again I wasn't getting paid, and I was frustrated. I wanted to give up. My mom needed my help, and I didn't even have the gas money to go see her, let alone enough money to eat food. I was living off protein shakes from the gym, and trust me there is such a thing as too much protein. My digestive system was a mess. I had all these thoughts of quitting in my head, and right then my phone rang. It was my manager. He said, "Yo, B, look out the window." I looked out the window, and my car was getting repossessed for late payments. Now car-less and basically stranded at the gym, I had a mental breakdown. I said to myself, "I have taken it as far as it can go; I gave my best ... it's time to quit."

It was the coldest day of winter, and I was walking outside the gym with no coat on. Right then my phone rang. It was William Schoettker, a guy I met in the summer. He had taught me a lot just the few times we talked, and he always had a habit of checking in on me at my darkest hours. I told him what was going on, and he encouraged me. He told me his rags-to-riches story, and I was inspired.

So I kept going. I heard Mr. Miller again—"be relentless." I refocused on my passion; I went harder than I thought was possible. I started listening nonstop to more personal development, reading Seven Figure Sam's training marketing emails, and finding different ways to separate myself from others. I developed a relationship with a trainer I deeply respected in Miami, named Armando Cruz. He encouraged me, and just the association alone helped me out tremendously—I was on fire.

After a month. I got the money to get my car back. I got dropped off at the car lot with just enough money for my car, walked in, paid my fees, went to my car with the confidence of a king, hopped in, put the keys in the ignition, turned it with a flick of the wrist, and nothing. Turned it again, nothing. The battery was dead. It wouldn't even start with a jump. I remember this day so clearly. It was snowing hard, and I had to walk two miles back to the gym to work.

Feeling like a fool and a loser, I heard the voice as loud and clear as if I had headphones on. God spoke to me in that very moment and scared the daylights out of me. He said, "By faith, not by sight." From that point on, I dominated life. I thought about it, and on my way to work, stopped at Kroger's and picked up a copy of the DuPont registry, and picked out two cars: a Range Rover and a black BMW 745. I told everybody at the gym this was my next car, and they laughed at me. They knew my situation, but I knew what I heard. I told everyone I was the top trainer in the world; I spoke about my dreams out loud with confidence and dared anyone to oppose me. I claimed everything I wanted in life that I did not have and rejected my present situation.

The next day I picked up a new client and got the money to get my car battery and more. From then on, I believed in greater things and I added the missing piece of my life that was stopping me from claiming victory, God. I was always a Christian on the outside, but I actually read the Bible and learned that I was doing it all wrong trying to follow Old Testament rules instead of letting my sprit guide my every decision. I got in fellowship with some stronger Christian brothers, Andrew Claybourne and Brian Mckee, who help take my faith to the next level.

Just months after not being able to get my car out of repossession, I was driving my own BMW 745—the car I picked out from the magazine. I went from having almost no clients to clients all over the United States. Some though online training, some actually flew me out just to train them; I was attracting everything I wanted in my life. I quit my job at the gym out of pure faith that my spirit was telling me to do so, and my income went from barely hitting $2K a month to over $8K a month in the same week. It's amazing because I wasn't killing myself like I was before. I was just being obedient to what my sprit told me.

I'll never forget I went out to Miami to meet Tammy Torres, a model I used to have pictures of on my phone wallpaper, two years prior. Now it was all about training, just months after not being able to find a single person willing to train with me in my hometown, not even for free. I was poolside at the Fountain Bleu hotel in south Miami with a woman I've seen in every magazine talking about exercises and projects she was working on. That changed my perception and took my faith to another level. Every goal I write down now gets accomplished, and I'm being mentored by Bob Proctor himself to be the next elite personal development coach. Make sure your dreams manifest as well so we can all live an authentik life—by faith, not by sight.

About Brandon

Brandon Oshodin is the owner and lead trainer of Authentik Fitness. He is world renowned for his approach to physical, mental and spiritual training. By offering these extra elements outside of the typical physical training, he brings his clients to a full and Authentik level of fitness. He lives by the motto: "By faith, not by sight." When creating Authentik Fitness, he had a vision of going beyond doing bicep curls and gaining size for his future clients. He had the vision of a culture of excellence, learning to overcome every struggle, and dominating not only in the weight room, but in the classroom, at work and at home. There is certain expectancy within Authentik Fitness; it is not your average training. This expectancy requires, at all times, being the best you can possibly be and living your dreams. Brandon has clients ranging from celebrity models and athletes to high school students who just want to gain more self-esteem or improve in their chosen sport to prepare for the next level of competition. Brandon strives to live and lead by example, following Jesus' words: "The greatest amongst you will be like servants." Brandon has been recognized as a top trainer for his unique approach to serving his clients and is being mentored and groomed by Bob Proctor to be the next leader in personal development.

CHAPTER 14

HEALTH IS THE CORNERSTONE OF SUCCESS: ACCELERATE HEALTH, ACCELERATE WEALTH

BY DIEGO FERNANDO SALDARRIAGA

In the past 2½ years, I have had accelerated success in the area of health and fitness. In June 2009, I had a work-related back injury, and as a result of a year and a half of inactivity, I was weighing 210 pounds. Since I'm 5 foot 7, my BMI (body mass index) was over 30, which means I wasn't just over weight, I was straight-up obese. I was now part of more than one-third of U.S. adults and approximately 17 percent of children and adolescents aged 2 to 19 years who are obese.

About a year and a half after the accident, the pain became bearable and I decided it was time to regain my health. Running had always been a hard thing for me to do and I needed a challenge. I decided I was going to train with a group, get coaching, and give myself a reason big enough to not quit, so I signed up to run a 10k race with Team in Training, to raise funds for the Leukemia and Lymphoma Society. That race was on Dec 5, 2010, and since then, I have participated in six half marathons, two marathons and five triathlons. I dropped 60 pounds in the process, and now I have a healthy BMI of 23.5. By the end of this year, I will have added a triathlon, a marathon, a 110-mile bike ride and a half-ironman distance triathlon to that list, with plans of participating in a full ironman next year.

Needless to say, I'm in the best shape of my life. I have healthy habits, and I enjoy a healthy lifestyle, but only a short time ago things were very different. In fact, for most of my life, this was not the case. I was never involved in any organized sports as a kid or a teenager, and my physical activity was limited to occasional bike rides and gym class, so I was chunky but funky. As I got older, I tried many diets and programs and would always achieve temporary success so my weight always fluctuated. It wasn't until I applied some key factors that I finally achieved a breakthrough.

While training for and participating in marathons and triathlons successfully, I began to notice a correlation between key attributable factors that I applied to my success in health and key principles that most of the wealthy people that I was learning from were attributing to their financial success. When I realized the blueprint I used to achieve accelerated success in health could also be applied to achieving accelerated success in creating wealth, I had a blueprint to take action and I was able to implement the principles I had been studying. It is through application of these principles that I was blessed with the opportunity to share space in this book with a man who I have the upmost respect for, best-selling co-author of Chicken Soup for the Soul series, Jack Canfield.

There are seven key principles to Accelerated Health and Accelerated Wealth, but because of limited space, I will only elaborate on three and I will give you free access to the other four at www.Iloveachallenge. com. While you're there, you can calculate your BMI for free, which I believe is one of the best places to start if you want to track and measure your success in health. I will also invite you to join me on a challenge to accelerate the process of maximizing your health. Though not in any particular order, the three key principles I will elaborate on are the ones I feel could make the biggest difference in your life.

PRINCIPLE 1: WHAT IS YOUR OUTCOME?

"It concerns us to know the purpose we seek in life, for then, like archers aiming at a definite mark, we shall be certain to attain what we want." — Aristotle

If you're unclear on what it is you want to achieve, you're going to scatter your energy, which will produce scattered results. When you get clear on your purpose, you are able to focus your thoughts and your energy. Persistent action toward a purpose with focused energy gets results.

I attended two conferences in 2008 that changed my life. The first one, "Unleash the Power Within," was in March. This was the same conference Oprah Winfrey attended in Los Angeles in 2011. The second one was "Date with Destiny" in December. By applying what I learned at these two events, I was able to break through one of the most challenging times in my life a year later: a 90-day period from April 19, 2009, to July 19, 2009, which I now call my 90-day challenge.

The man I had the privilege to learn from, and who masterfully delivered his profound wisdom from the heart, was Tony Robbins, to who I am in deep gratitude. There were two stories Tony shared that would become the fuel for my accelerated success in health. The first story was about Stu Mittleman, an ultra-distance running champion, who in 1986 shattered the world record in the 1,000-mile run in Flushing Meadows Park in Queens, New York. Being a Queens native, I had driven past the park many times while this event was going on and I would see people running at all hours for several days, but I just thought they were crazy and didn't know what it was all about. It took him 11 days and 20 hours, and he shattered the old record by 16 hours. Then 14 years later, in 2000, when he was nearly 50 years old, he embarked on 3,000-mile journey from San Diego to New York City, and he finished in 56 days, which is more than two marathons a day for 56 consecutive days. I was super impressed by his endurance, and I thought if this guy can do all that at 50, then I can surely run a marathon in my 30s, so I wrote it down in my notes.

The second story was of Sister Madonna Buder, aka the iron nun, who in 2006, at 76 years old, became the oldest person to ever finish an Ironman triathlon. She broke the record again in 2012, at 82 years old. She began training at age 48 and completed her first Ironman at 55 and has completed 325 triathlons, including 45 Ironman distances. Once again I thought if she can do it, starting at 48 years old, then I can do it and wrote "Ironman" in my notes.

Those two stories opened the doors of possibility for me, and it provided me with a vision. I became obsessed with the thought of accomplishing those goals. I didn't know it at the time, but I had established a definite purpose. I had a long way to go to accomplish these goals because I couldn't even run a mile, let alone swim any type of distance, but I started immersing myself in the topic. I subscribed to magazines, read books, watched videos, and looked at training plans. I started learning a lot about both marathons and triathlons, and I thought about doing it someday. But that was the problem–someday wasn't a specific date. I hadn't registered for a specific race, so I had nothing to train for. I felt that I had all the time in the world and that I would eventually get around to it, so I failed to take action on everything I had learned. I was missing a big why? A big reason to fuel that desire to achieve those goals and want them bad enough.

PRINCIPLE 2: WHAT IS YOUR BIG WHY?

"While we may not be able to control all that happens to us, we can control what happens inside us." — Benjamin Franklin

My big why came four months later, after one of the most challenging times in my life, which all started with a 90-day period that left me overwhelmed emotionally, drained mentally, and in pain physically. It all began on April 19, 2009, when my father passed away in Colombia at 69 years old due to complications from a stroke and type 2 diabetes. I always remember him having a rock-solid Buddha-type belly and he had no interest in physical activities. He lived a very sedentary lifestyle, and he had very unhealthy dietary habits, which led to obesity-related health issues. Unfortunately, we never really had a good relationship.

Then two months later, on June 3, my cousin Steve "Queso" Jimenez passed away in a freak car accident in North Carolina. He was only 31 years old, and he was full of life. To cap it off, the following month, on July 19, I injured my back at work and I was facing potential back surgery.

While still in physical therapy a year later, on July 3, I was off to Colombia again because my grandfather Jorge Gonzalez had passed away, at age 91, from a stroke. I had the utmost respect for my grandfather. He was a pastor, and I valued how he was a living example of spirituality, having a mission, living on purpose and having faith. He was a strong man, and

I remember him easily plowing down sugar cane fields with a machete in Colombia when he was well into his 70s. I was always impressed by his need to be active. He had also been a farmer, and everything my grandparents ate was grown on the farm. They were truly self-sufficient, and, as a result, very healthy.

During and after this turbulent time, I reflected on their lives and my life, and I asked myself a lot of questions. My father's life made me realize that I needed to change my lifestyle habits, and combined with my back injury, it gave me a new-found respect for my health. My grandfather's long life was a confirmation of the results you get when you combine an active lifestyle with good nutrition, and it was always an example of having a greater purpose and being of service.

My cousin Steve's death was a complete shock because he was very young. It made me think of the fragility of life, how tomorrow is never promised, and it reminded me to be grateful for every day you are blessed with. I thought about unfulfilled dreams and goals, and it made me realize that the time to take action on your dreams is now! It really gave me a sense of urgency. It was with these thoughts in the forefront of my mind that I decided to take action.

PRINCIPLE 3: WE BECOME WHAT WE THINK ABOUT; YOUR DOMINANT THOUGHTS CREATE YOUR CONDITIONS

"A man is but the product of his thoughts.
What he thinks, he becomes." — Mahatma Gandhi

When I set out to regain my health, I now had a clear purpose and a burning desire to achieve it. I wanted to handle grief and stress in a positive way and to lose weight and increase my energy, but the ultimate goal was to complete an ironman.

In the summer of 2010, I got a chance to attend a two-day running clinic in Central Park with Stu Mittleman, and it was a very encouraging experience. I congratulated him on his successes, and I told him about my goal to run a marathon, which was inspired by his story. I told him I was recovering from a back injury, and after analyzing me, he reassured me that I would be OK. He shared nutrition tips, he taught me how to train with a heart-rate monitor, and he analyzed my running form. He told me he wanted me to train within a certain heart range, and I stuck to the plan. I barely looked like I was jogging in that heart range, but I eventually burned a lot of fat because of it and I gradually improved my aerobic capacity.

By getting clear on my outcome I could focus my thoughts and energy toward taking persistent action. To complete an ironman, I would have to do a 2.4-mile swim, a 112-mile bike ride, and then a 26.2-mile run. I had always struggled with running, and I wasn't even running a mile, so I had a long way to go to get to the marathon. I would also have to learn how to swim for distance. I had never done any lap swims or anything—only hanging-around-the-pool-type swimming. And the longest bike ride to date was 71 miles, about 10 years before. I also wanted to do something for a good cause and make a difference because at the "Date With Destiny" seminar, I had decided to focus on growth and contribution, so joining Team in Training to benefit the Leukemia and Lymphoma Society was a perfect fit.

I signed up to run my very first race, a 10k in Central Park, on December 5, 2010, in memory of my cousin Steve. Team in Training provided the opportunity to train with great coaches that provided training plans, a group to train with, and a lots of support on race day. Being immersed in that environment, I was motivated to keep pushing forward. By attending all the practices, I started forming a habit, and I decided to keep training with them for a half marathon. Eventually, I started seeing myself as a runner, but it took a while to actually call myself a runner. After the half marathon, I trained with them for my first triathlon and the same thing occurred—by immersing myself in the process, I created habits and eventually I started seeing myself as a triathlete.

It wasn't until after I participated in two events that I started calling myself a triathlete, even though the coaches assured me that I was after the first. But that's what it's all about—the journey of becoming the person you need to be to achieve that which you desire. It's all about the journey. I also realized how important it is to have a vision and set big goals that pull you forward. Had my goal just been a 10k race, I may have just stopped running after achieving that goal and not given myself the chance to grow. As a matter of fact, 50 percent of new exercisers drop out in six months, but since the ironman has always been the bigger goal, it continues to pull me through countless smaller races along the way, compelling me to stay on course and thereby achieving accelerated success.

When applying these principles to accelerated wealth, it's an inside-out process: It's not about getting to a destination, about the psychological and emotional shifts that you have to make to feel wealthy and recognizing the true wealth in your life. Being wealthy and having financial success are two very different things. You could have all the money in the world, but if you are not grateful and you don't have love, happiness, connection, and good health to enjoy your success, you are not wealthy. True wealth originates in the mind and heart. My life is rich because of my beautiful, loving mother, my awesome family, my friends, my health, because I'm continuously looking for ways to make a difference, and because I am grateful for all the things that God continues to bless me with every single day. Gratitude makes you feel rich and abundant. When you live from this place and you provide more value and give, you accelerate wealth. Ultimately, your financial success in the information age will depend on how much value you provide, how much you give and collaborate, your willingness to be of service, and having the courage to be authentic and transparent.

ACTION STEPS

1. Get clear on your purpose and make it big so it pulls you toward success. Ask yourself what is my outcome? Once you're clear on your purpose, design a plan toward achieving that goal. Get mentors, follow proven systems and best practices, and work with a team.

2. What is your big why? Find a reason bigger than you to keep you on track when the times get hard; this is your fuel.

3. Break down the plan into smaller victories to focus your thoughts and energy toward taking focused, persistent action. Track and monitor progress, and don't forget to celebrate all the small victories along the way.

(To get steps 4-7 for free, go to www.iloveachallenge.com.)

"Your own resolution to succeed is more important than any other."
— Abraham

About Diego

Diego Fernando Saldarriaga started his first business in 1993 when he was 17 years old. He formed a partnership with his friend and started an independent electronic-dance music record label, and they promoted many events at the top NYC dance clubs of that time. Since then, he has started and owned several businesses ranging from parking enforcement companies to network marketing ventures. He is an avid entrepreneur and the owner and president of a real estate investing company he started in 2008. He suffered a work-related back injury in July 2009, and he was facing the possibility of undergoing back surgery. After a year and half of inactivity, he weighed 210 pounds and his BMI was over 30, putting him in the obese category. He decided to regain his health, and he became very involved with Team in Training to participate in marathons and triathlons to raise funds for the Leukemia and Lymphoma Society. Today, he is 60 pounds lighter, and he enjoys a healthy BMI of 23.5. His new-found passion for endurance events and achieving optimum health has led him to promoting Americas #1 Weight-Loss and Fitness Challenge, to encourage people to focus on their health and to promote healthy habits. He is currently working on becoming a Strategic Intervention Coach, an RRCA Certified Coach, and an ITCA Certified Coach.

To learn more about Diego Fernando Saldarriaga and about The Challenge, visit www.iloveachallenge.com or call (718) 740-0930.

CHAPTER 15

THE IMPORTANCE OF VISION IN A LEADER

BY DR. GATHER WILLIAMS II, "DR.G"

Vision is one of the most important characteristics of a successful leader. I love this definition of vision: "the act or power of imagination, mode of seeing or conceiving, unusual discernment or foresight." Ken Blanchard and Jesse Stoner define vision as "knowing who you are, where you're going, and what will guide your journey."

A leader must speak with clear vision and have the gift of influence, because no one wants to follow a leader who has no idea where he or she is going! I've heard it said before that a leader without followers is just a person out for a walk!

Great leaders are true visionaries. Before a leader can ever become great, she must be able to see herself as such, and I am convinced that a great leader will be able to see beyond the current moment or circumstances and see the desired outcome.

Without clear vision, men will dwell recklessly and aimlessly, trying every new "get rich quick scheme" that is presented, but a leader with a solid and clear vision does not wander, nor is he easily swayed like a weak tree limb!

A visionary leader must have a perspective of the journey and the goal that most of the time the people who follow will not understand until they start to see the results. However, a visionary and determined leader is not moved by this.

My colleague and co-author in *The Art and Science of Success*, Ken Blanchard, gives us two strategies to help us as leaders live out our vision:

1. **Always focus on your vision.** Your vision should be the foundation for your organization. If an obstacle or unforeseen event throws you off course, you may have to change your short-term goals, but your vision should be long lasting. Change is bound to happen. Unforeseen events are bound to occur. Find a way to reframe what is happening as a challenge or opportunity on the road to living your vision.

2. **Show the courage of commitment.** True commitment begins when you take action. There will be fears; feel them and move ahead. It takes courage to create a vision, and it takes courage to act on it. In the words of Goethe, "Whatever you can do, or dream you can, begin it. Boldness has genius, power, and magic in it."

That is excellent advice! If you as a leader are focused and committed to your vision, it becomes infectious and it becomes a lot easier to influence others when you are living and moving toward that vision!

Allow me to illustrate the importance of vision that a leader must have by using three "physical" vision characteristics of the tiger. To "have the eye of the tiger" is a statement that is used quite frequently. However, I wonder how many really know just what the statement means. Here are just a few illustrations and comparisons, which I found quite fascinating! They give new meaning to the phrase "having the eye of the tiger!"

1. **According to Tijgeritorium.net, the tiger's eyes are specially adapted to the dark.** Thanks to these adaptations, a tiger needs six times less light to see the environment than we do. This means that even the light of the stars at night is enough for tigers to be able to see what is going on in their environment!

Wow! As a successful leader, you need the ability to see where others cannot, and be able to adapt to the changes easily. The vision of a successful leader must be the same as the physical vision of the tiger! There will inevitably be dark times when your team or family that is depending on you will need more detail or light, and may even doubt the goals and visions that you have set before them, but you as a leader must be able to see in the dark and be able to continue to lead through it.

2. **Tigers hunt mainly during the evening and night, when the vision of their prey is compromised.** Let me encourage every leader—learn from the tiger! Don't be concerned about the people who doubt you and who just can't seem to see what you can see. You know the type of people I'm talking about, the ones who can only see what you are going through, instead of what you are going to! Keep hunting and stay focus on your goal and remain true to your vision because many people will be just like the prey of the tiger. They have limited vision and will never see you moving and achieving, especially in the dark times when it may appear to them that you have lost your way.

3. **Tigers have forward-facing eyes rather than one on each side of their head.** This provides binocular vision because each eye's field of vision overlaps, creating a three-dimensional image. Binocular vision enables them to accurately assess distances and depth, which is extremely useful for maneuvering within their complex environment.

As a leader you must exemplify laser focus on your target just like the tiger does, and you must fight to keep yourself from being moved by all the "white noise" in your peripheral. Like the tiger, your eyes as a leader must be set on your vision in such a way that even though you are aware of your surroundings and you hear the white noise, you have the ability to tune it out and maneuver through the complexities of your environment to reach your goals.

You must develop and communicate a clear vision! With a clear vision, you as a leader will know the following:

a. *How far away you are from the realization of your vision.* At all times, you must be able to gauge where you are!

b. *How to identify the people God has placed in your life to help you realize your vision.* As an author in the best-selling book *The Art and Science of Success*, I talk about how God's greatest gifts to us come in ships...relationships! Be sensitive as a leader to the people sent as gifts to you, to help you reach your goals.

c. *How to communicate that vision effectively and be able to influence your team to buy in to it.*

I love sports and I especially like to watch the dynamics of leadership play out. I can watch the leaders and captains of the teams getting everybody engaged and involved, and reminding all of them of the common goal and rallying them to victory or, many times, with bloody but unbowed heads, lifting them after a defeat, assuring the team that they will win the next one.

If you study the teams that win the majority of the time, you will find that there is a spirit and a culture of winning that begins with the owner but is shared with the whole organization, from the coach to every player. Great teams will not tolerate a player who's philosophy and vision is contrary to the team's, and it should be the same with you and your team. You will never win the "big game" or realize your vision if you compromise your vision for a player. Successful visionary leaders and champions alike have the ability to see the big picture because their perspective of the journey is much higher and their focus is not easily broken.

Max De Pree, the legendary former chairman of Herman Miller and author of *Leadership Is an Art*, said that in his visionary role he had to be like a third-grade teacher. He had to keep saying it over and over and over until people got it right, right, right! The more you focus on your vision, the clearer it will become and the more deeply you will understand it.

In the *Bible*, God told Abraham that he would bless him and that his offspring would be like the stars in the sky. Then God asked him if he could see it, because before you can ever hope to be it, you've got to see it! As the story goes, Abraham said that he could not see it! Well for starters, he was lying on his back in a low-hanging tent as God was revealing this to him, and he could not visualize beyond his environment. So God told him to go outside the tent and look up, and it was at that moment he could see the vision that was promised.

Sometimes as leaders we have to change our environment to see the clarity of our vision. Sometimes we are around "low-hanging tent ceilings," which can show up in our lives in the form of people, places, and things designed for one purpose, and that is to steal, block or kill our vision. We must be willing to crawl from under the weight of those "low-hanging tent ceilings" that are holding us back and blocking our vision, and step outside, look up and see our vision clearly!

Sometimes a leader can experience what my Pastor Mike Haynes calls "vision drift." You can start off well, and before you know it, find yourself off track. You must constantly be onboard correcting the vision. Here are four signs of vision drift:

1. Being in a constant state of busyness: Many leaders can find themselves doing more but enjoying it less, and appearing to really have a lot going on when, in fact, it's an attempt to fill the void of a lack of vision, or "vision drift!"

2. Justifying efforts when it is quite apparent that what you are doing is not working.

3. Spending too much time around nonleaders who can only see the low-hanging fruit and never lift their eyes for a greater perspective. Get with someone who is a great leader and is living his or her vision and dreams now!

4. A lack of ability to envision. Have you lost your ability to see yourself in it? What do you see and what does your life look like when you realize your vision? Remember, you must see it before you can be it!

Here are three things successful visionary leaders do:

1. They write the vision down and make it a plan.

2. They understand that without vision the people perish.

3. They realize that where there is more than one vision at the same time, it causes division.

These are all Biblical principals, which every successful leader knows and understands.

Take time to take an inventory of where you are right now:

• *Where is your vision statement written?* Is it easy to understand and explain? If not, start today by taking the time to think about where you want to be and how you will get there. Write the vision down and email it to your entire team. Place it in your office or home so it's before you every day. Develop that "bifocal vision" of the tiger so you can calculate how far you are from your target and what it will take for you to reach it.

- ***Does your team really understand your vision and the role they will play in realizing the vision?*** Are they invested? If not, take the time to have a meeting just on vision and ensure that each person knows their role and knows that they are important and play an critical role in the vision coming to fruition.

- ***Division must be resisted at all costs on your team.*** Many great companies and leaders with life-changing visions have never had those visions realized because the leader could not recognize that division lived in the ranks.

- ***Are you willing to change?*** Revision is OK! Sometimes leaders need to revise the plan, but that does not mean abandon it. There can many factors that can lead you as a leader to revise your plan. Your goal will not change, but the way you go about achieving it may. Have you ever written a paper or done a project that you had to go back and revise? Many times the paper or project is better than how it was first conceived! Take a look at your vision plan now, and examine whether or not you need to revise or fine-tune it in any way—if so do it!

- ***Can you identify the provision that has been made for you?*** What are your resources? The reality of your vision will be achieved through your ability as a leader to identify provision. Start today to write down the various connections and relationships that can help you achieve the vision. As we discussed earlier in this chapter, God's greatest gifts comes to us through relationships. I believe that when God gives a vision to a leader, he always provides the provision for the vision! Examine who and what can help you see this vision come to pass. Many times everything we need is already in our grasp, but we must take time to see it. I encourage you as a visionary leader to take time to do that right away!

In conclusion, the importance of vision in a leader is paramount. Without it, the leader and anyone who follows suffers. There will always be some level of vision in every organization, family, company, church, etc., because absent of a clear, concise communicated vision from the leader, there will be di-vision. I cannot emphasize enough the importance of creating a team of vision-invested people who will help you fulfill the vision, because no man is an island, and its takes a unified group with tiger-like focus on one vision to do big things! However, it begins with leadership possessing the influence and ability to dream, inspire, and lead people toward a common goal, through dark times and when the vision seems blurred.

Ken Blanchard states: "Leadership is about going somewhere. And if you and your people don't know where you are going, your leadership doesn't matter."

I have lived this philosophy in my career as many of you may have. I have been on a team where we were lost because our leadership was silent when it came to a vision. It is one of the most frustrating things to experience when you are working toward an unknown goal, when you have no ideal what as a company or group you aim to achieve.

I have also experienced being a part of a company with phenomenal leadership, where all the goals and the vision of the owners were crystal clear to our entire team. I will tell you that the company without vision went out of business within the first two years, while the company with the clear, communicated vision is still around today and one of the top company's in the world!

Over the years, I have studied the leadership style of some of the most successful leaders of our times—in many types of businesses, run by women and men, from many different ethnicities—and the consistent attribute that I found among them all was that they were people of great vision and influence. They possessed the ability to cast a vision and influence others to help see that vision realized! As leaders, I encourage you to model that kind of leadership and to use the information in this chapter to help you realize your vision.

About Dr. Gather

Over the past 25 years, Dr. Gather Williams II has lived a renaissance-like career, spanning across fields like business management and development, marketing, corporate training and speaking, coaching, consulting, counseling, writing, music production, and songwriting, as well as community outreach. He is one of the most diversified professionals and serial entrepreneurs in the world!

Dr. Williams is a best-selling author of *The Art and Science of Success*, Vol. 7, with author and millionaire Matt Morris; *Is Your Husband Married?* and the long-awaited *When All You Can See Is Water*, due out Fall 2013. He is also the Associate Producer and Music Score Director for the upcoming 2013 film, "Me and Bobby McGee."

He is also the author of three e-books: *Short Codes, and How to Use Them*, *The QR Code and Everything You Need to Know About It*, and *The Most Important Ingredient for ANY Successful Relationship*. And he is a writer for Examiner.com and his own blog, www.drgblog.com.

He is a Certified Self-Esteem Reinvention Expert, life, relationship, and business coach, and he holds a certification as a Christian Counseling Professional. He earned his undergraduate degree from Southern Illinois University and also attended several outstanding universities on the way to completing his master's and doctorate degrees, receiving the prestigious title of Graduating Diplomat from Friends International Christian University. Dr. Williams received his certification as an Expert in Self-Esteem Reinvention, as well as his Christian Counseling Certification from the ACCA. He is also ordained in the area of Sacred Music Ministry.

He is currently the CEO of Dr. G Inc., G-Dub Exotics.com, and New Cell World.com.

He has started, owned, or held corporate positions with over 50 different companies, and has been an executive coach for hundreds of business owners in many different areas of business. As the owner of the Dallas Christian Counseling Center (DCCC), Dr. Williams has counseled many adults through addiction, conflict resolution, and marital and pre-marital counseling.

He is the executive director for his nonprofit organizations: Boys to Men, which helps young men find and manifest their true passion and purpose; and The Lula Williams Hope Center, which is a rehabilitation center and safe haven for troubled teens. He is also a mentor for the juvenile system and a volunteer for "Lift," a literacy program for adults.

Dr. Williams is a both a member and holds or has held leadership positions within several organizations, including Kappa Alpha Psi International Fraternity, Alpha Phi Omega National Service Organization, Prince Hall Masons, 33rd degree, DFW Marketing, Dallas Interactive Marketing Association, the American Academy of Christian Counselors, Speaker Co Toastmasters, and the National Association for Self Esteem.

He is also a 30-year BMI writer and publisher, and is listed in the 2013 *Who's Who in World Business*. In addition, he will be inducted into the Academy of Best Selling Authors in September 2013 in Hollywood.

CHAPTER 16

DO YOU KNOW HOW TO TURN YOUR FAILURES INTO SUCCESSES?

BY JOSE GOMEZ, M.D.

"Now, when anything 'bad' happens, I remember that everything that ever happens to me has within it the seeds of something better. I look for the upside rather than the downside. I ask myself, 'Where is the greater benefit in this event?"
— Jack Canfield, author of *The Success Principles*

THE LAWS OF SUCCESS

Have you ever wondered why is it that some people seem to be so successful at almost anything they do, while others are always struggling and achieving very little in life?

This is why. There are laws of success that all the successful people in the history of mankind know and apply to become successful. Achieving success is like a combination lock: If you know all the right numbers and we apply them in the correct order, the safe opens. There are no other options. In the same way, if we know the laws of success and we apply them to achieve our goals, we will invariably be successful. There are no other alternatives.

MY FRIEND'S STORY

Approximately 25 years ago, I had a very intelligent friend who was attending the same medical school that I did some years earlier. Unfortunately, to his shock and amazement, at one point, he failed one of his classes. Because of this failure, he became very depressed, developed a very low self-esteem, and became obsessed with the fear of not being able to successfully complete other courses as well and, therefore, never being able to graduate as a doctor. He started avoiding relatives and friends who would be frequently asking when would he be graduating or if he had already graduated. His life turned into a nightmare of constant shame, guilt, fear and poor self-image. This kept going on for almost one horrible year until he decided to do something about it and take control of this highly emotionally disturbing situation.

Today, he has been a brilliant physician for over 20 years, and I will share with you in this chapter what he did to turn failures into successes and fear into courage so you can do the same. If you know the laws of success and you apply them in your life, the outcome has to be unquestionably great. It can't be anything else.

LAW OF SUCCESS NO. 1: INCREASE YOUR SELF-CONFIDENCE

This is what my friend did to increase his self-confidence, and you can do it too.

- When we have poor self-esteem, we tend to be sloppy in the way we dress and the way we carry ourselves in front of others. My friend took great care in making sure that he was always dressed very sharp and walked faster, taller and straighter, as if he was a very important and busy person who had no hesitation in speaking to others with great self-confidence.

- Change your mind-set: He was constantly telling himself that he was an outstanding student, who was going to be a great doctor (no question about it) and graduate in the top of his class (and so he did).

- Even though many times he felt like hiding in the back of the classroom, so he wouldn't be noticed by anyone else, he forced himself to sit in the front row and constantly raise his hand to ask questions or make comments in front of everyone else.

- Finally, he also decided to only hang around with the most brilliant students in his class who always made him feel that he was as good as they were and to prove it by carrying on intelligent scientific discussions with the group.

You, too, can do all of the above things to increase your self-confidence. You can pay more attention to the way you look and the way you conduct yourself in front of others. You can keep telling yourself what a handsome, nice, intelligent person you are, even if you don't quite believe it yet. Remember, when any statement is mentally or verbally repeated many times, our minds will start to believe it. Also, you can surround yourself only with winners and learn from them how to be a winner too.

LAW OF SUCCESS NO. 2: FOCUS ON THE POSITIVE

Whatever you focus on, it will grow—and you will get more of the same! If you focus all the time on the problems that you have, guess what, you are going to get more problems. But if you focus on solutions to your problems, you will find more solutions available to you. It is simple as that.

- Kill the ANTs: The ANTs are the **A**dverse **N**egative **T**houghts that we all have constantly going on in our minds. To be successful, my friend tried very hard not to pay too much attention or give any importance to those negative thoughts that were telling him that he was going to fail again. It was not easy, but after doing it over and over, the ANTs gradually diminished until they were almost eradicated from his mind.

We all have the power to choose what kind of thoughts we can entertain in our minds. Yes, I know it is not easy to control our thoughts, but I have good news for you—it gets easier and easier as we make an effort to direct them in a more positive direction.

- Tell yourself constantly how good you are: My friend sat down one day (and I encourage you to do the same) and wrote a long list of all of his skills, strengths, good qualities, positive values, times in the past when he was successful at something, and what other people said was good about him. And every night before going to bed, he stood in front of a mirror and told himself, in a strong, firm voice, everything that was good about him. He would end this daily practice by deeply looking into his eyes and sincerely saying to himself: *I love you.* This is a very powerful practice that I hope you will seriously consider using on regular basis to achieve great levels of success in your life.

• Another helpful daily practice that my friend was doing whenever he had a chance was "The Bragging Exercise." You can do the Bragging Exercise too. This is what he did to be able to focus on the positives about himself: He sat in a relaxed position and after taking three deep breaths, he asked himself mentally or verbally, depending on where he was and the degree of privacy he had, "What I admire and love most about myself is…," and then he attempted to complete that statement with as many answers as he could think of. When he ran out of answers, he paused for a few moments, took another three deep breaths and asked himself again: "What I admire and love most about myself is…." Then he started all over again by providing the same positive answers he did before or he came up with totally new answers to complete the statement about himself. He repeated the entire process several times in each sitting.

LAW OF SUCCESS NO. 3: DON'T DWELL ON THE PAST

Another thing that my friend did was to never tell his friends, family or classmates about his failed class. Negative thoughts and conversations other people have about you can create a negative energy that can prevent you from being successful in life.

You might want to deny the power that mental and verbal energy has. Although this has not been scientifically proven, keep in mind that science does not have all the answers to everything in this universe, and that there are many phenomena that science still doesn't have a rational explanation for. Therefore I urge you not to tell anyone about your failures in life, since their constant negative thoughts and words can make your future success in life more difficult.

Basically what my friend did was to keep absolute silence among his friends and start all over again from scratch with a new group of medical students, as if he was taking the failed class for the first time in his life, and it felt so good.

LAW OF SUCCESS NO. 4:
FIND WHAT IS YOUR PASSION AND WHY

My friend practiced the following at least once a week on weekends, and you can do it, too, to achieve success in any areas of your life.

STEP 1: He listed 10 things that he believed he needed to do or that he needed to become, to successfully achieve his goal of being a doctor. When you do this, make sure you use a verb word ending in "ing," such as: "socializing more with the top students in my class," "constantly recognizing my talents," "having more fun with the subject that I failed," "managing my time better," etc.

1. _____ 6. _____

2. _____ 7. _____

3. _____ 8. _____

4. _____ 9. _____

5. _____ 10. _____

STEP 2: Then he made a list of what he considered his top five most important things that will help him be successful. He chose them from the 10 things he had listed before.

1. _____

2. _____

3. _____

4. _____

5. _____

STEP 3: He rated each one of the above top five things by assigning a number from 0 to 10, where 0 meant it would not help achieve his goal and 10 meant it would help him a lot to successfully achieve what he wanted:

RATE

0 – 10

1. _____ _____

2. _____ _____

3. _____ _____

4. _____ _____

5. _____ _____

STEP 4: Finally, my friend told himself, mentally or aloud, and with all the details possible, why each one of the five things was meaningful and how he was going to put them into practice in his daily life. He began by considering the things with the highest numbers first, and then continued with those in the lower numbers.

To be successful in any area of your life, I would like to encourage you to practice this at least once a week, as my friend did to achieve his goal of successfully graduating from medical school.

LAW OF SUCCESS NO. 5:
SET GOALS AND KEEP THEM IN FRONT OF YOU

If you don't have clearly written goals of what you want to accomplish in life, you will never know where you want to go, or if you had ever even arrived there. It's like starting a long journey without a clear destination in mind. You will end up just about anywhere, and that will be very confusing since you did not know, in the first place, where you were heading to. Going anywhere is like going nowhere.

Some of my friend's goals were to study so many hours per day (enough to make sure that he would not fail that subject again) and to always immediately review the lesson from the class before and the one from that same day. That was his strategy, and it worked.

I encourage you to sit down (the sooner, the better) and set goals in the below seven areas of your life. Be very specific, stating for each goal how much and by when, so you can make your goals measurable, and include a dateline to be accomplished.

1. *Business:* job or career

2. *Finances:* income, profit, cash flow, investing

3. *Relationships:* your marriage, at work, socially

4. *Health and Fitness:* diet, exercise, addictions

5. *Fun and Recreation:* hobbies, vacations

6. *Personal:* spiritual growth, education

7. *Contribution and Legacy:* service projects

Another practice my friend did to achieve his goal of successfully finishing medical school was to complete the blank questions he wrote to himself (see below).

1. What is a difficult or troubling situation in my studies (for you, this would be in your family, job, finances, relationships, etc.)?

_____

_____

_____

_____

_____

2. What negative benefits or payoffs do I get for maintaining this situation?

_____

_____

_____

_____

_____

3. What is the price for allowing this situation to continue?

_____

_____

_____

_____

_____

4. What am I currently doing to maintain this situation?

_____

_____

_____

_____

_____

5. What am I pretending not to know in relation to this situation?

_____

_____

_____

_____

_____

6. How would I like to see this situation different?

_____

_____

_____

_____

_____

7. What important five actions will I initiate to change this situation?

1: _____

2: _____

3: _____

4: _____

5: _____

8. When will I start initiating these five actions?

ACTIONS TO BE INITIATED	BY WHEN: DATE / TIME

There are several ways you can keep your goals in front of you. You can write them on a piece of paper that you can read at least once a day (preferably when you go to bed at night).

You can also have a board (your "Vision Board") on the wall in your home or office, where you can cut and paste different pictures and other colorful and attractive material that will remind you of your goals. You can carry small cards with your written goals, which you can keep in your purse, wallet or pockets, and read them any time you have a chance during the day.

I would like to suggest to you that all the previous practices related to the Laws of Success do not have to be put into practice all at once. Just select those that resonate best with you and use them regularly and consistently; you can also switch them around and change them from time to time.

Remember, you can be very successful in anything you want in life. You don't have to wait for better circumstances or people to be present in your life, or hope for something other than you to bring success to your life. Simply follow the same Laws of Success my friend did, and, believe me, you will pleasantly surprised how simple and powerful they are in helping you successfully reach your goals. Good Luck!

"If you want to be really successful, and I know you do, then you will have to give up blaming and complaining and take total responsibility for your life—that means all your results, both your successes and your failures. That is the prerequisite for creating a life of success."
— Jack Canfield, author of *The Success Principles*

About Jose

For past four consecutive years, since 2009, Jose Gomez, M.D., has been awarded the qualification of one of the top psychiatrists in America. Dr. Gomez has been an extremely successful professional in helping people to enjoy happier and more successful lives. He is a dedicated teacher who has been a former professor of psychiatry as well as the Director of the Medical School at the Technological Institute of Santo Domingo in the Dominican Republic.

As a speaker, Dr. Gomez has conducted a large number of keynote speeches, workshops and seminars and has made many presentations to schools, churches and charitable organizations on topics such as Success Principles, The Drivers and Your Marriage, Time Management, Stress Management, How to Deal with Depression, Anger Management, Mental Peace and Happiness and Transforming Your Life Through Loving and Selfless Service. He has also spoken multiple times on the five most basic human values of truth, right action, peace, love and nonviolence to adults as well as to children living in the homeless shelter, Sulzbacher Homeless Center, in Jacksonville, Florida.

Dr. Gomez has been personally trained by the world-renowned speaker and author Jack Canfield, co-creator of the best-selling *Chicken Soup for the Soul* book series and author of the best-selling book *The Success Principles*.

His extensive work with helping couples to live fulfilling marriages began over 40 years ago when he was appointed medical director of a community mental health center in Louisville, Kentucky. Since that time, he has developed his own coaching system called The Drivers, used to teach spouses, business owners, teachers and ministers how to learn to meet other's needs in order to be able to create successful relationships.

Dr. Gomez is the author of the book *The Drivers: Turn Your Marriage Around in 30 Days* as well as the creator of an online 30-day course with the same title. He is a dynamic motivational speaker who has delivered many talks in the United States and other foreign countries, including India and the Caribbean.

Dr. Gomez has also dedicated large part of his time, for over 20 years, to provide free medical services as a physician in a rural hospital in India. He is a distinguished member of the Royal Society of Medicine in England and a Founding Fellow of the Institute for Coaching at the prestigious Harvard University Medical School. He is also a member of the Harvard Business Review Advisory Council.

Dr. Gomez can be contacted by accessing his website at: **www.MarriageAcademy.us**

CHAPTER 17

TRUTH OR DARE?

BY KAREN L. ROYAL

*For my sisters and girlfriends who taught me how to play the game.

THE GAME: Truth or Dare

THE RULES:

- Two or more players

- 1st player chooses another player, then asks a pointed question.

- The chosen player must either: a) answer the question truthfully or b) choose the dare.

- If the player chooses "truth," they will answer the question out loud in the presence of all players and their turn is complete. That player may then choose another player and ask a question of their choice.

- Should the player choose "dare" to avoid having to tell the truth, the 1st player will describe the details and instructions of the dare that must be carried out by the player; this action is the 1st player's choice.

- The player choosing "dare" must follow all instructions and complete the task, witnessed by one or all other players and in a timely manner, if not immediately.

Special note: All players *must tell the truth or take the dare.*

There are no exceptions, no excuses, no hesitation, and no changing the choice from Dare to Truth or vice versa once their choice has been stated.

It was mid-summer in the early 1970s. The heat intensified as the morning hours moved through the haze of humidity. The hydro lines buzzed with fervor. Laughter could be heard from a backyard on a tree-lined street in this small Southwestern Ontario town.

The laughter came from inside a large, golden-colored, heavy canvas tent. This tent could sleep a large family. However, on this day, as on most days, its function was to house us local kids who were entertaining ourselves. Most of our mothers had instructed us to "get outside and play in the sunshine and fresh air" after breakfast and to not return until dinner time.

The tent was a stopping place on the gang's daily journey. Stories would be shared, fears revealed, secrets told. The tent was often a shelter from the world that went far beyond protection from the rain and wind. Instead it represented a kind of sanctuary where we ruled our world—a magic, safe place that began upon setup at the beginning of summer and ended sadly when school started in September. The rectangular shape of dead lawn where it sat would be the only sign of its existence. It was my father who proudly set the tent up annually, and it was our backyard where it remained all summer long.

And there we would be. (I say "be" because looking back, that's exactly the state in which we were. "Be" in the full sense of the word, fully present in mind, body and spirit.)

And there we'd be on those hot, stuffy slow days of summer. We gathered and sat in a circle, with our feet at the center—pairs of feet that had been bare for weeks and were grass-stained and dusty—and the game would begin.

Usually, the older girls would start as the rest of us listened with fascination at their maturity and mystery. They seemed to know and had experienced things that we simply didn't know were possible.

The 1st player would then choose another, and we would hold our breath in anticipation for the question…."Did you kiss that boy? TRUTH or DARE?"… or "Do you 'like' that boy? TRUTH or DARE?"… or "Was it you who took Mom's cigarette butt from the ashtray that we all got in trouble for? TRUTH or DARE?"… or "Was it you who fed the dog chili that made him barf on the living room rug? TRUTH or DARE?"

And so it went on.

As thrilling as the questions were, the next rush was the choice. Would we hear the truth? Often, the resulting emotion of choosing the "truth" was a similar relief to going to confession, although judgment would occur that could sometimes be far worse than 10 Hail Mary's. Good or bad, at least your turn was over and complete under the rules of the game.

Choosing "dare" was truly when the exhilaration began. The dares could be anything from saying a swear word to approaching a stranger while pulling your nostrils up as far as they'd go, then shouting three times, "I'm a little piggy!" (This, of course, without fail, would send the rest of us into hysterics as we watched from a distance.) Furthermore, dares could range from wearing underwear on our head on the school bus (yes, some dares trickled into the school year) to eating dinner without using our hands until our mothers noticed and we were corrected with a smack!

Losing or failing was not an option; the mere fact of participating in the game meant we were immediately and automatically committed. The only unknown was how and what events would unfold. The known or sure thing was that events would occur and definitely be guaranteed entertainment.

All dares left us liberated, brave, proud, thrilled and fearless, and that makes perfect sense because we laughed and celebrated each and every success. We had an extraordinary support group who would push and prod and poke and whisper, "Do it! Do it now!" and their very presence was empowering. Their pat on the back with a "She did it!" was the win, the trophy, the success of the dare. The respect earned was a tremendous feeling, and we saw each other in a new light that carried us into adulthood.

DARE TO BE EMPOWERED

I hold memories to this day that empower me. Like anyone else, doubt still pops up for me, hesitation must be faced, and fear needs to be doused. Vincent Lombardi said, "Confidence is contagious, so is lack of confidence." This could not have been truer in the game and in my adult life today. Do you ever notice how you feel when you are near someone who exudes that "darer" mentality; how you become less hesitant?

I liken "the game of Truth or Dare" to life itself. We are here to participate. We are here to make choices. We are here to be an active player and to surround ourselves with a strong support group. We cannot play alone, and conversely we cannot reap the benefits alone. Often it's like jumping into a chilly body of water that takes your breath away. However, within seconds, we adjust to the new atmosphere and the cold forces us to keep moving as fast as we can, and then have fun! It sure beats sitting on the edge!

I like to think of DARE as an acronym.

D. Decide. Join in the game in your mind's eye. Enter the tent, sit in the circle with your dirty feet, and let the game begin!

A. Audacity. It takes a certain amount of audaciousness to even think we can do this or accomplish that. The world will challenge you on this. Be a little cocky! You may end up holding your nostrils up shouting, "I'm a little piggy!" but that's ok.

R. (I have a few "R" words for this one) Realize. You're a participant and an important one. React. No hesitation allowed. Rejoice. Celebrate often. Reject. Do not accept the idea that you've failed. That is impossible as a player. And finally, Resources. Choose your support group wisely and with great care. No "nonparticipants" allowed.

E. Enter. This is not easy. You will hear that voice in the back of your mind shout, "No way!" Jump into the cold lake water, and your body will adjust, then get moving as your fellow players are wowed and cheer you on.

DARE TO TAKE ACTION

I worked with a new, young sales agent not long ago who was astute, professional and held a lot of promise. He had a natural talent to communicate really well with everyone he encountered and was well liked and respected. He moved through training and studied hard. I noticed, however, that he hesitated to go out on his own for sales presentations. I knew he had the required knowledge, and I felt he was more than prepared to branch out on his own. We discussed his concerns that, to me, were unfounded. He was certain he would forget some piece of information or lack confidence that the potential client would feel. There was that hesitation that just cannot be allowed, so as a true "player," I pushed a little, prodded a little, and poked a little more, I whispered, "Do it, do it now! I've got your back."

Then the day came when he had his own appointment. There he was, about to take the leap. We double checked his presentation and all required paperwork. We spoke about a few different scenarios and discussed the questions most often asked by potential clients. He was definitely well prepared, and I shared with him the confidence I felt— that I saw in him a fine professional. As he stood in my office doorway, I wished him the best and with a big breath and chin up, off he went. He did it! He Decided to be a participant. With his chin up and new-found Audacity, he Reacted and used his Resources, and he Entered by jumping into the challenge.

The following day he entered my office, closed the door quietly, then turned to face me. The person I saw before me was transformed. He seemed a little taller, brighter and more confident. Upon hearing the story of his adventure, we laughed, and with a big pat on his back, he heard from me the accolade I knew all too well from my childhood game, "You did it!" He had successfully presented to the client who was very happy with the product offered and signed on the dotted line. This young salesman told me he had to contain himself until he was down the street and around the corner before he rejoiced in his success with a happy dance. He felt brave, liberated and fearless! Those old, familiar feelings welled up in me as I listened, remembering the butterflies in my stomach and the thrill of the game.

What was really fascinating to me was the manner in which he told his story. He focused more on the excitement of the details of walking into the client's office and how he felt in each moment while explaining the program and benefits of his offering and the client's interaction with him. He spent less time talking about the actual closing of the sale—that seemed to be just the icing on the cake.

DARE TO FEEL ALIVE

Sometimes we need a boost of encouragement to take the dare—to be brave. For me, I'll read certain books, pray or meditate and take actions to move myself forward. Even if it's a tiny step, it's still a step to build momentum. Another idea is to be conscious of people and things that allow us to feel encouraged.

There is a game I like to play with the sales agents with whom I work. I call it, "You know you're alive when…" This game is as simple as stating what makes you thrilled, fearless and/or liberated. During my meetings and sales training events, I often like to open with this game to warm everyone up and get them emotionally engaged.

Here is how it works: I'll usually start with "I know I'm alive when…" then fill in the blank. For example, "I know I'm alive when I walk into a room full of amazing people that I'm expected to amaze!" (The thrill of this challenge for me is the complete rush of daring myself to prepare and courageously stepping one foot in front of the other to carry myself into the room. Often, I'll imagine those childhood bare, grass-stained and dusty feet. This thought always reminds me of our childhood bravery and that some of the dares I had to complete were far more daunting!)

Some of the "I know I'm alive when …" statements have been fun, entertaining and deeply moving. For example, "I know I'm alive when I gaze into my newborn baby's eyes"; "I know I'm alive when I woke up this morning"; "I know I'm alive when I begin my presentation"; "I know I'm alive when I work hard, work out, get out of breath, jump, fly, sweat, tell the truth, think deeply, see clearly, love, believe" and so many more. I believe that somehow, someone bigger than us dares us to do these things. I am always left humbled and impressed after playing this game.

If you're new to this idea of a dare-style of game, start with a few small activities to get you going. The following is a checklist to encourage you. Remember, you can't lose once you commit to playing.

1. Begin with change. Something, anything—from a new hair cut to a different route to work to slightly adjusting your morning routine.

2. Commit to your life journey—be the player who has entered the tent. Events unknown will unfold; that's the sure thing.

3. Be creative in your choices, whether you're choosing Truth or Dare or deciding on the dare to be proffered.

4. Be open to and don't miss out on the entertainment factor. Whether it's from someone else's success or your own. To me, it is crucial to congratulate, celebrate, and revel in the thrill of the game.

5. Finally, your support group needs to offer a platform for you to be free and be yourself. As mentioned earlier, choose wisely and not necessarily folks just like you—that would be boring. Mix up the personalities, backgrounds and thinkers. Spice up the potential dares!

To this day, when I hear "I dare you!" my heart jumps. I feel that rush of a mix of butterflies in my stomach—my gut says, "yeah!" while my head says, "wait!" Exhilarating!

The world is waiting for you to show up in full regalia.

Come on, I Dare You!

About Karen

Karen is best known as an excellent educational and motivational speaker. With high energy, she is dedicated and engaged. She is often referred to as a real, down-to-earth visionary.

Karen's professional passion rests within the energy sector. She foresees a drastic shift as North Americans move into the new age of environmental and economical awareness. Overall, energy has become and will remain a hot topic that demands the attention, and in some cases, the immediate action of businesses. It is her mission to clarify, educate and motivate these businesses throughout the region.

It is with a fresh approach that Karen's firm moves to change the face of energy supply, generation and conservation. Through transparency, strong ethics and coherent options,

Karen surrounds herself with some of the most brilliant minds in the industry to advise business owners so they may move into this new era with confidence.

To learn more about your business' specific market and options and Karen's speaking engagements, you may contact Karen and her team at:

www.karenroyal.ca

Or email: kr@karenroyal.ca

CHAPTER 18

DOING THE RIGHT THING FOR SUCCESS

BY BERNARD WALTER, ESQ.

Our personal journey shapes our success that is unique in everyone, so please allow me a moment to introduce my journey and myself, Bernard Walter. Son of a U.S. Navy captain, I attended high school in Virginia, Portugal, and France, attended college in France, and then took pre-med studies at UC Berkeley in the '60s. Unfortunate disenchantment followed exposure to the money-machine side of doctors' offices instead of the healing arts, so I left Berkeley and spent nine years as a celibate monk under vows of poverty to find deeper meaning in life.

Seeking the best of both worlds outside the monastery, I spent a year in graduate school doing philosophy and then studied law at UC Hastings, San Francisco, with clerkships at the Court of Appeals and the D.A.'s Office where I worked in public service for seven years before private practice that continues to this day in California, Nevada, and Pennsylvania where I now live with my precious wife.

Now, I would like to share a few thoughts with you about "doing the right thing for success."

THE BOOK IN YOUR HANDS

Having this book, *Dare to Succeed*, in your hands right now puts you in the driver's seat of your life, distinguishing you from most people you know who are living mostly on automatic pilot, going through daily routines, meeting reasonable expectations in their work, relationships, and personal lives, but seldom stretching as you are now to cultivate success in themselves.

In other chapters, you see different success paths, which is important because success finds different expressions in everyone. The challenge is to find one's own way to success in big and little ways, but for now, let's focus on a common link between paths to success, "Doing the Right Thing," an extraordinary demand on us every mindful moment of every day.

YOUR KEY TO SUCCESS

Modern medical science supports a familiar phrase, "success is within you," and I use "mindfulness" as a neutral, inclusive term for that pivotal state of mind that every religion, psychology or motivational school of thought addresses where we center ourselves in prefrontal cortex activities. Located between the temples just behind our eyes, this is our brain's planning center for executive action, personality expression, and decision-making. It coordinates our actions to achieve our goals, *prioritizing* conflicting thoughts; *distinguishing* between good and bad, good and better, same and different; and *measuring the consequences* of our decisions and actions. For success, everyone starts here; then, "How much do we use it for confident hunches?"

This lights-on "choice center" in our brains stands between honoring intentional goals and unconsciously indulging in routine, habitual living and patterns of immediate gratification. Actually, "doing the right thing" instead of the easy thing is a choice for us every waking moment but available only when we are mindful, meaning when we are not mindlessly operating on automatic pilot. Automatic pilot supports our success, once trained, but otherwise it ignites familiar, old behavior patterns that return us to the status quo, presumably, what we want to change. When trained, our prefrontal cortex provides the mindfulness zone for knowing the right things to do for success and happiness.

Now, some obvious questions:

1. What is this mindfulness that recognizes the right things to say and do?

2. How can we shift from mindless living to mindful living and success?

3. Once we can shift into mindfulness, what's next?

The greatest leaders, visionaries and thinkers of all time answered these questions for the powerful, religious, atheists, and searchers of all kinds since the beginning of time, all in response to humanity's search for more than mere animal existence. My goal is not to offer more answers to ultimate questions but to encourage your search for a meaningful life that works for your success.

GUIDANCE ON YOUR PATH

Without prioritizing one way over another—each has its value—this much is clear: One key will not open all doors, so we can be grateful for what has brought us this far. Doors are ahead requiring different keys to new rooms and higher levels of success. The challenge is to use the keys we have that work for us individually, that optimize the mind-body connection, and that quiet our minds enough in this "Age of Distraction," surrounded as we are by televisions, telephones, radios, computers, and our own mental noise. Easiest access to the prefrontal cortex comes both in crisis and when our bodies are healthy, emotions undisturbed, and minds very quiet.

So where to start? You have *Dare to Succeed*; you have some Jack Canfield techniques available, and you have heard "there are no accidents in life," so this may be a good place to start. Try some practical exercises described in this book and find ones that work for you.

OUR TEACHERS

What results from actually following our parents' instructions (imperfect as they may have been in some ways), following suggestions in this book, or following the teachings of the greatest thinkers in history? We learn to set ego aside; to accommodate disciplines, goals, and schedules; to achieve little, then more, to enhance feelings of self-worth and then love, given and received. Instead of reinventing the wheel in isolation, teachers can expedite our progress to avoid other people's mistakes, instead of repeating them ourselves.

Teachers can be found at home, school, work, in religious and public service organizations, in films, and in many great books. You have vast resources for guides to doing the right thing for your success.

If you are married, the first place to look for help may be to your spouse who may coach you in what needs improvement and even partner with you in this book's guidelines. The single most important decision you make in your lifetime is most probably your life partner choice. For success, this partner choice is so much more important than your career choice, which job you take, where you live, how far to go in school, which car or house to buy, how much you weigh, etc.

No other decision impacts more dramatically on your quality of life, capacity for success, and feelings of having lived life to the fullest, moment by moment, until it's all over. Parenthood presents challenges, but is anything more difficult or more rewarding than establishing, sustaining and continuously enhancing one's marriage? If you are unhappily married, work to fix the problems.

If you are not married, do the right thing when it matters most. Marry the right person for the right reasons, and then know real success for a lifetime, something that all too few ever know.

A long-lasting committed relationship or marriage compels us to confront our blind spots, selfishness, egotism, insensitivities, laziness, and all the weaknesses and bad habits that obstruct our way to success. Enjoy the rewards of saying and doing the right things in this primary zone. Interestingly, our internal stripes follow us into our relationships and environments so divorce, changing jobs, changing teachers, or moving to a new location only provides external changes with no escape from the inner obstacles blocking our success. Partner/teachers help us work through those foibles, conquer them systematically, and progress by overcoming the limitations of our upbringing, bad habits, miseducation, and even some of our genetic dispositions.

Secondary relationships count, too, by surrounding us with good like-minded people seeking to do the right thing for their success.

MOVING THE EGO OVER

Reading this book, you have good keys, but here I invite you to take small steps within yourself. Success does not mean moving Napoleon off the throne but does mean moving ego over so the mindful master within you can take command of your life to do the right things at the right time with the right people for the right purposes. Look closely and you will see ego at the root of unhappiness, failure, divorces, crime, etc. Dropping ego out to do the right thing creates trust between people, brings success between spouses, brings parents close to their children to succeed, brings teachers to ignite love of learning for success in students' lives.

Kindness happens in small businesses where the dry cleaner or restaurant server seeks to make customers happy by giving a caring look, encouraging words, compliments, and friendly smiles. Income results and much more. This happens in big business, government, the military, and in every occupation, even among attorneys pursuing justice instead of just money. Everyone can feel road rage, negative judgments, and temptations to destructive habits of mindless living, including workaholicism, only to regret it later when the facts come in. Doing the mindless, easy thing is ultimately harder.

THE GOLDEN RULE

The Reciprocity Ethic or the Golden Rule is perhaps the closest thing to a universal key to doing the right thing for success. Deeply engrained in human nature, it finds expression in most cultures around the world throughout history as a consistent practical guide. Without reciting variations from modern aphorisms to ancient Persia, India, China, and the Native Americans, here is a version of Rabbi Hillel, an elder contemporary of Jesus, who said: "That which is hateful to you, do not do to your neighbor. That is the Torah (law) and everything else is only commentary."

This not only sounds good, but it works day to day for virtually anyone interested in doing the right thing for success. There is urgency in this familiar message as the world's communities converge to ever-closer proximity thanks to technology. This is the challenge of our times, learning to live together in peace. It starts from our personal inner resolution to do the right thing and step out of the petty ego-bound world of personal self-interest that blinds so many so easily.

Self-interest is natural, but whatever your present role in life, consider this test in your interactions with others: If the roles are exchanged, is it still the right thing, a win-win? The student can help or not help a fellow student with a problem. The plumber can see a shortcut to complete the job in less time and discount his work. A boss can chose his or her words carefully in a reprimand rather than explode. A stressed nurse can take an extra moment to listen to a troubled patient and share a caring look and touch. Every day we have countless ways to do the right thing for others and even for doing the right thing for ourselves with sufficient exercise, a healthful diet, some quiet time to unwind, and enough sleep. Will we do it?

Turning to the used car salesman who shares the bottom rungs with attorneys in public opinion surveys, he can fleece his customers, enjoy short-term profits, and endure long-term consequences in quality of life, but the used car salesman can also make fair deals equally comfortable for him on either side of the deal and do very well by doing good in his business. That's a win-win, doing the right thing that leads to greater riches than the quick buck.

MONEY AND SUCCESS

Only caring about money is the negative stereotype of lawyers and businesspeople, and that is true of some. A remarkably successful attorney, President Lincoln, advised lawyers as follows: "Discourage litigation. Persuade your neighbors to compromise whenever you can. Point out to them how the nominal winner is often a real loser in fees, expenses and waste of time. As a peacemaker, the lawyer has a superior opportunity of being a good man. There will be business enough." Lincoln thought deeply, consistently did the right thing, including litigation, and knew success far greater than most attorneys in history.

Whatever we do for a living, we can recognize the value of doing the right thing while acknowledging that we each have faults, make mistakes, and will make mistakes when we again fail to do the right thing, but the moment we touch into our mindfulness, good decisions and priorities emerge and the path becomes clear again. Work smart more than work hard, and remember: "No one on his deathbed wishes he spent more time in the office."

Working as an attorney with clients facing hard economic times, I sometimes tell them how lucky they are relative to other clients I've known with hundreds of millions of dollars, celebrities often living in a hell, not knowing who to trust, not recognizing their real friends, and trapped in empty feelings behind all the appearances of success. The poorer clients suddenly feel rich with relief that they can handle their problems.

NEXT STEPS TOWARD SUCCESS

The concept of "success" resonates with emotional relativity, of one being better than someone else based on popularity, athletic skills, money in the bank, occupation, looks, winning a contest, an election, or some other recognition, but note what each such success has in common: an inner feeling of having arrived, a contentment, a personal inner satisfaction with those circumstances. Taking an obvious example, think of Joe Blow muddling along one day and Joe Blow the next day, a lottery winner feeling very successful but still exactly the same person. The relevant change was in his feelings about himself, his contentment with his life as it is. How distant is that view of yourself at this moment with all you have? A shortcut: Flip your "success" switch within.

If you center yourself exactly where you are with who you are on the totem pole of life—ranging from starving refugees in Africa to a cancer patient facing death, to a rich, arrogant, emotionally abusive tycoon isolated in distrust of everyone—will your life look so bad? If we take away the blinders of judging ourselves, evaluating what is lacking, instead of soaking in with gratitude all that is good in our lives, instantly we know success, we know riches, and we love our lives. Radiating such energies, a positive magnetism results, luck smiles our way along with people around us, and doors open providentially.

"Everyone loves a winner," and having that rare energy of contentment within you resonates to everyone, inviting success and happiness to follow your inner balance. This dynamic contentment is not apathy but a charisma that attracts more success. Success is an inner state of mind available to everyone, including you right now as you apply the techniques, principles, disciplines, and external mechanics of generating the appearances of success that may impress some people but that are just frosting on the cake of the success feelings you cultivate within through that work on yourself.

CONCLUSION

You are unique; your experience of success will also be unique at different times in your life. This is true for everyone reading this book seeking success. There are all kinds of people, all kinds of outer success, and one inner glow of success that we can all treasure. Ultimately, success is not money, looks, or power, important as they can be; it is a state of mind. You can do it.

About Bernard

Bernard Walter is a best-selling author, a former monk, a former assistant district attorney in San Francisco specializing in prosecuting pimps, and now an attorney in private practice in California, Nevada and Pennsylvania, serving business clients, personal injury plaintiffs, the elderly and their families, and the public by trying always "to do the right thing."

In 1996, he started the legal side of a free medical/legal-aid clinic that has been serving the poor and disadvantaged virtually every Friday evening since then.

In 2003, concerned about the quality of legal services being provided to the elderly and their families in Luzerne County, Bernard founded the Elder Law Committee of the local Bar Association and served as its chairman for many years. He is now a member of the Elder Abuse Task Force, working to prevent and remedy the abuse of the elderly in Northeast Pennsylvania.

In 2006, working with the Building Industry Association and the Better Business Bureau, he created an attorney-less, user-friendly, fast and economical dispute resolution program for building contractors and their customers.

In 2007, he and several friends started Generation to Generation, a nonprofit corporation that studies ways to enhance communication between generations.

In 2011, he began working on a career mentoring project for K-12 students and found friends in the local school board and administration to integrate aptitude testing of students, counseling for career options matching those talents, mentoring relevant to career choices, etc. That project now includes a new senior project required before graduation: an individual half-hour oral presentation to teachers and local citizens on "My Career, Why and How" so students have good reason to learn in preparation for meaningful career paths awaiting them when they graduate to do the right things with their lives.

Dedicated to doing the right thing in his work, completing tasks as quickly, fairly and economically as possible, he now focuses on estate planning and estate administration where the estate attorney's primary duty is to serve the interests of justice in following the decedent's directions while honoring the decedent and enhancing relations between family members and beneficiaries as much as possible. The estate counsel needs to be the person everyone can trust to do the right thing.

He would welcome your suggestions and comments regarding:

1. How you recognize and do the right thing;

2. The keys you use to achieve your success;

3. How you tame ego-centered "self-interest" in favor of win-win strategies; and

4. Your thoughts, pro and con, relative to the American Bar Association affirming attorneys' affirmative duty to serve the interests of justice.

Contact Information:
Law Offices of Bernard Walter
1674 Memorial Highway
Shavertown, PA 18708-1498
(570) 674-9000
E-mail: bernardlaw@comcast.net
Website: walter-law.com

CHAPTER 19

FROM ONLINE TRAFFIC TO PROFIT:
MONETIZING THE EMOTIONAL DIMENSION OF THE SALE CONVERSION PROCESS

BY JAMES DATEY

A SHORT STORY

It was early morning and Sharon stood frozen. She realized that her laptop had been switched on when she clearly remembered shutting it down the previous night after briefly surfing the net. There was no one to suspect as her mother Mary rarely, if ever, touched her laptop. As she hurried through breakfast, she was preoccupied by thoughts of who could possibly be trying to gain access to her computer.

After suffering through a restless and sleepless night thinking about the perfect gift for her daughter Sharon, Mary was no closer to a solution. Sharon was turning 22 the following Friday, and Mary knew that if she went out to buy a gift, her overly suspicious daughter would suspect something and spoil the surprise.

Pragmatic Mary had always felt that online shopping was merely frivolous but with time running out she was now left reconsidering its worth and re-evaluating her prejudices. Her ignorance of the internet had bred fear, and she felt more trepidation than excitement as she went on Google and entered the keywords, "gift," "daughter" and "22 years old." Still uncertain of what she might find, Mary was pleasantly surprised to discover that the search engine had revealed items that she found very appealing. She browsed through them and found herself attracted to a site that seemed to have an excellent product selection as well as helpful gift suggestions. She was ecstatic to have found exactly what she needed. "Sharon will not only be surprised but will definitely love this," Mary thought to herself. She clicked on the order form, selected her product, and made some additions to the card, then found herself hesitating as she was about to click on the "pay now" button.

Mary noticed that her heartbeat was suddenly racing as many anxious thoughts began passing through her mind. "Is the price right? How good is the quality of this product? Will I even receive the product after I have paid for it? Is this a scam? Is my personal information at risk? Is this site secure? What will I do if my identity is stolen? Is this a legitimate business?" she asked herself. In a panic she was once again skeptical of the entire process and questioning her initial impulse to make an online purchase. Mary felt an internal tug of war between taking a risk she didn't feel ready for and giving her daughter a wonderful surprise. There was an obvious tension between her desire for the perfect gift and her growing sense of insecurity. With a heavy heart she left the site but failed to completely shut down Sharon's laptop.

On Sunday afternoon, when Sharon was in the backyard with friends, Mary's mind returned over and over to the laptop and thoughts of buying a designer dress online. Unwilling to allow her ignorance and fear to stop her, Mary reached for the laptop on Sharon's bed and began her search for the gift once again. Almost immediately she came across a niche form, and in one click she found herself discussing her doubts about online shopping with other women in the forum. She learned that most of them had been buying products online because it was quick, convenient and safe, provided it was done on legitimate websites that provided secure methods of payment. Mary's sense of female kinship could not ignore the endorsements given by the other women in the forum. With a heightened sense of self-esteem and courage, she was able to put aside her instinctive fear, called "online shopping." Confidently, Mary clicked on the "pay now" icon without the sense of foreboding that action previously carried and completed her online purchase.

As for Mary's daughter Sharon, her laptop mystery would be solved and all would be revealed to her on her birthday. Little did she know that her previously technically timid mother had decided to brave the world of online shopping with a new sense of confidence and satisfaction.

A TYPICAL EXPERIENCE

This story depicts the general stages that first-time customers would undergo in their online purchasing experience. Traditional marketers will state that the cornerstone of the buyer's trip is primarily the recognition of need, then the information search, followed by the evaluation of options. Only after successfully evaluating their options, will the decision to purchase follow.

My extensive experience of online marketing has shown me that when it comes to marketing online, the process is less logical. Events must happen in a certain sequence before a sales conversion happens. Before providing that blueprint, let's dig into the emotional fundamentals of an online purchasing experience.

FUNDAMENTALS OF THE ONLINE EXPERIENCE

It is well accepted that the purchase decisions of customers are driven by the functional needs satisfied by a product. The product must include functionalities that carry value from the perspective of the customer. However, the product must also generate and satisfy emotions in the customer.

In fact, in an online purchase, emotional considerations are more prevalent because of the physical absence of the product. In the online purchasing trip, the customer (Mary in the above-mentioned story) goes through the following emotional stages:

- *Optimism:* Optimism drives the customer to the web. The internet gives access to the entire world with the click of a button. Products are unlimited and windows of opportunity are omnipresent.

- *Excitement:* The internet search starts to give positive results. The customer begins to hope that a success story is in the making.

- *Thrill:* The search brings favorable results. The product is found. At this stage, the customer has a growing confidence in the system.

- *Doubt:* The customer is overcome by doubt and is sceptical of the offer being presented. This doubt may sometimes be accompanied with a sense of insecurity. Security concerns may be double-sided. There is a risk of identity theft but also the risk that the exact product ordered may not be received in the exact form envisioned, or lack to meet expectations.

- *Anxiety:* The tension between the satisfaction of having found the perfect product and the insecurity and doubt associated with the online experience creates emotional anxiety. The customer becomes confused and fearful instead of feeling secure and confident.

- *Desperation:* Unsure of whether to continue, the customer loses all drive and remains filled with desperation.

- *Capitulation:* The customer reaches the breaking point and leaves the site unfulfilled.

For traffic to lead to sales and, ultimately, to profit, the funnel—the system that channels the customer to the offer—must address emotional hindrances that the customer is subjected to initially. The offer, for instance, must be extremely compelling and irresistible and compensate for those hindrances, making the purchasing decision easy for the buyer. The funnel must also attempt to increase all positive experiences during the purchasing journey. The phase approach proposed here aims to satisfy these objectives.

MY 4 ACTION STEPS TO TRAFFIC FOR PROFIT

1. **Increase the site visitors' confidence level.** The site visitors' confidence level is increased through three specific activities: branding, influencer recruitment and communication.

   - *Branding:* When done properly, branding creates the foundation of a strong connection with customers and the general public. Therefore, not only do you get your company and its products known, you convert simple awareness to strong commitment. There are specific activities that you should conduct in your quest for branding. One of these activities is the development of press releases. Press releases allow you to get your company in the news. They are a very efficient self-promotion tool that not only helps position your company and product but also increases your website ranking. There are many press release companies, but my preferences are PRWeb (www.prweb.com) and Newswire (www.newswire.com). Both offer discount packages for frequent publishers. However, if you lack resources, you should use the services of a branding company. Many companies offer this service, but Celebrity Press (www.celebritybrandingagency.com) offers a professional and proven method for fast branding.

- *Recruit influencers:* Influencer recruitment is crucial in these days where word-of-mouth recommendations and criticisms spread through social media faster than fire in a dry field. Influencers are people who are active on social media and blogs. Consumers trust recommendations from a third party more often than a brand itself. An influencer is the mutual friend connecting your brand with your target consumers. When you align yourself with influencers, they bring their audience plus their audience's network. Through the loyalty of their audience, an influencer has the ability to drive traffic to your site, increase your social media exposure, and flat-out sell your product through their recommendation or story about their experience. Social media monitoring allows you to find influencers who advocate for your niche. Once you start finding influencers that seem like a good fit for your brand, put them on a Twitter list so that you can organize and follow them most effectively.

- *Communicate with CPV campaigns and free content.* With pop-up CPV (cost per view) campaigns, a pop-up is deployed on a computer screen when a keyword is entered in a search engine. The search returns the result for the keyword entered, but as soon as the researcher clicks on the search result, the pop-up is triggered. The pop-up generated is, in fact, a landing page requesting the researcher's name and e-mail in exchange for valuable free content. Once the e-mail is entered, the subscriber is included in an auto-responder with a pre-registered e-mail series and other valuable free content. This series of communications and free gifts provides information on the company and its products and increases the subscriber's confidence in the company and its brand. There are many companies providing auto-responder services, but I prefer AWeber (www.aweber.com) and GetResponse (www.getresponse.com) due to their high level of delivery. For the CPV campaign, registration to a network is necessary. Many networks are available on the market. I prefer Trafficvance (www.trafficvance.com) because of their responsiveness but LeadImpact (www.leadimpact.com) and Directcpv (www.directcpv.com) are also good options.

2. **Optimize your website.** Now that you have successfully drawn customers to your website, provide them with an enjoyable online experience.

- *Improve your website usability.* If your website is not easy to use, visitors will be unable to make a purchase and may leave in frustration to buy from your competitor. Your website must be intuitive-friendly and easy-to-use for your visitors.

- I*mprove your sales copy.* If your website copy does not clearly and compellingly present the benefits of your company/products/ services, then your site visitors will be unmotivated, unconvinced and unlikely to convert. The sales copy must be compelling enough to compensate for all the negative emotions that the site visitor may be going through.

- *Tweak your conversion funnel.* Every single step that your website visitors take is important from the moment they enter your website to the final click when they make a purchase or submit a lead form. Your conversion funnel must be analyzed and improvements must be made to increase the conversion rate.

- *Perform multivariate testing.* The most dependable strategy to increase conversion rates is to routinely and systematically test every important element in your conversion funnel—everything from headlines to buttons to page layout. A multivariate {split-testing} campaign for your website must be set up and continually managed to improve your website conversion rate.

- I*mprove website design.* Your site design must be improved to better communicate your message to your site visitors.

3. **Study your site visitors.** Use the following tools to study your customers' behavior:

- *Qualaroo:* This online survey tool provides a quick way to run short surveys of your site visitors. (www.qualaroo.com)

- *Direct chat interaction tools:* Olark (www.olark.com) enables you to chat with visitors on your website, which helps you identify what issues your visitor is facing. You could easily uncover common patterns and frequent problems you have to address to improve your visitors' experience.

- *Survey your customers.* Collect your customers' views and perspectives on multiple aspects of your sale funnel and your business. You can use SurveyMonkey (www.surveymonkey.com) to email three to four questions to your users and seek their feedback in return for sweepstakes. This is the quickest way to reveal hidden conversion issues. SurveyMonkey provides prebuilt survey questionnaires and analysis tools.

4. Retarget and track your site visitors.

- *Use traffic retargeting tools like AdRoll to improve the conversion rate.* With retargeting campaigns, you can show banners to users who leave your store without purchasing any product and drive them back to complete their purchase. This is a very powerful tool since you have the opportunity to follow them as long as you want. One advantage of AdRoll (www.adroll.com) is that it enables you to segment your site visitors based on the products they have viewed, how far in the purchase funnel they've been, or any other action you may find valuable. Sitescout (www. sitescout) will also provide you with retargeting tools with geographical segmentation.

- *Use Adwords Remarketing.* With this Google tool, you can target people who have already visited your website and show them customized ads when they visit other websites that are part of Google's Display Network. This can help drive visitors back to your website and convert them by giving them customized products on customized landing pages.

- *Track your visitors and analyze them.* New tools allow you to track and collect data on your site visitors right from their first visit. The information collected could include the history of their activities on your site, the context of those activities, the website they were visiting, the types of advertisement that brought them to your site etc. This information allows you to assess the performance of your advertisement campaigns with accuracy, including social media campaigns. In case of a lack of resources, many organizations could provide you with services in this area, but I prefer KISSmetric (www.kissmetric.com) for their global approach to online tracking problem solving.

Many online marketers tend to believe that traffic is the main issue when it comes to online marketing. But traffic is available on demand. The real issue is converting that traffic to a sale, which leads to profit. For this to happen, some specific actions need to be conducted in the proper order. In this chapter, we have discussed these steps, which were developed based on the emotional stages the website visitor has to go through in his online buying experience. The method is valuable not only to the major company with a heavy online presence which uses it to boost its profits but also to the individual willing to generate a consistent extra income online, as he could gain the unfair advantage and drive to vendors offers, traffic that converts.

About James

James Datey is the founder and CEO of Gettec Media Corp. Gettec Media is active in the development of internet solutions for businesses, particularly in the area of traffic generation and conversion. James is, above all, a seasoned online marketer, specialized in traffic generation and conversion methods. His approach to traffic generation focuses on nine different channels of communication with potential clients associated with a massive use of new technological tools (as shown in *The New Rules of Success*). James' approach to traffic conversion gives a great deal of consideration to the psychological and the emotional experiences of the online consumer as explained in this document. To learn more about the author, please visit his website at www.jamesdatey.com.

CHAPTER 20

7 GOLDEN NUGGETS OF "WISDOM":
WHAT MY PARENTS SHARED WITH ME THAT COULD HAVE DESTROYED MY CHANCES FOR SUCCESS

BY MURRAY MIDDLEMOST

DARE TO SUCCEED—INDEED!

Before I get into how my parents almost unintentionally sabotaged my chances for success, allow me to tell you a little about my path and some of the little things I've picked up as a dropout, husband, father, coach, personal trainer, fitness club owner, fitness business consultant, a physio clinic owner, and a web design and marketing company owner that have allowed me to feel fulfilled and successful.

I once heard T. Harv Ecker say that "All you know is what you live." You can read something, you can be told something, but all you truly know is what you've lived and experienced yourself." I know the information on the following pages will help you be successful, but only if you read the words and absorb them, making them your own and applying the information to your family, business and life in general. People have a tendency to say "I know that" when they hear a piece of advice or

189

information, and it may very well be true. However, when we say that, even if it is just to ourselves, we may be shut off to what comes next. That next bit, my friend, may be the gem, the bit, or idea that could have put you over the top. So all I ask is that you read the next few pages with an open mind, absorb the information, and then sift through and see how you may be able to apply these lessons to your life.

I believe that in order to ensure long-term success in any area of life, we have to always be assessing, asking questions, being honest with the answers and evolving. That sounds like a very simple thing to do, and it can be. However, I don't want you to mistake what is simple for what is easy to do because the questions that need to be asked in order for us to grow are often about ourselves, our behavior and our decisions. It's not always easy to be drop-dead honest with ourselves. I'm going to share with you some of my own personal discoveries from my life experiences and self-assessment. I want to take you through my own rough evolution. To me, success in life is *freedom*, being able to do what you want, when you want. Applying the following lessons to different areas of your life could allow you to be more successful and happy in your personal and professional life.

"Education is not the filling of a pail, but the lighting of a fire."
— William Butler Yeats

DROPPING OUT IS HARD TO DO!

I know, I know, you're probably thinking the same thing my parents were thinking. "Are you crazy?" "What are you thinking?" "You're throwing your future away." "You have no options if you don't stay in school." "Do you want to be a dishwasher your whole life?" I wanted to be an accountant or stockbroker (or so I thought), but I couldn't take it; I couldn't take school anymore. I felt smothered; I felt was being taught things I would never use, by people who had never applied these teachings themselves. So I quit!

And my parents were right. I washed dishes for a little bit, I served tables, and I was an assistant manager at an IT store. All three were amazing experiences but not financially rewarding enough, fulfilling enough or challenging enough for me to be either happy or financially comfortable. It wasn't until I left school and had a clear head that I realized I didn't even like accounting or the idea of living as a stockbroker. They were someone else's ideas. Neither drove me or got me excited. They just weren't me. I made the accounting decision for "standard of life" reasons and not "quality of life" reasons.

Dropping out forced me to truly figure out what really drove me, what made me jump out of bed and want to learn and work every day! Don't get me wrong. I'm not saying you have to quit something (least of all school) to have a clear picture; it's simply what I did as an uneducated, inexperienced and stubborn young man.

Dropout Lessons

- **Be true** to who you are and what you love! A person cannot consistently perform at a level that is inconsistent with their true being." I believe Zig Ziglar said that.

- **You don't know what you don't know,** especially at 18. But you and I know it is really true at any age.

- **You have something to learn from everyone**. You just have to want to, be open to and care enough sometimes to ask the right questions.

- **Be patient;** the lesson will become apparent.

"Your chances for success are directly correlated to the number of viable options available to you." — Brian Tracy

IF IT'S TO BE, IT'S UP TO ME...

That's a scary idea when you have just dropped out of school and everyone is tells you that "the world is over for you." Both my parents and Brian Tracy are right. However, what my parents failed to mention was that opportunity is everywhere if you are open to it. If you have a vision and goals, then you have motivation and, ultimately, lots of options. So I took some of the information I learned from school (a surprise for me) and a lot of information that I sought out from all over the place and was ready to apply myself. I opened my first business. It was called MetamorFitness. I still laugh at the name, and I know you can picture the logo. But without this experience, my life most definitely would not be the same. It was the ultimate; I loved fitness, I loved helping people, I loved not being told what to do. Most important,

I loved the pressure and need to always be growing and improving.

Entrepreneur Lessons

- **Execution and implementation** is not what you think or say; it's what you do. The idea is maybe 1 percent of the whole picture. It is what you do with the idea that matters. The 99 percent implementation—that's the hard part.

- **Goals**—you need to have them. They can be adjusted, but you must have them. Once you have set them, then everything you do must take you closer to achieving them.

- **Focus.** In life and business, there is always opportunities and distractions. There is so much opportunity that the most committed person can turn into the "next shiny thing" person. To be truly successful in sports, business and family, we need to focus on the most important goal: achieving opportunities.

- **Flexibility,** as I mentioned earlier. Be very clear about your goals, however, be open and flexible as to how to achieve them. Do not simply shrug off new information because it was not in the plan to do it that way.

"Many marriages would be better if the husband and the wife clearly understood that they are on the same side." — Zig Ziglar

YES, HONEY!

Those of you who are reading this are currently married, previously married, or have even lived with another human being know that it is not easy. You learn more than you ever thought you would about another person. Maybe just as challenging, and just as important, you learn more than you ever thought you would or could about yourself. When you are that committed to someone, it is easy to become complacent, comfortable, and even take your situation and spouse for granted.

Lessons Learned

- **Someone is always the boss of you!** Obviously, I say that tongue-in-cheek; however, what I mean is that I learned it is important, maybe even necessary, to have someone hold you accountable. For me, it is my wife. I am the idea person—the dreamer—and she keeps me grounded. She keeps it real! If we look at other aspects of your life, it may be worthwhile—both personally and professionally—to consider having a trainer, a coach, a consultant, a mentor or a mastermind group to bounce things off of, keep you focused, and hold you accountable.

- **Trust** with and by your spouse, clients, teammates and players. It's a fragile thing. Trust takes time, commitment and consistency. Your wife must trust you'll be there. Your client trusts you'll deliver every time. To be successful, you'll need to put your trust in people at some point in time.

"Nothing I've ever done has given me more joys and rewards than being a father to my children." — Bill Cosby

BUTTERFLY KISSES AT NIGHT

I'm a dad; this is the one thing I knew 100 percent I wanted to be when I grew up. I haven't grown up yet, but my wife has given me two amazing children anyway. If you're reading Rita, thank you!

I don't know if anyone is truly ready for becoming a parent. I also don't know how one measures their success as a parent. I do know that while I am supposedly molding and teaching these two young humans, they are teaching me and helping me to improve my communications, patience and life in general.

Life Lessons

- **Oh, my!** Some things that you want in life seem so big and scary that you feel you'll never be ready for them, so you put them off and put them off. The truth of the matter is there's rarely, if ever, a perfect time for anything. Sometimes you have to take the leap rather than waiting for it to be a perfect launch, and develop it as you go. Ready, fire, aim.

- **Take responsibility.** Obviously, you have to take responsibility for your children. I am speaking less about them right now and more about responsibility for our thoughts, words and actions. Own them both—good ones and the bad ones.

- **Be aware** someone is always watching you. I guarantee that your children are, and it is not always cute or funny when you see or hear them do or say something you know they learned from you. The same applies to employees, teammates and your competition. Be present, be an example and be a leader.

"To have long term success as a coach or in any position of leadership, you have to be obsessed in some way." — Pat Riley

WHO'S COACHING WHO?

Over the last 19 years I have coached a wide range of sports, athletes and professionals of all levels. My love for helping people, teaching people and seeing others succeed has been rewarded handsomely with their ongoing relationships and successes, as well as the wisdom that comes from communicating and working with such a wide range of people.

Coaching and Consulting Lessons

- **Lead and people will follow.** Speak with conviction and passion. Act decisively and with purpose. Recognize achievement and greatness in others.

- **Systematize** and maximize your time and resources by automating, outsourcing and regular training and tracking.

- **Have a plan** and follow it relentlessly. A practice plan, marketing plan, business plan. Heck, even a life plan!

- **Maximize** each person's potential by keeping them engaged and empowering them.

- **The numbers never lie** if you are tracking everything. The numbers will always tell you where your system is failing.

- **Listen** to everything. People do not always tell you exactly what you need to know. Pay attention to everything. Listen with every ounce of your being. It will be appreciated.

- **You're not alone.**

HERE THEY ARE: THE 7 GOLDEN NUGGETS OF "WISDOM" MY PARENTS SHARED WITH ME THAT COULD HAVE DESTROYED MY CHANCES FOR SUCCESS

1. **Don't talk to strangers.** I'm sure you have all been told this and even repeated this safety credo a number of times to your own children, if you have them. I certainly do not disagree that at a young age this is sound advice. My own personal experience was allowing this advice to govern my adult behavior as well. Any one in business or any person with hopes of professional success recognizes the importance of *networking.* "It is who you know." As we find our way into the grown-up world, I feel it is important to *speak to as many strangers as possible.*

2. **Never give up.** I am sure a number of you have seen the picture of the stork trying to eat the frog and the frog choking the stork so he cannot be swallowed. Not giving up in that situation is certainly good advice. The truth of the matter is successful people give up all the time. Giving up is necessary sometimes to focus your attention on your sport, family or business. *Successful people know what to give up and when to give it up.*

3. **Don't talk back or don't speak unless you're spoken to.** Maybe you haven't heard this yourself. This was probably just me, and I heard it a lot. I had/have a problem with authority. I still believe you should question everything. Don't accept anything. If you want to be successful, you have to *understand as much as you can,* and the only way is to talk back sometimes, professionally, of course.

4. **Don't put all of your eggs in one basket.** This is the craziest thing I have heard as an entrepreneur. If you do not *focus all of your effort and available resources* on the success of your project, chances are, it will fail or be much less successful than it could have been.

5. **Get a job/career.** OK, as a parent now it doesn't sound like bad advice. But I will be telling my children to *get a life instead.* Pick the life you want to live and what makes you happy, then make it happen. You are responsible for your happiness.

6. **You have to work hard.** There are times this is necessary and even fun. However, if life is about living and simple pleasures, and you're

working hard all of the time, then you miss out on those things because you are working hard or are tired. I say *work smart, automate and systematize* so you get paid over and over again for work you have already done.

7. Stop fooling around. Again, this may have just me. I am sure you were all very well behaved. As I said wrote earlier, I still do not feel grown up, and I really have no desire to. I say, have a blast, have fun wherever you can, whenever you can. That's why I think it's important do something that you love. So every day is an event, not a chore. *Be excited for the next moment.*

There you go. I hope you have learned something or have been reminded of something in this chapter that will help you in your ongoing journey to a happy, healthy and successful life. I wish you much success.

About Murray

Murray Middlemost is the president and CEO of MG WebCOM, a vibrant and quickly growing Hamilton, Ontario-based online marketing agency. Murray is a marketing professional with a unique point of view: He believes marketing should earn its keep. Meaning that it is measurable, relates to sales, and is efficient and affordable.

Murray specializes in bridging the gap between off-line and online marketing through the innovative and often automated use of leading-edge digital marketing software and systems. The aspect of working with Murray that his clients like best? He makes it simple. Many of Murray's offerings are "set and forget" so clients can manage their own marketing campaigns with little to no effort while seeing substantial ROI.

With 18 years of successful entrepreneurship under his belt, Murray is a highly sought-after fitness business consultant as well as the owner of fitness clubs and physio clinics. He is also a proven guru in the area of marketing that works for both small and large businesses.

Murray's most impressive credential? Clients who experience substantial and measurable growth directly related to his proven marketing systems. Additionally, Murray is a devoted husband to his fit, strong and extremely patient wife, Rita; a proud dad to two amazing children; and an active coach in the community. He is a genuine visionary when it comes to living life to its fullest and helping others reach their business and personal goals.

Find out more about Murray Middlemost by visiting MurrayMiddlemost.com or his company at MGWebCOM.com. You can also email him directly at murray@MGWebCOM.com to find out how your business can succeed through marketing systems that work. Look for Murray at the Simply Small Business Symposium in Hamilton, Ontario, 2013, where he will be the keynote speaker

CHAPTER 21

THE TRANSFORMED LIFE:
FINDING FREEDOM AND WEALTH

BY RANDY LAWRENCE

My journey of transformation took me from bankruptcy to wealth, through the discoveries that enabled my wife and I to make over a quarter million dollars in just four months! In our journey of life we are on a path of development. For certain people, it can also be a path of freedom, wealth, growth, awareness, and improvement, as well as a path of great joy. At times, you may come to the realization that you're not satisfied or restless with where you are, and then the question arises within you, "Do I want to change my life, and if so, how?" Often the pathway for this discovery of transformation, change or desire comes through the path of adversity, and I am no stranger to that path.

My transformation and the acceleration of freedom and wealth came into my life from the 2,000-year-old ancient truths I discovered during times of hardship and difficulties. When I applied these truths, it virtually transformed my life overnight and moved me from bankruptcy into living my dream life, and it can do the same for you. By tapping in to theses ancient secrets, you, too, can posses the keys to unlock the life of your dreams.

I discovered these keys amid the rubble of the economic collapse of the real-estate market and economy in 2008. Admittedly, at the time, I was living a life that I thought was on purpose. I had a good life, a successful real estate investment company, a ministry of helping people, a beautiful wife and family. Yet truth be told, I was not fully realizing my dreams.

My journey of transformation began in 1997 when I left behind my past—coming from a broken home and being a drug trafficker who destroyed lives—to becoming a man of God and a person committed to helping others discover their life path. At 27, I placed my faith in God and began the process of transformation, met my beautiful wife, became an entrepreneur, began seminary, and truly started moving toward my calling of helping people become free to enter their Promised Land of destiny. In my pilgrimage, I begin building a real estate investment company, and from 2003 to 2008, had built it into a successful company owning commercial properties, with 40-plus rental units in a three-county area in Florida. Unfortunately, those turned out not to be the best years to accumulate a lot of real estate because of the impending market collapse that began to unravel in 2008.

As the economy collapsed, the banks I worked with were losing millions of dollars through their defaulted development deals, and they begin to exercise the call provisions in my loans so they could began to set new terms for my repayment. As this unfolded, it immediately changed the financial picture for each of my properties. As each new term came out, it forced the properties into money-losing positions, and with each new agonizing meeting, I was suffering more and more losses. To add to the injury, the money I made from renovating homes evaporated as neighborhood prices fell so quickly that it almost became like trying to catch a falling knife. Even properties we could sell for a profit became more and more difficult as the banks changed their lending terms for new buyers, which made it virtually impossible for the buyers to get a loan. After all the years of struggle, it got so bad, I was losing over $10,000 per month, which eventually led to my bankruptcy.

The financial collapse, which I fought for over three years, and my ultimate bankruptcy, turned out to be one of the greatest blessings of my life. As the market collapsed and the banks called my loans, and I had difficult meeting after difficult meeting, I was forced to come to terms with the truth of my life and my thinking. Prior to the economic collapse, I thought I was free in following God, but I discovered I truly wasn't. I was following God, but I was not free from my circumstances, not free in my mind, and not free in creating the life I truly desired. I had more realistically just relied on faith to carry me and did not have a real crystal-clear vision of the life I wanted to live or even a plan to actualize my dreams. I discovered without vision, people perish, their soul emaciates, and the power for living disappears.

Through all the difficult meetings, the financial stress on my family, and the pressures on my marriage, I was determined to find a better way to live. There were times I felt like quitting and even wondered when God would bring about a change, even praying for a miracle.

The miracle happened when it all clicked one day while I was searching for answers while reading the Bible. I was reading a passage I had read before, but it miraculously leapt off the page and pierced through the veil of my awareness. It became so clear that "I had authority" over my life and, in fact, a God-given dominion and sovereign power to choose my life, to control my circumstances and my destiny. This became a watershed moment that led to my breakthrough and the discovery of the ancient truths that guided me through all the challenges, lifted me out of bankruptcy, and brought my wife and I into true freedom.

Once this happened, I realigned everything and began making the mental shifts to apply the keys I discovered. Those keys quickly brought me out of bankruptcy and led to my wife and I making over a quarter of a million dollars in only four months. I want to share my discovery with you and the simple step-by-step keys that brought me freedom so that you, too, can gain freedom and begin living the life you've dreamed about.

KEY #1: DEFINE YOUR DREAM LIFE

This is where you make a shift in your mind-set, to truly begin deciding what you want. Too many people think their desires are not in sync with what God wants. Those desires were created within you, and you have the divine power to embrace them and begin living them.

Realize you have a God-given right to live the life of your desire. God wants you to fulfill your purpose and those desires. He has given you the authority and the divine DNA to be able to master this life; you simply have to know how to begin to tap into it. Like I was before, many people are at the whims of fate and just leave things in God's hands and don't have a crystal-clear picture of the life they want. This opens the door for hardship and uncertainty. You must develop a clear vision of the life you want, what it looks like, what you're doing and have a detailed vision. A lot of times people know only what they don't want; for example, I don't want to do this, and I don't want that type of relationship. You have to become clear about what you do want by spending the time to truly decide and become crystal clear. When you only have a fuzzy vision of what you want, the result is you can't move toward it nor are you able to draw what you don't see for yourself. A great quote from my favorite book is "for lack of vision, people perish." That means they never achieve their dream and their spirit for living dies. As you define your dream life, begin living in authority, recognizing you were created to do this. The very fact that you're alive and the dream lives in you, means that it is meant to be!

KEY #2: MASTER YOUR INNER WORLD

Before you can truly master your outer world, you have to be able to master your inner world. As I was going through all those difficult bank meetings and foreclosures, I realized that there were certain fears, limitations and false beliefs that I had about myself and my circumstances. I discovered I had to change those so that I could change the outcomes I was experiencing. This is where, through your divine power, you start to take control of your thoughts and bring them into alignment with your desires and dreams.

Too many times people think they can't live their dreams or they may not have what it takes because they don't know how they are going to do it. You have to begin to make every thought captive to the obedience of what's best for your life. When you have a thought that is not supportive of your dream, you need to recognize the contrary thought, cast it aside, and be able replace it with a thought that supports your direction. This is a learned step-by-step process to achieve this.

During this process, you also uncover any false beliefs you may have and remove your internal hindrances. So many times people have limiting beliefs they are unaware of, and those beliefs are holding the person back. They are your beliefs, and you have the ability to change them.

Also people can have wounds inside that have happened in the past, yet they are still lodged deep down and subconsciously those wounds are them holding back. Through a step-by-step process of forgiveness, you can repair those wounds. Those wounds are burdens holding you back from flight. Begin taking control of your beliefs and learn to rewire them and support your new direction. Through the process of daily affirmation and thought control, you can begin rewiring your beliefs. By beginning to master your inner world, you are ultimately using your God-given power to control your actions and responses so that you can begin getting the outcomes you want.

KEY #3: LIVE AT THE TOP THROUGH RIGHT ACTIONS

First of all you have to begin to believe that you were created to be at the top. If you don't believe that you are to be at the top, it is awfully hard to receive it. Think about human beings and any other species on this planet; human beings are at the top of the food chain. In fact, it was in the dark times I was going through that I discovered that both the Torah and the Bible make the same declaration that God has created you to rule over the circumstances of this world and be at the head. Your destiny and your position are to be at the top; this is your purpose!

No matter where you find yourself right now, you were created to be at the top and the pathway to being there starts through giving. You have to be willing to give in your relationships, work and finances. That means creating value for the people you encounter in life. So many times people think, What is in it for me? However when you start approaching life with what can I do for you, you are fast-tracking yourself to where you want to be. You are moving to the top with ease. Learn how to begin framing your mind-set to think through the idea of value for others.

Also, modeling the right actions is critical, and this can be one of the biggest challenges for people, because we all want to do it our way. I was king of this. I would see someone successful in what I wanted to do, and then I would model them but do it my way and not get the same success they had. Finally, I realized through the difficulties and failure that I was going through there was a right way to go, and you can simply model the right actions and get the right result. This truth is as old as the sands of time. Just as one of the Apostles in the Bible said, "Follow me as I follow Christ."

KEY #4: CRUSH YOUR OBSTACLES WITH EASE

Life always has obstacles, challenges or pressures that can come at every level. Learning how to handle them with ease is a powerful key that gets you to the top and living the life you want! In order for you to crush your obstacle, you first have to know that you already have the victory. The obstacle is defeated because you've purposed to not let it stop you; God has already given you victory over it. It is also important for you to understand the purpose of the challenge. It is not intended to stop you; it is intended to refine you, elevate you, equip you and, ultimately, promote you. The best thing that happened to David was Goliath.

Understand that there are also different types of challenges: financial, emotional, spiritual and physical. You need the right approach in dealing with a specific type of challenge. Unfortunately, people make a mistake and use the wrong approach; they will use a spiritual approach to a financial problem. I'm sure all of us have experienced a financial challenge, and we prayed and prayed for a solution to no avail. I remember going through challenges and hoping praying and waiting for God to bail me out. In 2006, when I had a house that didn't sell, I was praying the economy would improve, praying banks would lend money to buyers, and that God would send me a buyer. Unfortunately, I still have that house today. I learned that I needed a financial solution, not a spiritual one, and later as I applied this principal, I easily sold all the houses we worked on.

To crush your obstacles with ease, you have to seek the solution, not just look at the issues of the problem but look at the ways to resolve it and get past it to where you want to go. I discovered the truth that there are specific solutions to the different types of challenges, and there is a path to finding them. We live in a universe with the law of polarity, meaning if there is a challenge there is a solution. Once you have your divine solution, then take bold action with faith, knowing that you have the answer—don't waiver on your way to victory!

KEY #5: CELEBRATE LIVING LIFE

You have to become relentless in keeping clarity on what your dream life looks like, not letting distractions, disappointments or even things that look good pull your focus away from the life you want. So often people get distracted as they are moving toward their dream life. You want to develop positive and powerful emotions anchored to the life you want. Begin practicing each day; visualize you and your family with abundance and you and your spouse together holding hands walking on the beach. Visualize helping people, and see and hear the gratitude of how you have changed their lives. Visualize you and your family living in the home of your dreams. Start speaking about it now—today as it is yours, not some distant future but right now!

Celebrate the victories with each step. So often people don't celebrate their progress and end up discouraged. I was a person who didn't really celebrate until I got to the ultimate goal, but when I went through all these difficulties and it was ongoing for three years, I had to learn a different way. I discovered that life is supposed to be a celebration of our journey, and I could celebrate each of my steps of victory. Begin celebrating the small steps of victory, knowing that they lead to your ultimate goal! God wants you to celebrate the journey—there is supposed to be joy in your life journey.

I am on a crusade to help 1 million people begin living their dream and having a positive impact on humanity. I want to invite you to step out in faith and begin using these keys to start living your dream life. Join me and others at www.getfreedomwealthnow.com who are living their dreams so that you can receive the life God has for you. I am here to cheer you on and be a resource that will enable you take the steps toward living your dream life!

About Randy

Randy Lawrence is known as the "Transformation Expert." He has been an entrepreneur for over 20 years, founding four successful companies, and he has been a pastor for over 12 years, helping to transform people's lives. Randy is also the founder of multiple life-changing ministries, and in the last six years, they have impacted over 30,000 people. He has been featured in the *St. Petersburg Times* and the *Tampa Tribune*, and also on CBN, NBC, and CTN—all focused on transforming people's lives.

He has experienced his own life transformations as well, overcoming an upbringing from a broken home and his life as a drug dealer since the age of 13, to becoming a successful entrepreneur, pastor, husband and father. His own journey of transformation is testament to the power of possibilities!

His latest transformation technology stems from the discovery of the ancient truths that are the foundation for the Freedom and Wealth Acceleration System (FWAS). These ancient truths came from his breakthrough discovery that lead him out of the economic rubble and financial collapse of 2008, and took him from bankruptcy to he and his wife making over a quarter million dollars in just four months, which lead to the founding of the FWAS.

His breakthrough system is based on a simple five-step process that can lead anyone into the life of their dreams and a life of abundance. Whether facing adversity or simply not living life on your terms, the FWAS makes the impossible become possible!

Randy is fulfilling his calling to help 1 million people awaken to their personal dreams and become equipped to enter their promised land of destiny. To find out more about Randy, visit www.getfreedomwealthnow.com. Look him up and follow him on Facebook, at Freedom and Wealth Acceleration System.

CHAPTER 22

SUCCESS BY NECESSITY:
THE STORY OF T-GRAM

BY THOMAS DIAGOSTINO

A child is born with no owner's manual or set of instructions on how exactly they should be cared for. In May 1988, my wife and I learned this lesson approximately eight weeks early, starting on a lifelong journey called parenthood after just marrying six month's earlier. Maegan Ann was born prematurely, weighing in at a mere 4 pounds, 8 ounces, leaving her new parents with feelings of wonder, fear and inadequacy. What were we going to do with this baby? This child is so frail; I can barely even hold my own daughter!

We quickly learned to adapt our lives to meet the needs of our daughter. Our whole world revolved around her feeding and bathing schedule. Some days, we would just stare at our tiny miracle and thank God for entrusting us to love, nurture, and raise this child to become a kind and productive member of society.

Maegan spent only 10 days in the hospital and was then released to us, now weighing a whopping 4 pounds and resembling a chicken. We playfully referred to her as our "chicken girl." We quickly learned that preemies do not sleep well, as they need to eat very frequently in order to grow, and that an uninterrupted night's sleep was a luxury of the past. The tag team method would be a key to our family's survival now—in more ways than we could ever understand at the time.

PERFECTION COMES IN MANY FORMS

The first-born child is imagined as perfect. We would soon learn that perfection comes in many different versions. Maegan was meeting most of her developmental milestones, especially in the cognitive category, but she was slightly delayed in the gross motor areas, such as walking. She was most comfortable sitting in a W position on the floor, which we just assumed meant that she was double-jointed and flexible.

As time passed, we became concerned that our little girl was not walking. She could get herself to a standing position but was unable to walk independently. Her favorite toy became a shopping cart, which would allow Maegan to get from point A to point B. At the time, we had no idea exactly how resourceful she was being. At about age 2, we began taking Maegan to medical specialists to try to figure out why she was having such difficulty with walking. The message for months from several doctors was that Maegan was developmentally delayed, simply trying to catch up. That is, until we met with Dr. Maria Pici. She looked right at my wife and stated, "This child has cerebral palsy; how did you not know?"

The news that day was devastating. Our perfect child was destined for a lifetime of leg braces, physical therapy, corrective surgeries, doctor's visits, and misunderstanding by so many. We were told on that day that Maegan would never make it out of a special education classroom, not be able to get on a regular school bus, never walk independently, and that the road ahead of us would be rocky at best. Dr. Pici told Ann to go home and love this child; advice that we are still heeding to this day. I was working, and that evening I got a call from my wife who had time to process this information and was so sad. When she told me, my response was: "We will go with what we got. We will take it from here. I promise we will one day walk her down her communion aisle, walk her down her graduation aisle, and one day, arm and arm, walk her down her wedding aisle."

On that day, my wife and I made that promise to each other and to my, Mae, to love this child. We promised that together we would walk Maegan into her first day of school, down the first communion isle, and, eventually and hopefully, walk her down the aisle on her wedding day. These promises were complex in that they require lifelong commitments of great magnitude, including unconditional love, courage, perseverance, advocacy, and strength of character. Not to mention, the bills that needed to be paid.

MAKING ENDS MEET—AND THEN SOME

To this point in my life, I did not know what it felt like to lose, and I was not going to find out now. As a small builder with a child with a pre-existing condition, it was impossible to get medical benefits, so my wife began working as the off-shift nursing supervisor at the local hospital while I took care of Maegan at night. Regardless of how the economy was, I needed to earn a living. I remember my wife stating half-jokingly that she did not care what I had to do. If I had to get a job at Burger King, the bills needed to be paid.

The first thing that I did was to expand my business from home building to spec builder. I was buying lots at the county tax sales, getting the titles cleared, and borrowing money on the lots and putting up homes. I also started including commercial remodeling, became the contracted builder for a lumber yard, and started bidding on municipal and government work. I even did window installation for a big-box store; no job was menial. I moved from site builder to project manager to business owner, doing several millions of dollars annually in this two-year period.

Throughout my whole life I had to focus on discipline, through the ROTC, to the military, to Wall Street, to project manager at a large construction firm. It became not about me but about us. Just about this time, our second child, Grace, was born.

The economy was horrible: Bill Clinton was running for president, and his political advisor, James Carvel, was telling everybody, "It's the economy, stupid." The economy did not matter to me. I kept reinventing my business model according to what the marketplace needed. I joined the National Association of Home Builders and was getting more education on marketing, product selection, and the latest on new technology and on how to become a better builder.

Leadership requires a vision, ingenuity and the ability to project this to the people who work for you. I only worked with the very best contractors. I introduced a standard of operation to all my subcontractors, streamlined my operation, and required all employees of my subcontractors to wear shirts with my company logo on all my jobs. Even with the economy in the tank, you could see 30 tradesmen wearing one of my shirts and shopping after work. Even with builders in my town working for 30 years, I became the builder of record; I even remodeled the church rectory! I was doing whatever it took to keep a roof over all our heads, and at the same time, my wife was working hard to keep the family medical benefits, because one month without medical benefits could have placed us in financial jeopardy.

Maegan was doing well. She was singing up a storm, wearing leg braces to help stabilize her gait, and she had undergone several eye surgeries. She was going to physical therapy, including horseback riding and swimming, and she was no different than anyone else. Frankly, we had neglected to mention to her that she was handicapped. Maegan loved her little sister, Gracie, and they were the best of friends. Business was great and expanding, and I was proud of my wife, and I loved my daughters unconditionally.

At this point, we began to put away money for the children's college education. The gift of education was one that we had committed to provide to our children, even before they were born. We had no doubt that we had a bright, whole, loving child, and that she and her siblings were going to walk down the graduation aisle. So we expanded our promise to one day walk her to her first day of school to one day walking her down the graduation aisle. At this point, the economy started to explode, and my wife became pregnant with twins and now needed to be a stay-at-home mom for a while.

All the time we were looking to help Mae walk better. We went to NYU to see if she would be eligible for a trial involving a spinal operation to help her walk better, but she did not qualify for this trial. Several years later, there was another trail for Botox injection therapy. She was not a candidate for either, but Mae was always a happy child. She enjoyed going to singing lessons and school, and being involved in special needs events. We were still always a happy family, but we were always looking for opportunities to make our baby girl perfect.

A BUSINESS IS BORN

With a wife and four kids at home, I was always looking for opportunities to increase our income. I stumbled upon a new business venture called

Superior Walls, the newest and greatest in foundation technology. Up until this point, I had never made a major investment, and I had never owned tractors, trailers or cranes. However, I had acquired a few trucks, tools, and a few employees, as well as a group of subcontractors. Nevertheless, I became a franchise owner in the largest precast concrete company in the United States and in one of the hottest markets in Northern New Jersey—T-GRAM was born.

T-GRAM stands for my family: Thomas, Grace, Rick, Annie, and the anchor of the team, Maegan. T-GRAM is "the why" I get up and go to work every morning—what drives me to work hard, achieve and succeed. I know that this investment is about the future and generational wealth.

Things were tight again, and Ann had to go back to work full time, now as a nursing director while I was trying to launch the new business. Time was passing by quicker now, and we knew that in a few short years, Mae and her brothers and sister would all be in college, and our promise was to finance their education times four.

Mae was doing great; she never let us down. The gift of her beautiful voice was filling our church as she was now a lead cantor. This is where she was most proud of herself; where at the end of mass the parishioners would tell her how her angelic voice inspires them each week and what a gift she is to our church. Ann and I were so proud; we were so happy our perfect little girl was an inspiration to others. It doesn't get much better than that!

TRIALS AND TRIBULATIONS

In June 2003, Maegan became critically ill and was rushed to the hospital. She had a combination of asthma and bacterial pneumonia, requiring her to be on life support. Maegan and I were home alone when she woke from a nap stating that she could not breathe. Ann raced her to the hospital while I stayed home with the three younger children. She was too sick for the local community hospital and required transfer to a pediatric critical care unit in Morristown, New Jersey. I called my mother-in-law and told her we needed help, and she and my father-in-law came the very next morning and stayed for over two weeks to help with the children.

Our parish priest drove over an hour to visit with us and administer last rights to Maegan. I do not ever remember a time in my life that I prayed so hard. My wife's friends and co-workers were there, each taking turns nursing our little girl. It was the toughest thing I had ever seen; my little girl on a respirator, while listening to the other parents in the ICU talking about how their child did not make it and our child was holding on for days on end. My wife and daughter were in the hospital together for nine days. Annie never left her side while I took care of the three little ones with the help of my mother-in-law. My father-in-law made sure to see the three little ones got off to school, and as hard as it was, I went to work every day, trusting in God. There was a rumor through Maegan's school that she had passed away, and when our home phone rang, my mother-in-law told the caller that Maegan would be home shortly.

After seven days of being intubated, Maegan turned the corner and started to breathe on her own. Several days later, she was home. She was too weak to make it up the stairs, so from that point on, all four of our children slept in the downstairs bedroom as the little ones felt compelled to help their sister and cared for her. This was just the start of trying times.

The following year Maegan needed lower body surgery to help her walk better as her feet and ankles were deformed and the muscles in her legs were spastic. Part of this surgery was experimental, and for us, cost was not an issue. This was what we worked our whole life for—the ability to find the miracle. She required 14 hours of reconstructive surgery and then months of intensive physical therapy. At this point, we needed to separate the family, and Gracie, Rick, and Thomas spent three weeks in California with their cousins so we could focus on Maegan's recovery. We each had a role to play that summer. Maegan's was to heal and rehabilitate, Ann's was to be a great nurse and mother to Maegan, and our extended family chipped in with love, support, and prayer, all of which were essential components in this step of our journey.

After a long hard summer, Maegan went back to start her senior year. One of the greatest phone calls I received that year was from Mae's gym teacher, Ms. Brennan. She called one morning to tell us that Maegan had just finished running the mile, which was a requirement for phys ed. She stated that it took Maegan over two class periods to accomplish this, but her courage and determination had left not a dry eye on the track that day. Completing a mile run to some may not be a big deal. For Maegan, it was like completing an iron man competition. Once again proving that with unconditional love, all things are possible.

MISSION ACCOMPLISHED

Today, Maegan is a college graduate, looking for work like many other college graduates out there. Gracie is a junior at Temple University and is on the Dean's list. Rick is an engineering major at Penn State, and Thomas who is Rick's twin is a freshman at Temple University studying international woman's studies; both are on the dean's list. Ann and I are still working hard to support three children in college. My business career has come full circle I am presently engaged in the business of tax lien investing at this point to develop generational wealth. My newest business venture is teaching and public speaking on my passion, which is tax lien investing. Hard work, perseverance, truth and integrity, coupled with the power of unconditional love and family, is the foundation of our lives all wrapped around our faith in the Devine. We will always have struggles; struggle is what allows us to appreciate life's gifts. The bottom line is that it's never about us; it's about commitment; it's about trusting each other; it's about unconditional love; it's about no excuses. It's about success by necessity.

About Tom

Tom DiAgostino grew up in the Monroe Housing Projects in the South Bronx of New York City. He started his college career at CUNY and then Pace University, both in the Army ROTC. At Pace, he did an internship at Reynolds Securities, a financial firm where he achieved a tremendous education in the markets, and has been heavily involved in the trading markets ever since. Eleven years later, he married his bride of 25 years and has four beautiful children. His business career started in 1988 as a project manager for Orenstein Construction. It was then he purchased his first batch of tax liens through the tax sale process. In 1992, he ventured out on his own and formed the company T-GRAM Inc., an acronym for Thomas, Grace, Rick, Ann and Maegan (he says he is the hyphen). He started as a site builder, then became a developer of small subdivisions, then bought a Superior Wall franchise that has set over 1,000 homes. In the last decade, Tom has been a rehabber, builder, and tax sale investor. His experiences entail every facet of real estate. Throughout his career, he has used tax sale properties for rehab projects, wholesales and rentals. Tom has kept current through education and seminars, adding new tools to his business practice to stay on top of the ever-changing marketplace. Tax sales are the foundation of Tom's real estate business.

CHAPTER 23

EMPLOYEE CONNECTION = MOTIVATION, INITIATIVE AND PROFIT

BY TONI FITZGERALD

It was just last year in the dead middle of the night that I lay wide awake, planning my escape. Under a poorly hung mosquito net, and on a thin foam mattress on the wooden floor of a school room in Nairobi, Kenya, I dreamed of the luxury beachside holiday resorts advertised in the airline magazine.

Laying around me, and in deep sleep from jetlag and emotional exhaustion, was the handful of my female travelling companions. In the next primary school room slept the men in our small group—husbands, boyfriends, sons or mates. Outside the door, alone, sat a very heavily armed security guard.

Had it only been three days since I left my home in Sydney and arrived in the slums in Africa? The putrid smells, the undrinkable water, nothing that turned on or off or flushed, the unrelenting poverty, and the biggest smiles from the widest brown eyes of 260 Matopeni school students who listened to our every word, curiously watched our every movement, and who wanted more out of life than this country was offering them.

Today, our group was leaving and moving on to villages in Uganda, and eventually Mali. Could I stand another four weeks living like this?

Hand sanitizer after their every touch or cough or sneeze, bottled water, meals of only ground nuts and rice, and that smell… If I was leaving the group, it had to be today.

Maybe it was the fear of failure, or being seen as a spoiled city girl… but I nervously dared to continue. I stayed on the path so very less travelled.

Through those weeks in Africa I experienced unbelievable animal encounters on safari, ate game at one of the top 50 restaurants of the world, taught school kids drama classes, met a Massai warrior chief's son, and slept on the ground under the stars next to noisy donkeys and camels in villages without running water and electricity. I met amazing people who are making a real difference. I graciously accepted a live chicken as a thank you gift, bought a family a goat for $25, travelled 90 minutes in a bus (and back) just to use a real toilet, danced into the night to African drums, and learned to drink vodka straight and hot!

I have so many vivid memories, none less impactful to me than that morning I decided to stay with my friends and continue on this journey. Packing our bags into a rickety old bus, I was acutely aware that I just couldn't wait to get out of there and away from the poverty, yet I watched Loretta, Liz, Alice, Kate, and big, booffy Laurie and Matt sobbing at the thought of leaving behind the smiling, laughing school kids who had touched their hearts and with whom they had formed some type of connection.

Was my heart stone? Why did I not feel this sense of connection? I wanted to leave the germs and the smells behind, yet I was now jealous of the emotions, passion and connection that my colleagues were feeling and I wasn't. In these few days, their perspective and what was important in their lives had changed.

MY TURN

Weeks later, in a Niamana village, it happened for me. I had met Kadiatou, a strong, educated local woman in her 30s, who was working to educate people, especially women, and turn them away from some horrible traditions and customs. Kadi had recognized that the only way her country could move forward was through the women. Women do everything. They grind the maize every day, look after the home and the children, and do whatever they can to earn a little money. And nearly always, the girls are kept out of school to help keep house. The cycle needs to be broken.

Kadi asked if Rae and I and some ladies in our now close group would meet with some women who wanted help and advice. This was arranged for after dinner as all the women had so much that had to be done before they could take a break. We waited under a tree. 9 p.m., 10 p.m.... maybe they weren't coming. Then, after 11 p.m., one by one, about 20 women arrived through the darkness. By firelight and torches I could see their weathered skin and the wanting in their dark, sunken eyes... but there was also eagerness, joy and life in those eyes that was only outshone by the array of bright, colorful fabrics in their Malian clothes and headscarves.

My life at home had so much, and theirs so little. I wanted to reach out and hug each and every one of those women. I felt connected, I felt alive, and that feeling motivated me to want to do something to help them, and especially their daughters, to a better life.

LEAVING A LEGACY

Back in Sydney, when telling my story to friends, they laughed with me, cried with me, and all said they were envious of this emotional experience, this connection that I had found, this "something" that was motivating me to do more. These friends wanted to follow me in this cause... and I realized, in every part of our lives, people are looking for leaders who have passion, who can show us something bigger than ourselves. Every single one of us wants to leave a legacy, wants to know that our life has had meaning and purpose.

Because it consumes so much time, for many, that legacy is their work. People are looking for passionate leaders and managers; they no longer want to be employees who just "turn up" to get their paycheck. Yet as a manager or business owner, you are probably still treating employees this way, and it probably frustrates you that there seems to be no caring from them. So you feel like a charity sometimes, or a parent.

Wouldn't it be great if there were some strategies that would help you get your people involved? Working with franchise groups and corporate clients, I have found that when people feel connected to the leader of the organization, their productivity increases by 20 to 30 percent.

For people who spend an average of 55 minutes a day on Facebook (believe it or not), your employees are actually searching for something you can give them, and it will also grow the profile of your company outside of your workforce.

Organizations must listen to their hearts. Most businesspeople and organizations today think that profits can only be driven from tactics. In an age where products and services can be compared with a mouse click, companies must not ignore their hearts; they must connect with the hearts of their employees by putting strategies in place that inspire them to want to follow their leaders.

Great company leaders must represent something that even their most junior employee can connect with. As a leader you need to wear some of your heart on your sleeve and stand for something bigger than profits.

Imagine your employees were making a YouTube video about you. Would that movie be about your heart's vision, or just your career achievements? If you died tomorrow, who among them would be at your funeral?

E-Myth author, Michael Gerber, says that every company, no matter how small, must have a "bust." Employees are longing to say, "That's our leader. We are proud to work here knowing that this company is achieving more than just building widgets." Today's leader makes no secret of his own past and present personnel struggles, which are reflected in seeing the organization now contribute to the well-being of a specific community or cause. Your employees will connect with you and the soul of the organization when they know who you are and what you stand for . . . not just your vision for the balance sheet. This connection fosters motivation by creating a culture of this being "a great place to work," resulting in increased productivity and employee retention.

As Stephen Covey, author of *The 7 Habits of Highly Effective People,* said when writing for Margot Cairnes, "Corporations today need both the 'minds' and the 'hearts' of their employees to succeed in the current marketplace."

Great working teams come from connection. When people know they are all working for something bigger than their individual paychecks, they create their own movement, which drives growth and company profit. This connection motivates them in different ways as they move through their own life cycle. Younger employees today want to work for companies that are seen as hip and also driving environmental responsibility. Smart executives and business owners know that motivators change as they progress in experience, formal qualifications, aspirations and family status.

Companies are increasingly realizing that what motivates an employee at recruitment will not keep them fulfilled over the years.

Are you making the mistake of thinking that more benefits or work challenges, more education and career growth opportunities are what employees need for their own fulfillment? This is just one area and does not apply to all people. We talk about work/life balance. People who know that their work efforts are truly making a difference in the world don't talk about this balance because their life already has meaning, and this results in higher levels of engagement, productivity and profit!

Being disconnected can cost you millions. Disconnected and disengaged employees are the silent killers of an organization. According to Gallup, $270 billion to $300 billion is lost to the American economy as a whole, with lost productivity and innovation due to low employee initiative and motivation. On the other hand, companies that encourage a culture where employees feel valued and a part of the whole success have higher numbers of self-starters and enthusiastic teams.

Work. Play. Connect. Savvy leaders are realizing that successful teams blur the lines between work and play. They do that when feeling valued and connected and are acting like a team, not soley a bunch of individuals doing just enough in their eight hours of time to be allowed back to do it all again tomorrow.

When speaking with companies to help them find their heart and a passion that can be shared with all employees, I first challenge them to "get disturbed":

- What wrong can they help right?
- What rules of the game should they declare unacceptable in today's society?
- Where can they make a difference to an individual?
- How can they change lives?
- How can it build their brand capital?

It must be a fit with the organization, or it will be seen as shallow and without heart.

After speaking at corporate events, I often meet business leaders who are contributing to the well-being of society through education, donation or volunteering. They share this information with me but have never thought to tell their managers and employees about their actions or their passion. By withholding this spark, they are denying their people this opportunity to be a part of that something that could be bigger than themselves.

I met the owner of a high-tech home theater retail chain whose youngest child was born deaf. The owner now personally funds major research into this condition and pays for hearing aids for families who cannot afford it. Imagine how many more young children could be helped if his organization as a whole knew of this passion, and it was strategically worked into the heart of the company. For even the newest floor staff, their perception would change from "working with cool toys that only rich people can afford" to one of "I am helping change the lives of children so that they can also hear these amazing sounds." He would be connected to the organization because it stands for something bigger than profits, yet at the same time, his connection would motivate him to actions that drive those profits.

My experience in Africa and my work with leaders of teams and entire organizations have shown me there are specific keys to building a connected workforce.

The 4 Keys to Employee Connection

1. **Vision:** At the heart of the organization there needs to be a vision that could inspire every employee, from the management to customer-serving staff. This is separate from the vision of corporate growth. This is the vision that allows everyone to see that no matter what their capacity is, they can contribute and affect change.

2. **Voice:** When employees feel that their company stands for something that contributes to society, they want to shout about it. The more connected they feel, the more they want to tell and do. The cause that started as just the passion of the leader becomes adopted in varying degrees by the individuals. This means the company must allow each employee the freedom to voice his or her ideas around the subject. This involves so much more than simply putting a suggestion box on the manager's desk. It often requires a cultural change at the heart of the organization.

3. **Value:** For the employees to feel connected, they need to know that their part of the contribution has value, their efforts are making a

difference, and their roles are important. They need to see a tangible link, a direct result from their input. When helping companies create these strategies, we look for constant and recurring actions, not a blanket yearly donation or event.

4. Victory: This serves as a reminder of the value and contribution that each person shares. Celebrate even the smallest milestones, share the team's ideas and achievements with the whole organization. Adopt the good news about what is being achieved as your own news and communicate this to everyone.

Now, imagine this...

Imagine a workforce that is so connected to the organization that at BBQs and family events, they want to talk about what change it is striving to achieve.

In my work with companies to help them with marketing via social media and online public relations, whether they are a one-city business or an international consumer brand, I have found that the power of employee connection when coupled with communication tools, such as Facebook, Twitter, Google and YouTube, creates workplaces where every employee is not just a team member but your advocate, your raving fan.

I never considered myself a leader. In fact, I failed John Maxwells' leadership class. Now, I am amazed and humbled how people so enthusiastically want to follow me when they hear my story of five weeks in Africa and how now we are changing lives, one little girl at a time. A message whose time has come and a platform for massive word of mouth will change the world.

What you as the leader of a team or an organization have at your fingertips for the first time in history is both the opportunity to stand for a message whose time has come and the power of social media, which is a platform for massive word of mouth. Organizations today truly can benefit when they dare to succeed with something bigger than themselves.

About Toni

Motivational Speaker • Social Media Marketing Business Consultant • Networking Trainer to Lawyers and Accountants

Toni Fitzgerald is an engaging and passionate motivational speaker, having worked in radio and with four major television networks, as well as gaining a real-world, bricks-and-mortar background in marketing strategy, advertising and promotion for B2B, retail and lifestyle companies. She is author of the marketing manual *Shoptactics*, two years in a row has been a senior judge for the Financial Review Internet Awards, and was named by the Australian National Newspaper as "One of the New Stars of the New Economy."

As the only Australian chosen to contribute to *Dare to Succeed,* Toni now shares her lessons on the value of connecting with both your customers, and perhaps more important, with your employees; and how savvy businesses are using this engagement to motivate their employees and foster their initiative. Toni speaks from the heart about lessons learned from the challenges in her career, from sidekick to Humphrey B. Bear on children's television, from national current affairs TV journalist to high-profile corporate marketing manager, and to the very ups and terrible downs as a business owner. Also, the stories of her challenges across her time spent in Africa are funny, sad and inspiring all at the same time.

Toni believes that the fast and changing pace of life today has left most of us not knowing who we are and what we want...and until we can connect with our own self, we cannot be happy in the job that we are doing or the company we are working for. Toni is not just a motivational speaker but has a strong focus on guiding businesses in developing sustainable, self-perpetuating and loyal relationships with both customers and employees.

As Toni says: "It's no longer business as usual." You can read more about her at www.tonifitzgerald.com.

CHAPTER 24

THE SCIENCE OF ETERNAL SUCCESS:
HOW TO SOLVE ANY PROBLEM AND WIN THE GAME OF LIFE

BY NAVEEN KHURANA

Permit me to begin with a few definitions of the key words we'll be discussing:

Science involves understanding a body of knowledge in a particular area and the laws and principles that govern that area. Observations, experiments and experience, then verify those principles and laws to be true in all times and situations.

Eternal includes past, present and future, with no beginning and no end.

Success means to accomplish a desired worthy goal or goals.

Science and laws are nothing new to us. Whether we realize it or not, we've been interacting with natural sciences and laws in physics, biology, chemistry and mathematics from our very first moments in this world!

When we were learning to walk, lost our balance, and fell down, that was an interaction with the laws of physics, gravity in particular. When we tried to grab a lit candle from the tip and got burnt, the physical laws of the elements made their introduction.

Just as science and laws exist in our physical world, they also exist in all of life's dimensions. In reality, there are laws and science that govern all areas of our life, including prosperity, relationships, health, wisdom, happiness and success.

And, as with other sciences and related laws, they are in play at all times; they are always affecting us, every single moment. They govern every action, word and thought.

The problem is, most people don't know these laws exist. But that lack of knowledge does not negate them nor exempt us from their consequences. Whether a child knows that fire burns or not, if she touches it, it will burn. In the same way, whether we are aware of these life sciences or not, we will be affected by them. Ignorance or intention will not excuse us from the law's effects.

If somebody jumps out of a plane and tries to fly using his power of intention, will he be successful? Science and laws cannot be overlooked or overcome. The successes, pains and pleasures we encounter are directly related to these laws and how we respect or do not respect them.

The good news is, this knowledge is not abstract, flowery language. Rather, it is tangible and anybody can learn it and use it to gain huge success today and from here on.

This knowledge has been in existence since time immemorial, and it can help the practitioner create wonderful outcomes in every sphere of life: physical, mental, emotional, spiritual, social and financial.

The key to transforming any life from a mixture of dissatisfaction and temporary happiness to eternal, thrilling awareness and pleasure is to understand these sciences and laws and integrate them into one's life. They are the single most important ingredient in the success of your life.

It is the struggle with these invisible forces that creates unwanted results. Imagine your frustration if you did not know about gravity and tried your best to fly. Try and try, and you will still not succeed. The same is true for all the laws that govern our interactions in life. Once you understand these laws, you can learn to use them to enhance your life and gain successes beyond your greatest expectations.

I've taken the initiative to boil down these laws to 101 that are the most relevant for our current situation and time. They cover the widest range of topics you'll ever come across in any life "success" program. Here are just a few of the topics covered:

The laws of:

- Pain and Pleasure
- Independence and Control
- Transmigration and Reincarnation
- Satisfaction and Dissatisfaction
- Karma—Action and Reaction
- Temporality and Eternality
- Material Nature and the Universe

There are 101-plus such laws that we are intimately associated with at all times on *www.scienceofeternalsuccess.com*, which are available as a free resource to help you live an enlightened and fulfilling life.

But just knowing them isn't enough. Without a road map that guides us through scientific implementation, objective information alone is inadequate. And, as in any endeavor, one must have a guide or teacher to really reach the highest stages of success. The endeavor for enduring and eternal success is no different. A mentor can point the way, point out the pitfalls and give you guidance and encouragement as you gradually traverse the path to everlasting success.

In addition, these laws hold the keys to giving you solid answers to all the important questions about life that you could ask. There are over 150 such questions that I share on our website at *www.scienceofeternalsuccess.com*. Again, this is a free resource to help you live a life with complete clarity, calmness and confidence for certain success.

Also these laws and answers to life's questions, when used systematically, bring about amazing transformations in our character and behaviors, mental and physical health, relationships and prosperity. The website *www.scienceofeternalsuccess.com* lists over 40 wonderful behaviors in ourselves and others that can be quickly manifest. The website is a free resource to give you practical and easy ways to uncover the best version of your amazing self.

Stay with me as we take a look at four core questions about life and some simple steps to help you begin to use this knowledge in your life.

CORE QUESTION 1: WHO AM I BY CONSTITUTION AND WHAT IS MY PURPOSE? (WHY WAS I BORN AND TO SUCCEED IN WHAT?)

By constitution you are an eternal person undertaking a human journey. By that I mean that you are an eternal being, who is taking the journey in this vehicle called the human body. Further, by nature not only are you eternal but full of knowledge and joy. And this joy and knowledge is ever increasing in the right setting. By constitution, this nature of yours cannot be changed by any means; it can only be covered over.

Here are some examples. Salt and sugar have their unique tastes by constitution. Water by its constitution is always wet. Fire by its constitution always gives off heat and light. Other examples can be given of many elements in nature that by constitution have certain characteristics and qualities that cannot be modified or changed.

However, the nature of these elements can be apparently covered over when they are mixed with other elements. For example, when salt is mixed with sugar, then it is hard to experience the true quality of either one. The true taste of salt is not experienced, nor is the true taste of sugar. Similarly, when water is poured on fire, then neither one can exhibit their true quality. Water may turn into steam and the fire may be extinguished. However, their *original* nature always remains unchanged.

Similarly, when you become an occupant in this body made of matter, then your original nature as an eternal personality, full of joy and knowledge becomes temporarily covered over. If you are a driver in an automobile, you as a person remain distinct from the automobile itself. You may get out of one automobile and become a driver in another automobile; you, as the driver, remain the same; only the vehicle changes

Similarly, you as an eternal person are an occupant in your current body. At some point in time you will be vacating this body and will become an occupant in another vehicle or body. This is called the Law of Transmigration. There are more than 8 million types of bodies that we can become occupants of, in thousands of species of life. You can observe this.

Your purpose then is to reclaim your true and lasting position as an eternal person full of joy and knowledge The mechanics of this scientific process can be easily tapped into, and you can then use this knowledge to fully exploit your gift of advanced intelligence and propel yourself toward a successful human life, today, tomorrow and forever.

CORE QUESTION 2: WHAT IS THE NATURE OF THIS MATERIAL UNIVERSE AND ITS PURPOSE? (AND HOW DO I MAKE SENSE OF IT ALL?)

This material universe is admittedly very vast and seemingly unlimited. It consists of countless galaxies, planets and stars situated in a vast expanse of space.

Although one may see infinite varieties of manifestations within the scope of the creation, including mountains, valleys, oceans and streams; the sky, the earth and the clouds; trees, plants, and so many varieties of vegetation; and the almost endless variety of birds and animals, reptiles and aquatics, there is one thing in common. All the different varieties of creation are composed of these five elements: earth, water, fire, air, and ether in different combinations. If you ask any scientist to characterize all the rudiments that make up anything on this planet, ultimately they would have to break them down into these five essential ingredients. The *living* creatures, however, have these additional characteristics: mind, intelligence, and a sense of self, or soul by which their living symptoms or consciousness are expressed.

Further we see that everything within this creation is constantly changing: The trees in the forest start out as seedlings, grow over the years by taking up water and sunlight, produce flowers, fruits and seeds (which produce new seedlings) and maintain themselves in this way for some time, then gradually the tree begins to dwindle and finally die. If you analyze any living creature within this world, you will see that it goes through these six kinds of changes. Those creations of nature that are inanimate, such as rocks, stones and metal don't "die," but they do dwindle and become destroyed with age. Even rivers and lakes dry up. In other words, nothing is permanent within this creation.

Our own bodies go through the same phases of life: birth, growth, maintenance, reproduction, dwindling, and then, finally, death. Again, I said, "our bodies." This law of impermanence only applies to the body and not to the occupant of the body, or the soul. Only the body goes through the cycle of birth, aging, reproduction, disease, deterioration and death. You, the person and soul within the body, remain separate and aloof from this cycle of change.

This, then, is the evidence of the impermanent nature of all matter in this universe. By extension, not only your body, but all things and persons related to your body are temporary by nature. Just as the body comes to an end, all relationships also come to an end. All the possessions connected to the body, whether homes, cars, bank accounts, or any of hundreds of others, cease to have any relationship with the body, or you, the previous occupant of the body.

This world is, therefore, described as a temporary "refugee camp" for us. It is not our real home but a temporary place of much pain and suffering wherein the miseries of the mind and body, from other living creatures and beings, and from natural forces are a regular unwelcome experience.

In summary then, the purpose of this universe is to give us enough unwanted situations so that we should want to find a better home, as covered in the next section.

CORE QUESTION 3: WHAT IS THE NATURE OF OUR ETERNAL HOME AND ITS PURPOSE? (AND WHAT CAN MY AFTERLIFE BE LIKE?)

There is great detail about the features, activities, nature and experiences in the eternal realm, our eternal home. Stemming from our lifestyles these days, our toxic, clogged-up and unclear intelligence, mind and senses, with their diminished capacities, get in the way of experiencing this reality.

If we embark on the journey to detoxify our bodies, mind, intelligence and senses, using the knowledge of the laws of success, and integrate those laws gradually into our lives, this awareness and experience of the timeless life in the eternal realm will become progressively clearer to us. This is not religious or sentiment but experiential science.

This process of going from theoretical knowledge to personal experience is called scientific experience. An example will help here. Let us say that there is a jar of honey on the table before us. I may have never tasted honey before, and my friend may try to describe to me the taste of honey. I may listen attentively and "think" I know what she is describing, but until I take the lid off the jar and begin to dip into the honey myself and taste it, I cannot experience it. Similarly, this knowledge about permanent and eternal success versus short-term and temporary success can quickly be experienced as true knowledge as we begin to use it and integrate it into our lives.

The description of our eternal home is amazingly appealing and attractive. As we "detoxify" ourselves, we increasingly remember and recollect this reality. This complete reality satisfies us physically, emotionally, mentally, intellectually and spiritually, in every way. Actually, we become fulfilled in ways that we cannot even imagine at this time!

In our eternal home, there is no birth, no disease, no aging, and no destruction or death. There is no anxiety or stress of any kind. There is no lack at all in any way. All our relationships (yes, there are wonderful persons there, so there are wonderful relationships!) are completely happy, satisfying and fulfilling. Desires are fulfilled instantly. Every word we speak or hear is a song, just like divine music. Every step we take is an amazing dance. Every moment is a thrill in every way. There is no ignorance, only full and complete knowledge. The happiness there is like an unlimited ocean as compared to that of this material world, which is like a drop in the ocean. By our constitution, this is where we belong.

In summary, the material world in which we now live is a perverted reflection of the real world. That means that everything that we experience here has it's origin in its "pure" form in the original world. In the real and original existence, there is no birth, no death, no old age and no disease. There is no anger, no envy, no lust and no greed. There is no stress or anxiety. There is only ever-increasing eternal abundance, harmony, joy, complete satisfaction and happiness.

CORE QUESTION 4: HOW WILL ALL OF THIS HELP WITH MY CURRENT NEEDS AND PROBLEMS? (SO I KNOW I HAVE LIVED A THRILLING, SUCCESSFUL LIFE)

The key is to use this knowledge in a systematic way. As we live more in alignment with the laws that govern our lives, our current desires, while in this present life, are fulfilled in the easiest and fastest way. Problems reduce or disappear, prosperity comes easily, peace and tranquility become ever present, and we are protected from all kinds of mishaps and unwanted situations.

We live at peak levels of physical, mental, emotional, spiritual and intellectual health; confidence and clarity about any matter or issue in life helps us make good decisions; pain is minimized and pleasure is enhanced greatly. Harmony and friendliness prevail in relationships. Life is as good as it can get.

5 DAILY ACTIONS TO BUILD SUCCESS TODAY, TOMORROW AND ETERNALLY

To strengthen your desire and mind and to expand your capacity and capability to increase awareness, knowledge and wisdom, as well as to tap into higher experiences of pleasure and success, take a few minutes each day as follows:

1. Engage in activities to detoxify and expand and/or enhance your mind and intelligence as well as your sense of taste, hearing, smell, touch and sight.

2. Reduce and eliminate activities that create toxins and contamination and have a diminishing effect on your capabilities and strength.

3. Pay special attention to what you eat and drink as these affect your entire body and senses, mind and intelligence. Foods and drinks that come from pure sources and in the form of gifts from nature are very cleansing and nourishing.

4. Use scientific meditation practices, which are very powerful for cleansing and awakening new capabilities in the body, senses, mind and intelligence.

5. Commit to acquiring this priceless knowledge and reclaiming your thrilling life of perpetual peace and prosperity.

Please visit *www.scienceofeternalsuccess.com* for more and free resources to reclaim the thrilling life and success that is likely lying somewhat dormant in you.

About Naveen

Naveen Khurana was born in 1947 in New Delhi, India. His father was a highly respected doctor and he was educated in the best schools and universities in India and lived a comfortable life.

His journey to learn about success, freedom, the higher truths and pleasures in life began in his early childhood when his parents would frequently take him to visit Gandhi and other successful leaders. Visiting these persons and hearing from them had a profound impact on him.

After graduating in 1970 from the elite Indian Institute of Technology (IIT), he enrolled at the University of Illinois in the United States to pursue graduate studies. While in graduate school, he often found himself discussing the "tough" questions about life with his friends and professors; questions about success, life's purpose, self-knowledge, karma, reincarnation, yoga, meditation, etc. He was in discussions with bright and educated persons; but he found that solid or satisfying responses were hard to come by. He made many wonderful friends, but observed how the predominant focus on temporary and fleeting success, and happiness based on short-lived pleasures, left them, including himself, dissatisfied and unfulfilled in many ways.

In 1972, he took the search for true success and a meaningful life very seriously. He began exploring different schools of philosophy, modern teachings on self-improvement, yoga, meditation, and different religious doctrines. He graduated in 1973 with two masters degrees and entered the corporate world in Detroit and rapidly rose in his profession. He did very well financially and retired in 1978.

Soon after, he had the good fortune to study and learn in the private chambers of very successful "life" scientists and mentors, and he received solid answers to every question he had about life. He practiced scientific processes for true and lasting success and experienced indescribable joy and satisfaction that created a huge "paradigm" shift. He also had access to extensive private libraries with hundreds of publications that specifically deal with life success and elevation. Interestingly enough, he also came under the guidance of one of the mentors of Gandhi.

For over 40 years now, with more than 50,000 hours of study and daily practice, he has given his major focus to absorbing and using this "Science of Eternal Success."

He has distilled this vast body of knowledge into three categories: 1) The 150-plus questions that open the mind to complete knowledge, 2) The 100-plus Laws that shape true lasting success, and 3) the 40-plus qualities and behaviors of highly successful and happy persons.

His wife of 30-plus years, Michele, has been his constant companion and partner. They have a genuine understanding and experience of success, both temporary and eternal, and have used this knowledge to live a lifestyle which includes financial independence and the freedom to use their time as they choose. They know how to "succeed" in the easiest way both for the "now" and the "future," as well as how to balance the two needs very well. They live a prosperous and pleasurable life in peak health and with wonderful relationships.

Please call us toll-free at (888) 628-3368 or visit us at:
www.scienceofeternalsuccess.com for more information.

CHAPTER 25

DARE TO PLAN... FOR RETIREMENT

BY PATRICK MUELLER

Does anyone really want to be the Wal-Mart greeter? Is this really the life they had planned on living during their golden years? Are you going to be the next Wal-Mart greeter? Maybe this sounds harsh, but these are the stories I see and help people avoid every day. Most people spend more time planning their next vacation than they do on their financial plan for retirement. Why? Because it's boring and confusing!

I never envisioned myself being an investment/retirement advisor. It's not something you dream about becoming when you are a kid. "Mom and Dad, I want to be a retirement specialist when I grow up."

"That's great, son, let me feel your forehead and see if you have a fever?" When I was growing up I had visions of becoming a professional baseball player until my parents bought me my first drum set when I was 13, and then I was destined to be a rockstar! I absolutely fell in love with the drums, and this became my No. 1 passion and is still a big passion for me today; I still play professionally in Atlanta. I went through the school of hard knocks at age 19; I lost a restaurant and had nothing but a car up for repossession and sheer determination. I had to claw my way to the top. I found an opportunity with an insurance agency that helped small businesses with insurance benefits, and I was able to sink my teeth into that business. A series of promotions led to my own successful insurance agency, which I headed for 13 years. Along the way, I helped train hundreds of agents and helped thousands of individuals with their insurance needs.

Over the years I started seeing a big disconnect with the financial professionals servicing the retirement community. Friends that I knew in the financial services industry were either stockbrokers acting as advisors or I had friends that were in the insurance industry acting as advisors. So, immediately, I saw that people were getting biased information everywhere they went because "advisors" were benefitting from them financially based on what products they were selling. I didn't see anyone doing real planning for people and designing a retirement plan that fits with what was in their best interests. So I started to study with a lot of industry experts to get to the bottom line, and the more I dug in, the clearer it became as to the large amount of bad advice that people were receiving. Other than wanting to be a famous drummer playing to huge audiences, my big passion is helping and educating people. So it has become my mission to help families build the retirement of their dreams so that they can focus on what they really want to do and become in their golden years.

So enough about me, how do we make sure you don't become the next Wal-Mart greeter! Unless you really want to be?

Let me begin by walking you through the three phases in your financial life.

1. **Accumulation Phase (years 20 to 60, approx.):** This is the phase we all start in, where we start saving all our nuts up for the future. We open our first savings account, and when we start our working career, we start a retirement plan through work (401k, 403b) or maybe an individual retirement account (IRA). This is where we are introduced to different investments vehicles and start investing our hard-earned money in the hope that it will grow. Stocks, bonds, mutual funds, real estate, etc. We put our money into these types of investments and hope that over a period of time that our money will appreciate, and we will have accumulated enough money to live on in retirement. Since you are younger during this phase and have more time to wait, you can afford to be more risky in your investing choices.

PHASE 1 EXPERTS:

- **Brokers:** Most brokers deal in primarily managed money or investments that require constant monitoring. Although you are at the risk in the stock market, you can achieve the highest return from the types of accounts that most brokers specialize in. Brokers (such as money managers from firms like Merrill Lynch, Edward Jones, etc.) make their money by the continued management of the funds they sell to their clients. Without money to manage, they do not make a fee/commission.

2. **Preservation and Income Phase (age 60 to death):** During this phase, you should concentrate on preserving the assets you have worked all your life to accumulate. Time is growing shorter and shorter, and you now have less time to get back what you may have already lost. Since timing is so important, you must understand exactly how much risk you can afford to take. Based on your income needs as well as the goals you have set for your hard-earned retirement dollars, you must invest accordingly. Keeping your money safe during this phase is a key component to achieve a stable income plan, one that you cannot outlive and can always rely on.

PHASE 2 EXPERTS:

- **Retirement and Estate Planners:** Financial professionals that focus their energy solely on retirees or those soon-to-be retired deal with investments that focus on the preservation of assets. Planning for retirement is a tricky business that many investors do not have a sound plan for. Rather than accumulation of assets, the preservation of what you accumulated plays a significant role in providing you with the income that you need during your retirement years.

PHASE 2 COMMON INVESTMENT VEHICLES:

- CDs, Insured Deposits, Government Bonds, Fixed Annuities, Fixed Indexed Annuities, Fixed Income Models

- True Diversification (safe investments with risk tolerance according to individual situations)

3. Distribution Phase: This is the phase that determines where everything that we have accumulated over our lifetime, that we haven't consumed, will now go. Choices include our loved ones or a charity. For those who properly plan to have assets left over for their heirs, it is important that you develop a distribution (or "estate") plan for when you walk out on life.

PHASE 3 EXPERTS:

- **Estate Planning Attorneys and Retirement Planners:** The most important objective once you have passed away is the distribution of your tax-deferred accounts (IRA, 401k, etc.) to your heirs in the most efficient and tax advantageous way possible.

PHASE 3 COMMON INVESTMENT VEHICLES:

- Wills, Trusts, Power of Attorney, etc.

- Avoiding Probate and Estate Tax

Now that you understand the three areas of your financial life, I will show you how to how to create a rock-solid retirement plan for the preservation and income phase.

The harsh facts are that almost 60 percent of retirees run out of money before they run out of life, because they have not altered their investment strategies upon entering retirement. Imagine getting on an airplane and the captain comes on the intercom and says, we have beautiful weather and beautiful, clear skies…and we have a 40 percent chance of making it to our destination—would you stay on that airplane?

Let me walk you through a scenario of the average couple we see in our office: Jim and Wanda are excited about retiring and starting to live life and do all the things they have dreamed about when they reach this Promised Land called retirement. Now that Jim and Wanda are no longer receiving paychecks, they need to start taking money from their savings to maintain their lifestyle. What could affect Jim and Wanda?

Common mistakes we see:

- They have not saved enough to maintain their current lifestyle.

- They don't keep track of what their lifestyle is really costing them.

- They have money invested in a place that can potentially suffer a significant loss.

- They have their money invested in places that are not designed to produce the income they need.

- They encounter unforeseen health-care expenses.

One of the biggest retirement myths I see is that you cannot make a modest return on your money unless your money is at risk, and this is absolutely false. When you are nearing retirement, it is much more important to protect yourself from any loss than it is to try to get your money to grow.

Example: If we have a $1 million in the stock market and the market drops 50 percent, leaving you account value at $500,000, what rate of return do we need to get to get back to our original $1 million? Answer: 100 percent!

You need a 100 percent return on your investments just to get back to even!

Are you scratching your head? Let me explain. If the market drops 50 percent one year and comes back 50 percent the next year, wouldn't you be even?

No!

The reason is you are not earning off of the original $1 million you invested. Your current value is $500,000, so a 50 percent return would bring you back up to $750,000. That's why it takes a 100 percent return to get back to your original $1 million! So how often does the stock market go up 100 percent?

I'm not down on the stock market, but I am down on people taking too much risk. If you are in your 20s, 30s, 40s, you still have time for the markets to recover. If you are nearing retirement or are retired, time is not on your side. This scenario gets even worse if we need to use this money to maintain our lifestyle during our retirement years when the market is down.

Cash flow is king in retirement. Hail king cash flow! I don't care how much money someone has accumulated, it's all about cash flow in retirement. I have families who have millions and are on a crash course for disaster because of their lifestyle. I have families who have accumulated very little in assets but have an incredible cash flow and will never have anything to worry about.

The first step we need to take when we retire is to learn to replace your paycheck. So we need to figure out how much income we need to maintain your lifestyle.

1. **What will be your income sources?** Social security, pension, rental income (use only if it's consistently rented). How can these income sources change in the future? We know that if Jim or Wanda dies that we will lose one of the Social Security incomes and the surviving spouse can keep the higher of the two Social Security incomes. Now if you have a pension and when you die, what will your spouse continue to receive? I see quite often people who have great pensions, but when the owner of the pension dies, the spouse gets no survivorship benefit. One of the fastest-growing poverty groups in the country is widowed women. So unless you plan to go out like Romeo and Juliet, we have some planning to do.

2. **How much is your lifestyle?** This is an area where almost everyone is wrong. Most people wing this and try to guess what their expenses are or try to itemize their bills: Here's what the mortgage is, light bill, gas bill, etc. This process is painful and boring and almost always wrong, because there are a lot miscellaneous expenses that generally are not accounted for.

So here is a simple process we walk our clients through. Most people have one or two checking accounts where all the bills are paid out of checks, ATM withdrawals and credit cards. On the front of your bank statement each month it shows you how much came into your account and how much came out of your account. You want to add up how much money came out of your accounts each month and add up the last 12 months. This will give you a pretty accurate idea as to how much your lifestyle really is.

This can be a very eye-opening experience; on average, most people we see are off by about 30 percent. So if we want to make sure you don't outlive your money, is this a pretty important figure to know? I recently sat down with a couple and they told me their expenses were $90,000 a year. I asked them where they came up with this figure, and they said, "We think that is what we are spending." When they added up their bank statements, they were really spending $160,000 a year! Now your situation might not be this extreme, but bottom line is you need to know your numbers.

Let's use an example with Jim and Wanda:

- *Social Security:* $25,000 annually

- *Pension:* $10,000 annually

- *Total Annual Income:* $35,000

- *Lifestyle Expenses:* $75,000 annually

- *The Difference:* -$40,000 annually

Now we know that if Jim and Wanda want to maintain this lifestyle, they will need $40,000 a year to be generated from their retirement assets.

If you are going to build a house, the first thing you need to lay down is a solid foundation to build on. The foundation in your financial home is your lifetime income plan. Once you have your foundation in place, we can start to build the walls and roof of the house. How many times have you had to replace the foundation in your home? Not many. But you may have to repaint the house or reshingle the roof. However, if you have a solid income plan, then you will have nothing to worry about in your financial home. To create a solid foundation for your financial home, your income plan should have three components.

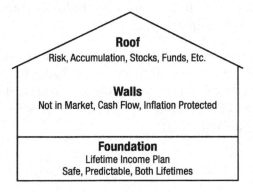

Roof
Risk, Accumulation, Stocks, Funds, Etc.

Walls
Not in Market, Cash Flow, Inflation Protected

Foundation
Lifetime Income Plan
Safe, Predictable, Both Lifetimes

1. Safe: The money used for the foundation needs to be safe. If the money you need to live on is in a place that can lose value, this can devastate your retirement.

2. Predictable: The income generated needs to be predictable. We need to know how much income is being generated and when we can expect it to arrive.

3. Both Lifetimes: The income needs to last for your lifetime and your spouse's lifetime.

Once you have built your foundation, it's OK to take a little more risk and build the walls and roof of your financial home.

There are not a million ways to construct a lifetime income plan. In fact, there are only a handful. Most of the families we serve like to create their own personal family pension, where we leverage the assets through an insurance company and guarantee that you cannot outlive your income. I listed some common vehicles that are used in these plans but cannot get into specific details as to what would be best for you because there is no such thing as a one-size-fits-all investment, and everyone's needs are different.

Most of these financial instruments have to be done through a licensed professional. When seeking an advisor, you want to make sure they specialize in preservation and income planning. They need to have a license that specifies they have a fiduciary responsibility to you, meaning they have to do what is in your best interest. This sounds like common sense, but most so-called advisors that are out there carry licenses that state they are only held to a suitability standard, where they just have to show how the investment is suitable for you, not what is actually the best option for you. If you are not in my industry, most people would never know to ask these questions.

Knowledge is only potential power; you have to take action and put that knowledge to use. So take the time and walk through these simple steps and find a good advisor to help you with the process. I wish you much success with your life's adventures, and I don't want to see you greeting me when I walk into Wal-Mart!

About Patrick

Patrick Mueller is a highly regarded retirement/investment planning specialist. He founded his company, Bella Advisors, in an effort to fill a niche that was not being addressed properly in the retirement planning field. Bella Advisors specializes in helping pre-retirees and retirees navigate the ever-changing financial landscape and striving to ensure everyone has peace of mind in their golden years. Over the last 17 years, Patrick has trained hundreds of agents, helping thousands of families and businesses across the country with their financial needs.

Patrick is also a professional drummer, spending much of his time writing, recording and performing. Music is one of his biggest passions.

Patrick resides in Roswell, Georgia, with his daughter, Isabella, whom his company is named after.

You can learn more about Patrick Mueller at www.BellaAdvisors.com.

CHAPTER 26

FROM FOOD STAMPS TO FREEDOM: THE 5 STEP FREEDOM FORMULA

BY MATTHEW LEE

By the time I hit my senior year in high school, I was considered a model for success. I attended St. Thomas Academy, an elite, all-boys Catholic military school. I remember that year's military ball like it was yesterday. I stood there at 6 foot 7, an athletic body frame, all decked out in my class A military uniform, next to my high school sweetheart. To any observer, I was the privileged son of a doctor, a lawyer or business executive.

By that time in my senior year, I blended in quite well in the elite private school environment. My resume was dense with accomplishments. I was a first-team all-state basketball selection, a candidate for the Mr. Basketball Award, and I had a division 1 basketball scholarship. Heck, I even turned down opportunities to go the naval academy and an opportunity to attend an Ivy League college.

While everything on the outside seemed to match my elite private school environment, I quietly held onto the secret behind the façade: I didn't come from a privileged family, nor was I a straight A student. In fact, I was quite the opposite. At 5 years old, I was not totally sure what, "laid off" meant, but I soon found out Christmas would be different that year.

As the oldest of my mother's three kids, I had to sacrifice so my brother and sister could get more toys that year. As a single parent, my mom worked as many as three jobs at time to make ends meet. I never forget the humbling experience of walking into a store and my mother pulling out food stamps to pay our grocery bill. I can remember deciding not to go with her again for fear of being seen using food stamps. Prior to this experience, I must have thought I was Eddie Murphy in school joking about other kids and how their families were on welfare. Now, I was afraid of becoming the joke.

I thought the food stamp experience was bad enough, but on more than one occasion our family was visited by the "foreclosure" ghost between my eighth grade and senior year of high school. I don't know anyone who likes moving; imagine the fun of moving in the middle of the winter in St. Paul, Minnesota. Was this normal? I guess it was...at least it was for me, but I held my head up high; I was proud of the values my family instilled in me. I could have felt sorry for myself, or said to myself, "Why does this happen to me?" Instead I looked at it as a game to turn these obstacles into fuel for my success?

A BLUEPRINT FOR SUCCESS

Like most people I had once believed success was executing a perfect plan. During a recent interview for a TV show, I was asked, "What makes you a success?" When I paused to think about it, every picture I had going through my head of true success had way more to do with my ability to overcome obstacles and turning adversities into opportunities. That interview helped me formulate the "5 Step Freedom Formula." These were the core five steps I found at the foundation of any success, even in the face of adversity.

It wasn't long ago that the "5 Step Freedom Formula" was put to the test. In 2008, when banks stopped lending due to the mortgage crisis, our real estate company was forced to close our doors. No perfect business plan or MBA class could have prepared us for this. While most real estate professionals let these adversities stop them, we decided to turn adversity into an opportunity and reinvented our business. The result was The Path to Home Ownership Blueprint™, a system to empower renters through financial education, to become homeowners and create a foundation for wealth creation. While most media outlets were telling the public about all the obstacles of home ownership, we were breathing life and hope into our community. We did such a good job that the local Chicago Fox Affiliate did a full-feature TV segment on the success of our program. All this during the worst financial crisis since the Great Depression. The "5 Step Freedom Formula" passed the test with flying colors, and we not only turned a failed business around, but we were empowering people, transforming lives, and revitalizing our local community. Our company's new goal and commitment is to grow our program nationally and empower 100,000 renters to become homeowners while building a foundation for wealth.

Ever face obstacles and adversities and wonder how to succeed despite the odds? I invite you to grab pen and paper to outline your goals, and burn these steps into your memory. I am going to share with you the 5 Step Freedom Formula I've used to overcome obstacles and turn adversity into opportunities. I am going to illustrate the 5 Step Freedom Formula by using an example of how we help clients in The Path to Home Ownership Blueprint™.

THE 5 STEP FREEDOM FORMULA

Step 1: Believe in the Possibility and Be Committed to Your Success

The first step to home-ownership success for the renters we work with in The Path to Home Ownership Blueprint™ program is to control the conversation happening in their head. They either have a story that says becoming a homeowner and creating wealth is really possible, or they have a story filled with excuses and reason why they can't afford to own a home. When I point out to renters that by paying rent they are simply paying their landlord's mortgage, almost instantly they make a shift and suddenly see the possibility of home ownership as reality for them. The real problem is not believing in the possibility but combining it with the commitment to take the actions and make the sacrifices necessary to have success.

I understand how these renters feel because when I wanted to buy my first home I had horrible credit, and I didn't have a lot of money for a down payment. While I probably was saying in my head that I couldn't afford to fix my credit, I had a mentor that challenged me to think differently about my situation. First he simply asked me, "Are you interested or committed to buying your first home?" I asked for clarification, and he said "When you're interested, you will only do what it takes when it is convenient, but when you're committed you'll do whatever it takes to succeed." That caused me immediately to change the conversation in my head from "I can't afford it" to "How can I afford it?" He also showed me the math, and I realized it cost more money to continue to rent and miss out on the tax benefits of home ownership than it did for me to pay the cost to repair my credit. Let's just say all of a sudden I became very committed!

Step 2: Create Your Master Plan

The next step is to create your master plan by figuring out how you will get from where you are now to becoming a homeowner. We create the master plan by taking pen and paper and answering some thought-provoking questions. We write out the answers to the following questions:

When it comes to the goals of home ownership and having a solid foundation for wealth creation:

1. What will your life will look like when you've accomplished your goal?

2. How will it feel to know you've accomplished the goal?

3. How will achieving this goal impact your family and other loved ones?

These are important questions to answer because every renter has a different answer that is important to them. This also helps them form a crystal-clear picture in their mind of their goals being accomplished. The more they focus on this picture, the harder it is for them to get discouraged by all the obstacles that will get in their way during the process of obtaining their goal.

The next question is very important also:

4. What are 5-10 specific things that must happen, and by what date must they happen by for you to be happy with your progress?

By answering this question, renters will now have the milestones they will need to accomplish and the date they must happen by in order to achieve their goal home ownership. These may include credit repair, saving for a down payment, paying off collections, and finding an ideal neighborhood.

The master plan is your road map for success. Without it you are simply taking a road trip without a map. This master plan also allows you to measure your progress along the way and know when you are close to accomplishing your goal. With your master plan in place, you now are ready to go on to Step 3.

Step 3: Create a Dream Team

To be successful in any goal, it is extremely important to have a Dream Team to help analyze your plan, give feedback, and hold you accountable. Quite often I have clients who come into The Path to Home Ownership Blueprint™ where this is not their first attempt at home ownership. They've tried this process on their own or with the help of someone else, with no success. These clients are sometimes the most difficult to help.

One example we see often is that the clients have attempted and failed to repair their credit. They either try repairing their own credit or they hire a credit repair company. In both cases, they didn't get the intended result in order to be able to buy a home. The problem is, either one or a combination of the following problems: They lack the knowledge and experience to repair their credit issues, they hired the wrong credit repair company, or they simply lacked the training to put together a sound spending plan and emergency savings to support a good credit repair regimen. Without taking these things into account, most people are taking a shot in the dark at best.

In our program, we help clients overcome this by assembling a Dream Team of experts and coaches that help to guide their steps to ensure they take the right steps, in the right order, and at the right time. Many people never realize trial and error is the most expensive training you can get. The return on investment of a Dream Team is priceless. Their valuable guidance, feedback, and accountability will be an investment that makes you money!

Step 4: Take Bold and Decisive Action and Hit Your Goal

The harsh reality is every renter will hit obstacles and adversity, but this is when they must embrace that part of the progress and remind themselves of what their life is going to look and feel like once they hit their goal of home ownership. The Dream Team helps them navigate the challenges that occur while implementing vital steps, such as getting their credit in order, helping them get money for a down payment, getting them pre-approved for a mortgage, assisting them with finding their dream home, and building a solid financial foundation for wealth creation. One of the most powerful things the Dream Team helps them do is overcome procrastination, avoid perfectionism, or keep a positive focus. Be bold, take action!

Step 5: Improve Your Success and Create Bigger Goals
You've successfully turned adversity into opportunity and become a homeowner. What a feeling! So what's next? Don't forget to celebrate the progress you created. After putting in so much effort and overcoming so many obstacles to become a homeowner, the last thing you want to do is revert back, but that is exactly what happens for most new homeowners. So the next things you should do is spend some time reflecting on what you did right and what things you would like to improve going forward in the process of building a foundation for wealth creation. In our program, becoming a homeowner is the starting point of new goals to solidify your foundation for wealth. It's about making financial success a lifestyle.

For most of our lives we are taught about success as if it's a destination. That couldn't be further from the truth because once you have achieved your goal, it is now time to make a new goal. So when you are ending one goal, you are really beginning your next goal. The most important thing you achieve in hitting a goal is not the goal itself, but it's the person you become in the process. It's the skill sets you develop; it's the greater appreciation for hard work and discipline; and it's the confidence you give to yourself to create more success. So don't stop here, decide now to continue to grow by creating bigger goals.

There are some who might say this 5 Step Freedom Formula is farfetched and won't work in their situation. I'm not here to convince you of its power, only to expose you to it. There have been many instances in my life where I faced insurmountable odds, and maybe I should have given up. Looking back I would have been unable overcome those odds if I wasn't open to the possibility that new information and new approaches to life could yield new results. I am passionate about this formula because I've been using it even when I didn't know of its existence.

When I was accepted to the eighth grade class of St. Thomas Academy, there were only two months before class was set to start. There was no denying the fact my family couldn't afford to send me to St. Thomas Academy. I could have gotten discouraged at that point and given up hope. Instead I called the admission director so many times that summer he might have thought I was a bill collector. Fortunately for me, he didn't see this as nagging him; instead, he saw my determination and shared my story with a wealthy donor. That fall I entered St. Thomas Academy. The donor decided to invest in my dream and agreed to pay for my education through my senior year in high school. There were two conditions for receiving the scholarship: 1) to keep up my grades, and 2) to pay it forward. I share this 5 Step Freedom Formula with you so you may have success in your life, but in the back of my head is the hope that you will use your success to pay it forward, just as I am by sharing the formula with you.

About Matthew

Matthew Lee, also known as "America's Home Ownership & Wealth Expert™", is a best-selling author and business growth coach who is regularly sought out by the media for his out-of-the-box insight on real estate, credit scoring, business growth, wealth creation, and personal growth. Matthew is co-founder of The Path to Home Ownership Blueprint™. The Path to Home Ownership Blueprint™ is the only program of its kind to help renters overcome credit and down payment challenges to become homeowners while they build a foundation for wealth creation. The idea for creating The Path to Home Ownership Blueprint™ came out of the need for middle-income Americans not just to buy a home but to really learn the fundamentals to get ahead financially and secure a better financial future. The Path to Home Ownership Blueprint™ is a five-step proprietary process that uses a multipronged approach to help clients become homeowners while simultaneously helping them develop the skills necessary for wealth creation and helping them gain access to a team of experts to help them in fulfilling a successful financial plan.

Critically acclaimed as the "The Concierge System for Home Ownership & Wealth Creation", The Path to Home Ownership Blueprint™ is just that, because there is no other system that combines education and expert guidance in a simple system for the average American to get ahead financially.

To learn more about Matthew Lee, America's Home Ownership & Wealth Expert™, www.ThePathToHomeOwnership.com.

CHAPTER 27

6 KEYS TO SUCCESS
(AND THIS MAY SHOCK YOU!)

BY DR. MARILIZA LaCAP
AND DR. DARREN W. TONG

My husband and I are both dentists, and we just finished opening our second dental office in Tappan, New York. Great location......it's just a 5 minutes drive from my house. People around us thought we were crazy for taking on such a risk during a down economy when people were losing jobs and big businesses going bankrupt. We decided to open a second location because we felt there was a need for "our kind of dentistry." This was apparent in the amount of patients we were seeing and referrals we were getting. While other businesses were firing employees, we were hiring and expanding our services. Our patients actually love going to our office. Not love, but LOVE going to our office.

We are LOVED, and we are popular. How can being a dentist make you popular? After all, 22 years ago when we opened our first office, there was not a day that went by that someone said to me, "Don't take this personally doc, but I hate dentists." Are you kidding me? Don't take it personally? Of course, I took it personally. People hated my profession, they hated me! Something had to be done.

How did this hate turn into love and what do I mean by "our kind of dentistry"?

The answer is simple: We followed the universal truths of success.

First, let's talk about some of the *lies* about success:

- You must compete and win at all cost.
- You need to step on many people to get to the "top."
- For every winner, there must be a loser.
- You must sacrifice and suffer until you get to the "top."
- It's lonely at the "top."

Yes, these are lies, and they are not the keys to success. You will be shocked at what I will reveal. You might not even believe me because of its simplicity. Once you get it, it is very enlightening.

THE 6 KEYS TO SUCCESS

The first three keys have to do with you. It has to do with your belief systems and who you are.

Key #1: Create, Don't Compete

There is no need to compete because there is more than enough to go around. Believe in abundance instead of scarcity. You don't have to compete, but you must *create*. Be creative and think outside the box. If you are worrying about the "competition," you are wasting energy in something you have no control over, not to mention you are creating negative energy around you and not allowing your brain to think clearly about what you do have control over. Think in a world of abundance. There is more than enough to go around. This type of thinking allows your mind to expand and doesn't place a ceiling on what you can achieve. The possibilities become limitless.

Everyone would agree that there is something special about a creative person. You would also agree that after doing anything artistic, a person feels a profound sense of accomplishment that feels unlike any other emotion. The emotion created when someone is in the act of being creative or just the observance of someone else's creativity is staggering. There is an attraction to creation.

So many people in the world today focus on being "competitive," when what people really want is creativity! To "compete" means that you are average—you are the same as everyone else. To "create" is a game changer! You are beyond competition. Creativity is the most stimulating and magnetizing of all the human emotions. Creativity is the factor that brings you in and makes you want to engage in time and resources.

So, are you the same as everyone else in a "competitive" world, or are you "creating" a stimulating and magnetizing experience with anyone you come into contact with?

Key #2: Give More in Value Than the Price of What You Are Offering

Value is not the same as price. The value can be in the form of good advice, guarantees or even friendship. When a person feels they are getting more in value than what they pay for, you have created a winning situation for everyone. What people really want and need is a "trusted advisor" or person to help them understand that the "value" really is greater than the price.

Everyone's value system is different. Time saved for a busy person is priceless. This value is given by running on time, finishing ahead of deadline, or adding services that buys time. Information given to the right person at the right time is invaluable. This information can enlighten and unburden someone who has been misinformed. Expert advice during a pivotal decision-making process can change a person's future. A life-changing decision that was influenced by your expert advice is priceless.

Simply put, we should always exceed the expectations of others and build value.

The best of the best seek to exceed expectations at all times. With prospects, clients, peers, family, and strangers, it's always the same. This is not a workstyle, it's a lifestyle. This should be who you are.

Ask yourself, "What would it take—what can I do to make a person's day?" From there, go beyond and create a "wow" factor that can quickly move from experience to memory.

Key #3: Always "Give Forward," Don't Just "Give Back"

This is the "who" of "you." It is not the "tit for tat" concept of you give me something, and I'll give you something in return. There should never be an obligation or contract—explicit or implied. There should never be any condition or expectation. Simply give forward without any expectation of anything in return. Most people would be shocked at how often opportunities to give present themselves. The best way to give is to give without question and without an alternate agenda. When someone is giving for the right reasons—and the correct reasons are essential for this belief to work— then people pick up on it. You become highly attractive and trustworthy. There is a special aura and glow about someone who gives forward. To give and have no intention of looking for a reward or to make a sale is unique and special in today's world, regardless of where you live and the language you speak. Giving comes in all shapes and sizes. It can be basic and monetary in form. It can be physical, a presence that is there when needed, and it can be the use of a talent on behalf of another.

Put caring for yourselves and others at the very top of your priorities in life. Demonstrate caring for others in very attentive and physical ways and have the guts to ask for care when you need it. Let caring be a continual life practice, not a touchy-feely concept. Approach this area of your life with a mastery mind-set, and the result will be a life filled with vibrant emotion. If you're not making a point to be caring of others in your life, the people around you don't feel cared for, loved, appreciated, respected, or engaged by you at the level of the heart. So, naturally, they contact you less frequently, trust you less, buy from you less, follow you less, and leave you more. In all human relationships, it's a remarkably easy formula to figure out: care more, connect more.

"We make a living by what we get. We make a life by what we give."
—Winston Churchill

Once you have the first three keys (beliefs) in place, the next three keys are promises made to the person you are doing business with.

Key #4: An Attitude of Gratitude
This is very counter-intuitive. Let the person you are dealing with know that you are grateful, appreciative, and thankful for their time, effort, work, and even their very existence. In its purest form, it is the beginning of a relationship based on an "Attitude of Gratitude."

Of all the emotions possible, the one that bonds two people—or organizations—more than any other is the grace of gratitude. The Attitude of Gratitude creates a bond that builds and builds with no end in sight. It becomes a connection that glues people together indefinitely. A bonding occurs when there is an obvious and sincere thankfulness expressed for a person's presence and very being. It is an attitude that becomes magnetic, compelling the recipient to bond with you on subconscious levels. The first action is not to attack or take the high ground. The first act is one of humble grace that will sincerely bond you to whomever you are doing business with.

> *"Gratitude unlocks the fullness of life. It turns what we have into enough, and more. It can turn a meal into a feast, a house into a home, a stranger into a friend."*
> —Melody Beattie

I love this quote because of the ending. The "attitude of gratitide" can turn a "stranger into a friend." All the people you come in contact with at work now become your friends you are helping, not just customers you are doing business with. It changes positively the way you will do business.

Key #5: Clear Education
After establishing a bond through appreciation and gratitude, you begin educating.

- **Be Concise.** One secret is to never pick more than three things to talk about. You see humans typically only remember three things from any given conversation or presentation. So pick three things that you need to educate your audience on and lightly, ever so lightly, cover those three things. The goal here isn't to impress them with facts, figures, and reams of data. It is about building trust. Here's the truth. The people you are talking to, the very people you are trying to convince, those you are trying to get to take action, don't care what those three things are. And they don't really want to know. What they want to know is if you are trustworthy.

- **Be Compelling.** Can you be trusted? Can they trust you? If so, then they can trust what you say and what you haven't said. People's lives today are in a state of constant crisis. Most people are either in a crisis, leaving a crisis, or running to a crisis . . . they certainly don't need more crises in their lives. So what they really want to do is trust you with their success once they believe they have the good news that you are the expert and can trust you. What they clearly never want to do is become the expert themselves. People just want to know that you are the expert, and they will recall enough to justify that you are who you say you are, even if you have not said that much. Don't take this trust lightly. What people want is peace of mind that your are the one to be trusted.

- **Be Clear.** People may only remember 6 percent of the three things that you say, but they will remember everything they feel while they are with you. They will recall 100 percent of how you made them feel after they forgot most of what you said.

- **Go Back to Basics.** The three C's are important. Be clear, concise and compelling when speaking.

Key #6: Ease of Business

Ease of Business is actually an emotional response to the trust they have in you. Why?

People are busy and already feel their lives are complicated. Most people and businesses live from one challenge to another. What they need is someone who is going to make their life a little bit easier. If what you offer makes it easy, simple, and crisis free, they will engage in it. This generates an emotion of relief, like a vast burden has been lifted from their shoulders. You want them to think, "Wow, when I am with this person, it is so easy!" The relief someone feels by knowing their life is easier because of you is overwhelming to some.

So ask yourself…is what I am doing for this person an emotional relief because I am making their life easier, or is it just another crisis in the making?

If you can become their bond of "calm," built on a trust that you are the educated expert they need, and complete it with the relief they seek through an easier way of doing business, the flood gates will open and people will begin rushing toward you and seek what you have to offer.

So there you have it: the 6 Keys to Success.

WHAT IS OUR KIND OF DENTISTRY?

This is the last question I left unanswered, so here's the explanation: "Our kind of dentistry" is the kind that goes beyond our patient's expectations because in creating the two locations, we've incorporated the 6 Keys of Success. Because we've done that it is a place where patients feel safe, comfortable and well cared for. By following the 6 Keys of Success, we've transformed an experience that is traditionally *hated* into an experience that is *loved*.

We have an Attitude of Gratitude. Every patient who walks through our doors are valued and respected. We are grateful because they have placed their trust in us, and we don't take that lightly. To show our gratitude, we have cookies in the waiting room, overhead TVs, massaging and heated dental chairs, paraffin hand treatments during cleanings, and a warm towelette to freshen up at the end of treatment.

Our office gives forward by holding two days of free dentistry for both adults and children. We are committed to helping the community around us through donations and free dentistry where needed.

We offer clear education by explaining treatment from the heart. We truly care about the patient and explain the treatment to them in a language they can understand, need and deserve. We let them know they are important and deserve to be healthy.

We provide ease of business by helping our patients afford the dentistry they need through different financial options. We offer workmanship guarantees, on-time guarantees and satisfaction guarantees.

We give more in value than the price. This value is demonstrated in our team members who surround our patients and are 110 percent dedicated to providing services that will go beyond our patients' expectations. There is value in the education we provide. The guarantees to our many patients are priceless.

We create ways of providing dentistry where it is painless. Going a step further, creating an experience in the dental office where people love coming to us because it is fun, enjoyable and relaxing.

About Dr. LaCap and Dr. Tong

Dr. LaCap

Dr. Tong

Dr. LaCap and Dr. Tong, also known as the Dynamic Duo of Dentistry, have both been creating beautiful smiles through exceptional care in their Bergenfield, New Jersey, office, Washington Dental Associates, for over 22 years. They just opened a second dental office in Tappan, New York. They have created a dental experience so comfortable that they had to open a second location. Dr. LaCap and Dr. Tong first met in dental school at Columbia University School of Dental and Oral Surgery. In fact, they were anatomy lab partners. Was it love at first sight? You'll have to ask them.

After over 22 years of working together as dentists, they still share the same passion for creating beautiful and healthy smiles. Their shared vision for Washington Dental Associates in New Jersey and Smile More Dentistry in New York, have both materialized into an exceptional dental experience, where patients feel comfortable, well taken care of and safe.

The experience in their office and their dentistry is so exceptional that they are known as the "Mercedes Benz" of dentistry within their community. Both have appeared on NBC, CBS, ABC and FOX affiliates, as well as *USA Today*. Dr. LaCap is also an Amazon best-selling co-author of *Secrets to Total Body Health*.

Another passion they share together is for each other and their five children. Their free time is spent volunteering in their children's school or church. Dr. LaCap lectures at St. Pius Church and is a Girl Scout leader for her daughter's troop. Dr. Tong is an assistant soccer coach for his two younger boys. Currently, the family's favorite destination is Disney World.

Dr. Mariliza Lacap and Dr. Darren Tong both received their dental degree from Columbia University School of Dental and Oral Surgery. Dr. LaCap received an academic scholarship. Academically and clinically, both doctors were in the top 10 percent of their class. They both received extra training in cosmetic dentistry at New York University Dental School.

They are both members of the American Dental Association, New Jersey Dental Association, Academy of General Dentistry, Bergen County Dental Society, Bergen County Implant Study Group, International Congress of Oral Implantologists, and American College of Implantologists

Their awards include Excellence in Orthodontic Award from the American Association of Orthodontics and Excellence in Periodontics Award from Northeastern Society of Periodontists

To learn more about Drs. LaCap and Tong, please visit www.SmileMoreDentist.com or visit their two locations:

19 Legion Drive
Bergenfield, NJ 07675
(201) 384-2425

140 Oak Tree Road
Tappan, NY 10983
(845) 359-1763

CHAPTER 28

LITTLE PINK HOUSES

BY KEN NUNN, ESQ.

Yes, I really did live in a little pink house in a run-down neighborhood in southern Indiana. I lived in that little pink house for three years. Today, as I dictate this chapter, it is hard to believe that I could ever be a lawyer and the owner of a large, very successful multimillion-dollar law practice. My first car only cost $75. Today, I own two new Rolls Royce Phantoms; one is a sedan and the other a convertible. How did all this happen?

EARLY YEARS

I literally grew up on the wrong side of the tracks on the poor side of town. I was raised by a single mom who did the best she could. When I was 6 years old, we lived in a three-room house with a bathroom out back. It was common for our lights, heat, and water to be shut off for weeks at a time. It was common to be evicted for nonpayment of rent. Sometimes we would only get three or four day's notice. I still remember the sheriff coming to the door, giving us the notice to move. My mom would scramble to find another house with low rent. We were evicted from about a dozen different houses in the next 10-year period.

I can remember once when our heat was shut off during a cold winter when I was about 9 years old. I would take my little red wagon throughout the neighborhood and collect tree branches and pieces of wood. When I had a wagonload, I would take it back to the house and start a fire in our stove so that we could have some heat that night. Sometimes I would take my little red wagon out two or three times in one night. One night I came upon a saw mill that had a whole trash can full of little 2x4 pieces of wood. I couldn't believe my luck.

Beginning at age 12, I went to work to help my mother pay our bills. I had two paper routes: one in the morning before school and one after school, and I also delivered newspapers on Saturday and Sunday. In the evenings, I would set pins at the local bowling alley for 7 cents a game. I learned from an early age what hard work was.

HIGH SCHOOL DROP-OUT (BUT NOT FOR LONG)

I didn't like the high school I was going to. My grades were awful. My attendance was awful. I was only there about half the time. So I decided to quit high school when I was 16 years old, and to my surprise, my mother did not object. I did not attend school for one whole year. I had a part-time job that paid 50 cents an hour. It was about this time in my life that I got into some trouble. I stole two sets of golf clubs from the trunk of a car, which was owned by a lawyer, Dixon Prentice. I spent two weeks in jail, and I was on probation for a year. I made a promise to myself that I would never do something stupid like that again. I've kept that promise.

When I got out of jail, I went to the lawyer's office and apologized. The lawyer was very nice and accepted my apology. I didn't see attorney Prentice again until 15 years later. When I did, I was shocked and surprised!

I don't think I would have ever gone back to high school, or ever graduated from high school, had the next thing never happened. We were evicted from our house again for nonpayment of rent, and once again my mother scrambled to find an inexpensive house to live in. That house was located in a neighboring city about 10 miles away. We packed up everything and moved into the next rental. I had about a dozen new friends, and that summer was fun because I was the only one who had a car. My friends asked me if they could ride with me the first day of high school, and I was too embarrassed to tell them that I had no intentions of going back to high school, so I said OK. That was truly a new beginning for me. I went to the principal's office and filled out some paperwork. I was a high school student again.

I worked my way through high school at a part time job at Kroger. I stayed at Kroger for three years and learned a lot. I never missed a day of work in the three years I was there. I remember during my senior year in high school, I only had one pair of pants to wear. I wore these pants to school, to work, and everywhere else. They were black. I routinely laundered them, and they would gradually begin to turn gray because of the laundering and ironing. So, for 25 cents, I would buy small packages of black RIT dye and redye the pants again and again. I only had three long-sleeved checkered shirts, and I rotated those throughout the year. About two weeks before graduation, I purchased a new shirt at Kroger for $1.67. The first day I wore my new shirt to school, one of my teachers commented that she liked my new shirt. I was so embarrassed because I thought no one noticed that I wore the same clothes all the time throughout my senior year. I thought it was my little secret. I guess it wasn't.

I finally graduated from high school when I was 19 years old (the oldest in the class).

THE COLLEGE YEARS

I spent eight years in college getting my undergraduate degree and my law degree. I worked my way through college. During my second year of college, I was married and later had two wonderful children. Our incomes were very low, and it was a very tough time for us. We lived off of credit cards, and I still remember Standard Oil taking my credit card away from me because I did not make my payment on time.

During my sophomore year at Indiana University, I saw the movie "To Kill a Mockingbird," which is about a lawyer in a small town. I left the theater that night determined to be a lawyer. I checked out the law school the next day and I was told that my grades were not good enough to get me into Indiana University Law School. I worked really hard during my junior and senior years, brought my grade average up, and I was accepted at Indiana University Law School. I barely made it. Accepted... by the skin of my teeth.

I worked as hard as I could in law school. I studied 14 hours a day during my first year. The second year was a little easier, and the third year was about like the second year. I graduated from law school at the bottom of the class. I was just glad I graduated. I passed the bar exam the first time around. However, upon graduating, I was deep in debt and flat broke.

I was very proud to be a law school graduate of Indiana University. Shortly thereafter, I was sworn in before the Indiana Supreme Court. At last…I was a real lawyer.

THE EARLY DAYS IN MY LAW OFFICE

I opened my own law office shortly after I was sworn in 1968. I started my office with a fold-up card table and four matching fold-up chairs. I had no other furniture. There were days when my phone would not ring. There were days when I would have no cases to work on. It was during a time that lawyers could not advertise as they can now. I handled anything and everything: divorces, bankruptcies, criminal law, wills, probate, fence disputes, contracts, everything. It was not an easy kind of practice. I was still learning. It was common for me to come home at the end of the week and tell my wife "there's no money this week." It was also common for my wife to give me lunch money each day. It was tough to be a new, young lawyer in a city filled with lawyers who are gray-headed and very experienced. I was the new kid in town among all the lawyers. All the other lawyers seemed to be doing great, and I wasn't.

I recognized quickly that I was not the smartest lawyer in town. But I made up for that by being highly organized. It was common for me to work into the evening and on weekends. I just simply outworked my opponent. I would spend hours with witnesses and clients preparing them for trial. I would file every motion that I could think of to keep the other side busy and off balance. I did the unexpected in the courtroom, and I won lots of cases. I finally decided to focus on injury and wrongful death cases only.

In 1978, a new law changed my law practice. That was the year when lawyers could advertise legally. Up to that time, it was against the law for lawyers to advertise. I had always been taught throughout law school that a "real, successful lawyer" didn't have to advertise. That's not true! I got a lot of ridicule from other lawyers for advertising. I still get ridiculed!

THE OWNER OF THE GOLF CLUBS

The lawyer I stole the golf clubs from was appointed to the Indiana Supreme Court. As a young lawyer, I appealed and argued the case before the Indiana Supreme Court. When those five judges in their black robes walked into the Supreme Court to listen to my case, I spotted Justice Prentice immediately. He knew who I was…and I knew who he was. A mutual friend had alerted us both. To get to argue a case before Justice Prentice was exhilarating. I had come a long way since he last saw me. By the way…I lost the case.

MY LAW CAREER TODAY

I am currently the owner of a very successful multimillion-dollar law practice in Bloomington, Indiana. We are statewide. I have 92 staff members, including 15 lawyers. The Ken Nunn Law Office is ranked No. 1 in the State of Indiana for spending the most money on advertising. Our law office is ranked No. 1 for doing the most jury trials for injured clients in the State of Indiana. In fact, our law office has been ranked No. 1 for the past 12 years. We fight big insurance companies every day to get justice for our clients!

Our law office has the No. 1 largest jury verdict for a wrongful death case in the State of Indiana, in the sum of $157 million. We also have what we believe to be the largest jury verdict in our home county, in the sum of $15 million. Last year was a very successful year fighting for new clients against big insurance companies. In 2012, our law firm obtained many million-dollar settlements and multimillion-dollar verdicts. I am one of Indiana's top-rated lawyers, rated AV Pre-eminent in *Martindale-Hubbell*, a rating system established in 1887. My rating is the "highest possible rating both in legal ability and ethical standards." I'm proud of my rating!

People ask me when I'm going to retire, and my response is always the same…"when I can't work anymore." I love practicing law, and I look forward to coming to the office every day. I'm having the time of my life. I truly love helping my clients, and I can still remember my roots and the rough time I had growing up. My clients who have been injured or clients who have lost loved ones deserve justice. I am always anxious and ready to fight the insurance companies to get back for my clients what they lost.

One of the major reasons for my success is that I have surrounded myself with excellent staff. Some of my staff has been with me for 10 to 35 years. I have also surrounded myself with great lawyers. The lawyers in my office are respected statewide and are very distinguished. They are amazing. They fight hard and they win big settlements and judgments against insurance companies. I am very proud of my staff and my lawyers.

One of my principles of success is to always look out for my staff. I help my staff when they need help. That same principle applies to my clients. I always look out for my clients, and I am there when my clients need help.

Here are some more reasons for my success:

1. Helping injured people with difficult cases that other lawyers wouldn't take.

2. Being highly organized.

3. Teaching our staff about the Indiana's new laws and how to fight for our clients.

4. I wrote a book titled *How to Double or Triple Your Income in the Next Three Years.* I never published the book, but I did apply its principles to the operation of our office. We did triple our income in five years. We didn't hit our mark in three years, but I'm happy with the results after five years. Maybe I need to publish the book.

5. As each day begins, I believe today will be the day I write the best letter ever. Today, I will say the best words ever. Today, I will come up with a new idea that is better than any I have ever had before. Every day is an opportunity to outperform myself. I realize my real competition is myself. I do not compete with other attorneys or law firms. I compete against myself every day.

6. Staying focused and reminding myself on a daily basis what I want. There was a time when I wanted a big, new house. So I cut out a picture of a house that I liked, and I taped it on the mirror in my bathroom so that I could see that picture every day. I worked hard every day. Now I have that big house. I did the same thing with my law office building. Today, I have a new, and very large, office building. Set goals and focus on the goal until you succeed.

7. Return phone calls to clients…this shows respect.

8. Don't keep a client waiting in the outer office longer than two

minutes.

9. Don't let a client on the telephone be on hold for longer than one minute.

10. At the end of every conversation with a client, either in person or over the phone, always end the conversation with "do you have any other questions?"

11. Believe in your client. Don't spend too much time on negative thinking. Instead focus on how their case can be won. Believing you can win is the key to winning. The lawyer must put his heart and soul in the case. When that happens in our office…we win big.

12. I have never forgotten my roots. You can't teach hungry.

13. I love what I do. I love to get justice for my clients. And I love helping the little guy.

14. I believe and I follow the Golden Rule.

About Ken

Ken Nunn is the owner of the Ken Nunn Law Office, located in Bloomington, Indiana, which limits its practice exclusively to personal injury and wrongful death cases. For more than 45 years, the firm has built a strong reputation as a defender of victims' rights, having represented over 25,000 injury and wrongful death clients over the past four and a half decades. The law office currently consists of 91 staff, including 15 attorneys, as well as six retired state troopers who serve as investigators for the firm.

The Ken Nunn Law Office has been ranked No. 1 by the *Jury Verdict Reporter* for the past 12 years for doing the most jury trials in Indiana for injured plaintiffs. In 2009, the firm obtained a $157 million judgment for a wrongful death case, the largest jury verdict in the history of Indiana and the sixth largest nationally that year. That firm also obtained $15 million on behalf of an injured child, the largest jury verdict in Monroe County, Indiana.

Ken received his bachelor of science degree in business in 1964 from the Indiana University School of Business, and he received his Juris Doctor degree in 1967 from the Indiana University School of Law. At that time, he was admitted to practice law in all state and federal courts in Indiana.

Ken is a member of the Million Dollar Advocates Forum, the Multi-Million Dollar Advocates Forum, and is listed in the Top Trial Lawyers in America®. He has been listed as an Indiana Super Lawyer, and is a member of the American Association for Justice, the Indiana State Bar Association, and the Indiana Trial Lawyers Association. He and has been a guest lecturer at Indiana University, both to undergraduates as well as students at the I.U. School of Law. Ken is one of Indiana's Top-Rated Lawyers, rated AV Pre-eminent in *Martindale-Hubbell,* a rating system established in 1887. His rating is the "highest possible rating both in legal ability and ethical standards."

Married for 50 years, Ken and his wife, Leah, have two children, Vicky and David, and two grandchildren. Vicky currently serves as a litigation attorney in the Ken Nunn Law Office. Ken was listed in the 2012 edition of *Who's Who of America,* and was also commissioned a Kentucky Colonel by the Governor of the State of Kentucky.

CHAPTER 29

DARE TO SUCCEED WITH PERSONAL BRANDING USING LINKEDIN

BY GREIG WELLS

It's a brand-new world out there.

"We are all going to become head marketers of the brand called YOU."
—*Fast Company* magazine

I learned this lesson the hard way. My goal in sharing my story is to help you save hours and years of frustration, by giving you a shortcut to success because you Dare to Succeed!

For the first 12 years of my career, I worked as job recruiter. I helped software companies in Boston find and hire the best technical employees and leadership talent to grow their business. When I called on a potential new client to offer my job placement services, there was very little that would differentiate me from the hundreds of my competitors who were calling on the same people and offering the same thing.

Differentiating yourself is the biggest challenge faced by any service provider, job seeker, leader or business owner. The challenge is that we all look the same on paper. Our websites all look the same, and the things we say in our sales calls all sound the same to the decision maker. So why should someone choose to do business with you or hire you over your competition?

The obvious answer is that I make the difference. People choose to do business with me because of me. It would seem then that investing in yourself is the best way to influence your success. For many years, I devoted myself to mastering my craft, and I also immersed myself in personal development, which leads to success through word-of-mouth referrals. I was very capable of doing a great job, and when I did, people would tell their friends. In return, these warm referrals led to more business.

You have to be great at what you do to succeed, but investing in yourself alone is not enough. When I approached a client that did not know me without this warm referral and without them knowing I was the best, my success rate was significantly less. Everyone was saying they were just as good as me, but how could anyone tell that I really was the best?

This inability to convince people I was the best came to light when I had to change jobs as a recruiter, because I moved from Boston to Tampa. I had to start from scratch and win over new clients without knowing anyone in this market. How can I stand out from the crowd is the issue every job seeker faces, just like every salesperson faces.

My breakthrough came while listening to Jim Rohn's protégé, Ricky Rainbolt, speak, and he said: *"Brand will always win over talent."* Just like me, you have often been the most qualified to win a client or to get the job offer. When a client chooses someone else, it's often because that person did a better job of marketing themselves. They did a better job of showing how they were the solution to the problem that was being faced. They won through a personal brand, and that's exactly what you need.

A personal brand is what influences people to choose you over your competition. So what the heck is a personal brand? Most so-called branding experts cannot answer this question in a single sentence, yet they will tell you that the essence of your personal brand is that you are expressing yourself in a single sentence. I find that ironic.

My expertise is the ability to simplify things into easy-to-understand concepts. So here is a simple yet effective definition for what a personal brand is: *A personal brand shows how you are different and better than your competition.* When you use a personal brand to position yourself as different and better than your competition, you favorably influence their decision to choose you.

There are three steps to building a personal brand to help you Dare to Succeed:

1. Place your personal brand in a place where people can easily find it online on LinkedIn and on Google.

2. Use LinkedIn groups to identify the major problem being faced by the person you are trying to influence, and use your LinkedIn profile summary to position yourself as the person best uniquely qualified to solve this problem.

3. Create examples, stories and frameworks to show proof of how you are going to solve the problem via your LinkedIn work experience and LinkedIn recommendations.

A brand does not exist just because you say it does. You can't just call yourself the world's best at whatever you do, because anyone can say that. A brand exists when you are consistently reinforcing it with proof. The proof can be online, in the things you say and do, and in what people say about you.

Your identity is based on the message people see when they find you in Google search results. So Step One of personal branding is you need to control the messaging people see when they find you in Google search results. People are already searching Google for your personal or business name on a regular basis. You may already be losing business every day based on what people see when they Google your name.

One of the simplest ways to influence what people see in Google when they search for your name or your business name is by having both a personal and business profile on LinkedIn. **LinkedIn profiles almost always show up at the top of the Google search results.** Google is by far the number-one place people go to search for information about solutions to their problems. However, if a business wants to find a person to solve their problems, the number-one place they go to search is on LinkedIn.

Having a personal brand on LinkedIn enables you to be found in Google and LinkedIn search results, which are the top two places businesses search for people to solve their problems. Companies and recruiters love LinkedIn because it has both the active job seekers, as well as happily employed people who are often perceived to be the better qualified candidates. Your LinkedIn profile summary is the ideal place to show off your personal brand, because it is the first thing people will read when they find you online via Google.

Step Two in building your personal brand is to position yourself as a solution provider. When people are looking to hire you or your company it is because they have problems they need solved. People will feel that you understand them when you can describe their problem better than they can.

In building your personal brand to show how you are different and better than your competition, you are first going to state what you do in terms of the problems you solve for your customers or clients. For example, rather than me saying, "I offer recruiting services," I would instead state that "I will help you grow your businesses by finding and motivating talented leadership to work at your company."

I've identified the reason a business owner is seeking my recruitment services in the first place. It's likely because they need talent and leadership to grow their business. I am then expressing what I do in terms they relate to, and by me restating their problem, I show the business owner that I understand their perspective.

Identify the reason someone would want to hire you or your company; what is the major problem they need you to solve? The most effective way to tap into your business's audience and find out what problem they need to get solved is to use groups on www.LinkedIn.com. There are LinkedIn groups for every possible industry, profession, and around every business topic. You should join these groups and monitor what people are saying for hints as to what major problems they are facing. The key is to join groups that your customers are in, not just groups related to what you do, which are likely to have your peers in them.

In LinkedIn groups, you should ask this question to get people to directly tell you what their number-one problems are: "What are the biggest challenges being faced by (insert your target audience)?"

So, for example, if I sold information technology (IT) services or was looking for a job in IT, I would join groups that have IT directors, and I would ask them: "What is the biggest challenge being faced by IT directors?" When your target audience answers this question, they are giving you the problem you need to solve through your personal brand. It is very important that you do not look internally to determine what problems you are going to solve, and build your personal brand instead around the problems of your target audience.

The number-one mistake people make when building a personal brand is to look internally or guess at what problems their audience needs solved because then you might wind up building a brand no one needs. For example, if I looked internally at myself and what I have done for most of my career as a job recruiter, I would likely come up with a brand statement that says: "I will find for you that employee that no one else in the world can find." That is what I have done most of my career, but this would likely fail as brand statement because finding people is not the major problem being faced in today's troubled economy. In this job market companies have no problem finding employees; the problem they now have is sorting through candidates to find the great ones.

You need to adapt your brand to show how you are solving the current needs of your target audience, not just focusing on the main results you have gotten in the past. Positioning yourself as a solution provider for the number-one problem being faced by your target audience is the first key in building a personal brand that will result in you being chosen over your competition. Once you have developed this brand statement, the ideal place to put it is in the summary and headline of your LinkedIn profile.

The final step three in building your personal brand is to show how you can solve their problem differently and better than everyone else they are considering. People are not going to choose you just because you state the problem and say that you can solve it, because your competition is likely saying the same thing. When you show them how you are able to solve their problems, they will then start to believe your claims of being the best.

There are three ways to show how you uniquely solve a customer's problem using your LinkedIn profile:

1. **Tell the origin story of how you became who you are through your LinkedIn profile.** If you think about some of the most popular superhero movies, we all want to know how Spiderman got his powers or how Superman came to be—these are the origin

stories. In your LinkedIn profile, under your work experience, you want to show how you progressed into your current role. Talk more about the skills you developed and still use in your current role rather than talking about specific work experiences, which are not as relevant.

For an example of this you can look at my LinkedIn profile, which I link to in my bio section. You will see that I had a job in customer service. I talk about the skills I learned and still use today as a successful business owner and recruiter. The skills are relevant to what I do today, even though the experiences may seem like they are not.

2. **You want to tap into the intangibles that make you unique at what you do.** Our LinkedIn profiles and often our resumes focus too much on just skills and experience. You should assume everyone being considered for a job has the qualifying skills and experience. However the truth is, there are many common attributes in hiring a person or business that you can reflect in your LinkedIn profile. You can do this through your personal brand, to gain an edge over your competition in getting the client to choose you.

For example in the recruiting business, an intangible trait would be honesty, because many recruiters are perceived as being as trustworthy as a used car salesman. So in my LinkedIn profile, I tell the following story to build my personal brand as an honest recruiter: "People always tell me I'm the most honest recruiter they have ever dealt with. They tell me at times it feels like I am trying to talk them out of taking a job I got them. But that is just because I pride myself on finding the best true fit for both the job seeker and the company." You see how I have made it into a story that seeds the idea of me being honest into your perception of me, without just saying I am an honest recruiter. This would have no credibility. I have worded it so that it doesn't sound like I am being boastful.

TIP: To craft a branding story for yourself, use this framework: "People always tell me..." then insert the story with what you want to brand yourself as.

3. Use LinkedIn recommendations to get other people showing how you solve problems uniquely. The third key to showing how you solve the problem differently and better is to leverage social proof. This means to get other people talking about how you previously solved the problem for them. In the end people will only give so much credibility to what you say about yourself; it is much more powerful and believable to get other people saying how you solve the problem. A LinkedIn recommendation is written by other people about you and shows up on your LinkedIn profile for everyone to read. A LinkedIn recommendation is only valuable if it is talking about the same themes and problem solving that is consistent with the branding in your profile.

TIP: When asking for a recommendation, use this framework: "Can you please recommend my skills in area X and Y, and talk about how I specifically used them on project ABC?"

The key to getting quality LinkedIn recommendations is to make very specific and direct requests. For example, my personal brand is now focused more on teaching LinkedIn than on recruiting. So when I ask a recruiting friend for a recommendation on LinkedIn, I need to phrase it as: "Can you please write about my success on LinkedIn and specifically how I helped show you how to use LinkedIn?" This covers my topic, which is LinkedIn, but also the recommendation will show my teaching ability. This is exactly what I want for my personal brand.

In this chapter I have shown you why you need to have a personal brand that shows how you are different and better than your competition. I have also shown you how to build a personal brand using www.LinkedIn. com.

To recap there are three steps to building a personal brand to help you Dare to Succeed:

1. Place your personal brand in a place where people can easily find it online; for example, LinkedIn and Google.

2. Position yourself as the person best uniquely qualified to solve your client's biggest problem.

3. Create examples, stories and frameworks to show proof of how you are going to solve the problem in a unique way.

About Greig

Greig Wells is an author and expert on personal branding, specializing in using www.LinkedIn.com.

Greig has been featured on NBC TV, CBS Radio, the *Wall Street Journal Marketplace,* and *Fast Company* magazine. He has been an international speaker and trainer, teaching LinkedIn strategies that get you to the top of search results on LinkedIn, which results in you being found and hired fast.

As part of giving back, Greig has trained over 55,000 job seekers on using LinkedIn through his free webinar training, "LinkedIn Insider Secrets to Getting Hired Fast," which you can register for at www.JobSearchSmarter.com.

For more info on helping your business generate leads and get new clients using automated software on LinkedIn, visit www.GreigWells.com.

CHAPTER 30

PASSION, PERSEVERANCE AND THE POWER OF LEARNING

BY GERALD LUCAS

When I was four years old and noticed a price tag inside a children's book I was reading, I proceeded to copy the entire book page by page (words and pictures) and then went door to door on my street trying to sell "my book" to neighbors. I suppose this was my first failed business venture. A few years later, I started a landscaping business that I ran until I graduated from high school. I can remember coming home exhausted, dehydrated and covered in grass clippings after a long day working in the hot sun. I used to put the cash that I earned into an empty fish bowl until one of my parents could take me to the bank to deposit the money into a savings account. My parents always provided for me, so I didn't work out of necessity. The money I earned from landscaping gave me a sense of accomplishment and allowed me to buy the things I wanted with my own money like a radio, a tennis racket and eventually a car.

I was competitive and wanted to do a better job mowing lawns than the big landscaping companies that operated in my neighborhood. I started mowing lawns in diagonal patterns when an experienced landscaper told me that cutting this way prevented thatch build-up. I used to start every landscaping job by cutting around the shrubs, gardens and perimeter of the lawn before meticulously cutting the remaining portion in straight diagonal lines. Over the seven years I landscaped, I saw the advantages of working with passion. I was passionate about doing the best job possible and it showed—my customers tipped me on a regular basis, and they recommended me to other people they knew. I liked the fact that my customers trusted me, often paying me before I finished and sometimes in advance if they went away on vacation. Cutting lawns year after year showed me how important perseverance is to successfully completing a job as well as overcoming obstacles like angry dogs, sweltering heat, allergies, rain and mosquitoes.

Learning from my mistakes and imitating experienced landscapers was also critical to becoming skilled and efficient. Looking back over all my life experiences, I realize that I've accomplished the most when I was able to combine passion and perseverance with constant learning and improvement.

Like many people, I wasn't sure what I wanted to do when I graduated from high school. Before I settled into the real estate business I've run for over a decade, I held more than a half dozen different jobs. Ultimately, I wanted to run my own business like I'd done as a kid. When I was accepted into the graduate business program at MIT, I focused my energy on entrepreneurship. While at MIT, I worked with a local internet start-up company that manufactured internet kiosks. I graduated from MIT in the middle of the dot-com boom and went to work for several internet companies based in New York City.

A CAREER IS BORN

I began my career as a real estate investor unintentionally, with a little help from my Mom. My mother, who is an accountant, had been telling me to start looking into buying a home. I thought it was a good idea but kept procrastinating and putting it off. Lucky for me, Mom persisted, visited me on her week off from work and found a local real estate agent to help find property. I had no savings, but made an offer to buy a small tenant-occupied condo anyway. When my offer was accepted, I had to use a credit card cash advance to come up with the down payment and closing costs.

While I waited for my tenant's lease to expire, I noticed that similar apartments in the neighborhood were renting for significantly more money per month than my tenant had been paying. I realized that if I became a landlord and increased my tenant's rent, his new monthly rental payment would cover my new mortgage and condo fees, plus leave me with some extra money at the end of each month. At that moment, a light bulb went off in my head—I had discovered a viable path to financial freedom. Real estate became my new passion. I wanted to buy more property but felt that I lacked the knowledge to do it successfully. I tried to learn everything I could about real estate investing, first by reading books and listening to a real estate audio course my Mom had. I also sought the advice of experienced real estate investors in my area. The steady investment of both my time and money into learning has given me an edge over other real estate investors and played a major role in my successes.

A COSTLY MISTAKE

Billionaire stock market investor Warren Buffet says that "the road that leads to great success is usually paved with a ton of mistakes." I made one very expensive mistake after one of my most profitable years as an entrepreneur. I was approached by a fellow real estate investor about buying an apartment complex he'd come across out of state. He said that he was interested because this complex's rate of return was much higher than the rate of return we'd likely get for a similarly sized apartment complex in our area. Still, he had some reservations and didn't want to buy an investment this big by himself. After my windfall year, I was brimming with overconfidence and somehow convinced myself that my past success and experience would allow me to handle a huge investment in a real estate market I wasn't familiar with hundreds of miles away. When we purchased the property, we hired a local property management company, immediately began making surprise visits to our new apartment complex, and instituted an on-time rental-payment bonus system to encourage our tenants to pay their rent on time.

Despite all our efforts and the years of combined property management experience we both brought to the venture, the apartment complex we bought was a bad investment. Unfortunately for us, bad investments rarely improve with age. The icing on the cake was that we paid too much money for this bad investment. I've learned over the years that a bad deal is worse than no deal at all and overpaying for real estate is one of the most dangerous mistakes you can make as an investor.

Two other factors that were completely out of our control made matters even worse:

1. The price of oil hit an all-time high; our buildings were heated by oil, and as landlords we were obligated by the state to provide heat to our tenants for nine months of the year.

2. A lawsuit brought against the local water company tripled the cost of our quarterly water bill. Despite trying every cost-saving strategy we could think of, we were losing on average well over $10,000 a month. In order to sell the apartment complex after several failed attempts, we had to make good on a threat to our lender to stop paying our mortgage if the lender didn't allow our buyer to assume our $1 million bank loan. By the time we finally sold the complex, my business partner and I had lost over $400,000 each.

Two months after we sold the apartment complex, Lehman Brothers filed for bankruptcy protection, the world's monetary system almost collapsed, and real estate transactions ground to a virtual halt. As hard as it had been to sell the apartment complex before, it would have been almost impossible to sell in the middle of the global financial crisis. So as painful as this episode was for both of us, our perseverance in bargaining and negotiating with our lender and the many buyers we entertained paid off because our losses could easily have been much greater.

LESSON LEARNED

An experienced investor told me early in my career to make sure I thoroughly knew and understood my local real estate market. Since then, I've always tracked and monitored home prices and inventory levels on a monthly basis in the local areas where I normally invest. When I noticed home prices peak in Spring 2006, after years of unsustainable expansion, I knew that the market was about to change. As the real estate market declined, banks stopped lending, unemployment rose and the number of unsold homes grew. Homeowners were struggling, and even very successful real estate investors I knew were experiencing financial hardship. I increasingly found myself answering questions from friends and fellow investors who were struggling to make their mortgage payments. I was infuriated by the unscrupulous tactics banks often used on homeowners to try to squeeze more money out of them.

My company, Performance Property (www.performanceproperty.com), became a passionate advocate for homeowners and investors who'd fallen behind on their mortgage, negotiating with their lenders so they could sell their homes when they'd made the decision that a short sale was their best option to avoid foreclosure. Since the buyer in a short sale transaction normally pays the closing costs, our service was and still is free to our short sale customers. To help inform clients and other struggling homeowners and investors, I began posting free educational videos on my company's YouTube channel (www.youtube.com/user/performanceproperty). I also started writing articles that eventually lead to my first book, *Short Sale Specifics*.

Both patience and perseverance is required to successfully negotiate real estate short sale transactions, which, in some cases, can take years to resolve. Continuous learning is also crucial because banks often change the way they process short sales. I was and still am a passionate advocate for my short sale clients. Our clients really appreciate the resolve and passion that we provide on their behalf, and they express that gratitude regularly through the heartfelt testimonials they write us.

OPPORTUNITY KNOCKS

Around the time I released *Short Sale Specifics*, I was approached by an Australian pension fund looking for new investments for their clients. The pension fund was interested in U.S. residential real estate because they wanted to buy into the market before prices started to rise again and because real estate provided a good hedge against Australia's inflated currency.

Over the years, I've noticed that successful people don't find opportunities—they create them from possibilities we all encounter on a regular basis. This Australian pension fund had presented me with a possibility that I needed to transform into an opportunity.

In less than two weeks, I developed a comprehensive strategy and written investment plan and handpicked the initial team of real estate professionals to implement it. This required a great deal of passion, perseverance and focus to get everything and everyone lined up in time to execute the plan. I had to use all the knowledge, learning, personal relationships and skills I'd developed over the previous decade. After I convinced the pension fund to invest in my local market, I worked collaboratively with them to form a Real Estate Investment Trust (REIT) and produce an investment prospectus that was based on the two-day presentation I'd initially prepared and presented. I was named chief investment officer of the REIT, and I travelled to Sydney, Melbourne, and Canberra, Australia's capital, on a one-week whirlwind tour to pitch our investment plan to the pension fund's investors. The investment tour was a huge success, and in a matter of a few months, we'd raised over $100 million.

SHARING THE KNOWLEDGE

Achieving your own goals is satisfying but I find that sharing knowledge with others so that they can maximize their potential is even more personally rewarding. I've had the pleasure of working both as a real estate investing coach and a college professor, teaching people step-by-step how to start their own businesses. My students have worked in a wide variety of professions. I've taught firefighters, salespeople, teachers, doctors, farmers, accountants, pharmacists, builders, truck drivers, realtors and financial planners.

I teach the same success principles that have helped me survive during hard times and thrive during good times. I post free real estate investing instructional videos on my company's YouTube channel (www.youtube. com/user/performance property) to help my coaching students and

Gerald's FIVE Success Principles in Real Estate and in Life

1. *Passion, perseverance and learning are the keys to success.* Passion gives you the spark to get started. Constant learning gives you knowledge and expertise, and perseverance gives you the strength to endure temporary failure and frustration.

2. *A bad deal is worse than no deal at all.* Bad investments, whether personal or financial, rarely get better over time—if you can't fix them, you have to get rid of them as soon as you possibly can.

3. *Past success does not guarantee future success;* every investment you make must therefore stand on its own merits.

4. *You don't find opportunities; you must create them.*

5. *There's no shame in admitting you don't know something.* Recognizing where you need improvement makes it easier for you to learn. Everything that you now know, you learned at some point along the way.

other aspiring investors. Every individual is unique, so I start out all coaching relationships getting to know each student so we can individually tailor the coaching sessions to focus on accomplishing the student's specific goals. I've found that it's easier and safer to learn from other people's mistakes than it is to learn from your own mistakes. Because I encourage them to focus on small, incremental steps, many of my students have avoided making some of the mistakes that I've made as an investor. The key is breaking problems down into manageable pieces. One of my former college students now runs a successful nonprofit, and many of my coaching students have enjoyed the extra income and enhanced financial freedom that real estate investing can provide.

THE KEY TO REALIZING GOALS AND FULFILLING YOUR DREAMS

Passion, perseverance and an unending commitment to learning have allowed me to meet life's challenges and achieve financial independence. Both my struggles and my triumphs have convinced me that most people can use these three principles to realize their goals and fulfill their dreams. When our short sale clients get discouraged and want to give up because their lender is being unreasonable, we point out that patience and resolve today will pay off for them down the road financially if they stay the course and continue to work with us to eliminate their mortgage burden. When my coaching students let temporary hardship or the fear of failure overwhelm or paralyze them, I remind them to think about the financial freedom they desire and encourage them to focus first on taking just one step beyond where they are today.

We all possess the capacity to achieve and luckily all the skills that are necessary to be successful can be acquired. We just have to learn how to develop our abilities and take advantage of our potential. There are few things more satisfying than overcoming the odds, achieving your goals, and building a better life for yourself and for the people around you. The best part is that success has its rewards, and when you achieve success, you get to choose what those rewards are.

About Gerald

Gerald Lucas is a real estate investor, author, coach and professional speaker. Gerald is the author of *Short Sale Specifics: An Easy-to-Read Homeowner's Guide to Short Sales,* which draws from his experience successfully negotiating hundreds of real estate short sales. A landlord and condominium developer, Gerald has owned and managed properties that range in size from condos and single-family homes to big apartment complexes.

Always eager to pass his knowledge and experience on to others, Gerald has coached hundreds of students throughout the United States and Canada on how to invest in real estate. A former college professor, Gerald designed, developed and taught the small business certificate program at Hudson Community College in his hometown.

In 2011, Gerald partnered with an Australian pension fund to form a Real Estate Investment Trust (REIT). Together they raised over $100 million to invest in residential property. Gerald developed the REIT's entire investment strategy, handpicked the REIT's initial team of professionals (attorneys, title company, property manager and leasing director), and oversaw the first $20 million of all property acquisitions.

Gerald is currently Managing Director of Performance Property, LLC, in Jersey City, New Jersey, and is a licensed Realtor. Gerald holds business degrees from Howard University as well as MIT's Sloan School of Management. Gerald is a long-time musician and singer-songwriter who regularly performs in the New York City metropolitan area. Gerald actively supports Big Brothers Big Sisters as well as Project Homeless Connect.

CHAPTER 31

WANT TO BE SET FOR RETIREMENT? WALK THE ROAD LESS TRAVELED

BY CHRISTOPHER SCALESE

We've all seen the advertisements and commercials. They are so prevalent that we've almost become immune to them. What I'm talking about are the ads from all the Wall Street brokerage firms that continually deliver one message—and one message only: How to Grow Your Money! And when you think about it, who can blame them for beating the same drum over and over again. Making loads of money in the stock market is fun and exciting and can even be described as sexy. But I feel there is something flawed with this message. Now, don't get me wrong: Growing your money is a great thing. But growing your money at all costs, ignoring all the risks and without a plan, is a recipe for disaster. And here is where I feel many brokerage firms are doing a tremendous disservice to the investing public.

The way to achieve true financial security and independence is simple, but it's not easy. If it was easy, everyone would be able to accomplish it. You need a true financial plan. And implementing a true financial plan goes well beyond just calling up Charles Shwab or Vanguard and having someone on their 800 number pick some investments for you. It requires time and effort, patience, and diversification, which means not always using the stock market (which Wall Street hates by the way). And it may require paying a professional for assistance. This is not the road that the major brokerage firms want you to take. But sometimes the road less traveled is less traveled for a reason. But for those who have the courage to break away from what the masses are doing and forge their own way, the rewards can be beyond anything you could have imagined.

WHY GROWTH AT ALL COSTS DOESN'T WORK

As someone who has worked in the financial services industry since 1992, I have seen firsthand the devastating effect that a "growth at all costs" mentality can have on someone's financial situation. On the surface, the message seems reasonable. While you're working, you try to grow your money as best you can, and then when you retire, you simply live off the nest egg you've accumulated. Wall Street even has a formula for how you can live off your nest egg when you retire. Their advice is to keep a mix of 60 percent stock and 40 percent bonds. They then suggest that you withdraw approximately 5 percent a year from your nest egg, adjust your withdrawal annually for inflation, and— *voila!*—you're set for life.

But here's where things get interesting. What they don't tell you is that this formula, tested over about 50 years, gives you approximately an 83 percent chance of never running out of money during retirement. Now I don't know about you, but when I retire, I want to be 100 percent certain of never running out of money, not 83 percent. Would any of you get on an airplane that told you the chances of reaching your destination safely is 83 percent? I doubt it! So why take the same chances with your financial health.

And things are getting worse. Last year, Wall Street experts lowered their recommended withdrawal rate from 5 to 4 percent because of the extremely low interest rate environment we are in. And this year, a new study came out and said the chance of success using a 4 percent withdrawal rate is now down to 48 percent. So the new recommended withdrawal rate is now 2.8 percent. Think about that for a minute. Wall Street recommendations have basically cut in half the amount of income they recommend you take out in order to have a successful retirement.

Let me give you a real-world example to illustrate how this formula could be devastating to a person's financial situation. I met recently with a couple in their early 60s who retired in 2004 with $1 million in their nest egg. At the time, they told their broker that they needed $45,000 of income from their portfolio for retirement. Their broker told them since that was only 4.5 percent of their total assets, they were in great shape. But as anyone who has lived through the 2000s in the stock market can attest, it has not been kind to investors. Between 2004 and 2012, this couple saw their nest egg shrink from $1 million to $500,000. Sure, they withdrew $45,000 per year from their investments, but they've also seen their nest egg cut in half. At this rate, they could be completely out of money in the next seven to 10 years with no hope of recovery.

DO YOU HAVE A "MAYBE" INCOME PLAN —OR A GUARANTEED PLAN?

What doomed this couple is what happens to a lot of folks I see. They had no guaranteed income plan for their nest egg. I know it's a cliché, but it's true. Those who fail to plan, plan to fail. This is the first, and most important step that should be taken when putting together a successful retirement plan: Have an income plan. The couple in the above example had what I call a "maybe" income plan. This simply means that their retirement income "may be" enough to last them through the rest of their lives. The "maybe" threshold is insufficient. When you are putting together your income plan, it should be a *guaranteed* income plan, not a "maybe" income plan. And while we're talking about an income plan, you also have to make sure that the income plan addresses the needs of the surviving spouse once the first person passes away. Let me illustrate what I mean.

Another couple I met with recently are enjoying a very happy and secure retirement. Between the husband's $36,000 in pension income, $18,000 in social security income, and the wife's $10,000 in social security income, their combined income of $64,000 is more than sufficient to meet their lifestyle needs. But here's the problem: There is no survivor benefit for the husband's pension. This means if he passes away first, his wife is going to lose his $36,000 pension, plus she'll lose her $10,000 social security income, but she will assume her husband's $18,000 in social security. In other words, her income will go from $64,000 down to $18,000. And she told me there is no way she could survive on $18,000. Because they recognized this problem while the husband was still alive, they were able to take the necessary steps to make sure the wife would not have such a huge drop in income should her husband pass away first.

5 STEPS TO SUCCESSFUL RETIREMENT PLANNING

The first step of the income-planning phase of retirement that needs to be addressed is inflation. The reason this is important is that the average retirement is going to last between 25 and 35 years. And what that means is that the income you may need today will probably be woefully insufficient 10, 20, or 30 years from now. Consider that at the average historic inflation rate of 3 percent, your income need will more than double by the end of your retirement. So if your income plan does not factor in inflation, you will probably find yourself in financial trouble sometime down the road.

The second step of a successful retirement plan is a tax plan. Because in the end, it's not what you make but what you keep in your pocket after taxes that really matters. Consider this comparison of two different retirees. One has $1 million in their nest egg, while the other has $600,000. On the surface, you would think that the person with $1 million is enjoying the better retirement. But let's take a closer look at their situation. The first investor has their entire nest egg in bank CDs that are currently yielding 1 percent interest. So the income that is being generated is about $10,000. Also, because this investor is in the 15 percent tax bracket, he's really only making $8,500 after taxes. The second investor has his nest egg in a tax-efficient portfolio earning 5 percent, so his income is $30,000. And because his portfolio focuses on tax efficiency as well, he's only paying $500 in taxes on his $30,000 of income. In other words, the person with $1 million is netting $8,500 after taxes while the person with $600,000 is netting $29,500 after taxes. Upon closer inspection, it's pretty clear which person is probably enjoying their retirement more. This is why having some kind of tax plan is so important, because without it, you may be paying more than your fair share to the government.

The third step of a complete retirement plan is a long-term care plan. Unfortunately, almost all of us has heard a horror story of someone who needed long-term care and ended up spending all their hard-earned money to pay for that care. This is where having a solid plan could mean the difference between a successful retirement and one filled with financial worry. I know that one of the biggest reasons a lot of people don't consider long-term care insurance is because of how expensive it can be. And this certainly is a valid argument because the typical long-term care plan can average between $4,000 to $8,000 per year in premiums. When you throw in the "use it or lose it" risk associated with most plans, people tend to get very hesitant on moving forward. What I mean by "use it or lose it," is that if you pass away without needing long-term care, then all those premiums you've paid over the years are basically wasted. Consider a $5,000 annual policy that you were paying for 20 years, and you're looking at $100,000 of money that you received absolutely no value from.

Again, this kind of risk really makes people think twice about protecting themselves from long-term care expenses. But a way to get around this "use it or lose it" risk while still protecting your nest egg is to look at insurance that will pay out a death benefit in the event that you never need long-term care. Let's look at this a little deeper. Let's say a typical long-term care policy costs you $5,000 a year and will give you total long-term care coverage of $250,000. Though the $250,000 of coverage will go a long way in protecting your nest egg, the risk of feeling like you wasted those premium dollars should you not need long-term care is preventing you from taking the coverage. But as an alternative, you can look at a similar policy that will cost you the same $5,000 in annual payments, with the same $250,000 of coverage, but it will give you a life insurance death benefit if you never need long-term care. In other words, if you pass away without using the long-term care coverage, your beneficiary will receive the $250,000 as a tax-free death benefit. So you are essentially eliminating the "use it or lose it risk." If you need long-term care, you're covered; if you don't, then your beneficiary receives the money. Either way, someone is benefitting from all those payments you made over the years.

Speaking of a death benefit, this leads us to the fourth step in a successful retirement plan: an inheritance plan. Without proper planning, a big portion of your nest egg is going to be paid to the IRS when you pass away. Let me give you an example of how big the potential tax bite could be. A couple I've been working with for several years wanted to start doing some estate planning. We started by looking at a worst-case scenario should they do no proactive planning. Based on the current tax laws, we determined that their $2 million portfolio could be reduced to $1.1 million because of taxes and penalties. So overnight, their nest egg would be cut almost in half. A proper inheritance plan will go a long way in ensuring that the maximum amount will be paid to your heirs, with as little going to Uncle Sam as necessary.

Finally, after putting together 1) an income plan, 2) a tax plan, 3) a long-term care plan, and 4) an inheritance plan, it's time to tie it all together with 5) an investment plan. Only after you have the first four steps in place, can you finally pick the proper investments to make the overall plan a reality. This is where Wall Street gets it wrong with their message of grow, grow, grow.

How does growth at all costs give you a guaranteed income for life, for your spouses's life, and adjusted for inflation? How does growth at all costs make sure you are paying the least amount of taxes? How does growth at all costs protect you from long-term care expenses? And finally, how does growth at all costs get the maximum amount to your heirs? It doesn't. I'm all for looking for some growth but only after you've taken the time to put together a detailed and personalized plan based on your specific needs. This is the crucial step that Wall Street misses, and therefore, the general investing public is going to miss as well. I challenge you to walk the road less traveled. Dare to be different, dare to be brave, dare to succeed.

About Christopher

Christopher Scalese is the president and founder of Fortune Financial Group, a financial planning firm exclusively dedicated to servicing and educating retirees. Since 1992, Chris has helped over 600 individuals and families achieve their ideal retirement. He works directly with his clients in building, protecting, and preserving wealth for their retirement years. Chris accomplishes this through advanced retirement income planning, risk management, and tax reduction. Chris frequently writes financial columns for various publications, has made numerous television appearances, can be heard each weekend on The Financial Safari Radio Show, and appears weekly on "The Financial Safari" TV Show. His first book, *Retirement Is a Marathon, Not a Sprint,* was published in 2012.

CHAPTER 32

OVERCOMING "BAD GENETICS": THE REAL TRUTH ABOUT YOUR HEALTH AND WEIGHT LOSS

BY DR. CHARLES LIVINGSTON, DC

My story isn't one of rags to riches, I'm sure you've read quite a few of those already. My story is about personal triumph and mastery of my health, weight loss, weight gain and fitness. This is a passion that I have now shared with over 100,000 people around the world.

My journey officially began in junior high. I come from Milan, Indiana, which is a town with a population of about 1,000 people. I was the only Asian kid in my class and 1 of 2 in the entire town. Because of this, I always felt a bit out of place and self-conscious. It didn't help that I was cursed with "poor genetics." I was the shortest kid in class, one of the skinniest, and I had a giant head. Pretty much, I felt like one of those little gray cartoon aliens running around my little town.

I was average, at best, in sports. Too short for basketball, I was a terrible shot, and I was way too skinny for football. Peers would often tell me "you could be the football!"

Well, as you know, junior high isn't easy on anyone, but it's especially hard on us short, skinny kids. I was getting to the age where I would notice girls, but they certainly didn't notice me. I started to lose confidence because I faced rejection after rejection. At that age, it seems like an eternity, and I thought this is probably how my life would always be. On top of that, add the fact that I had a raging case of acne—which, to most teenagers, is a death sentence for our self-esteem.

With these odds stacked against me, I did what any skinny Asian kid would do . . . I started martial arts. Yes, very cliche, but it was a pivotal moment in my life, not just because I could defend myself but because it changed the way I thought about myself and about life. It taught me to:

1. *Look at things as a whole and not as individual parts.* Everything is connected in one way or another, therefore, the decisions you make now can affect your future. In other words, don't miss the forest by staring at the tree in front of you.

2. *Look at problems from different angles.* Nothing is ever one dimensional.

3. *Be a solution-based thinker, not a problem-based thinker.* Whenever I look at any obstacle in my life, I find three solutions to solve the problem, instead of wasting time complaining about it.

4. *Look for patterns—patterns in people, patterns in behavior, patterns in yourself.* By discovering patterns, I was able to understand and predict the outcome for many of the events in life that used to cause me problems. A pattern can also equate to a habit that you have or that someone else has.

Armed with this knowledge, I started to apply it to my situation. This started my journey into natural health, fitness, weight gain, and eventually, weight loss.

I was ready for my plan of action . . . it was fairly easy to figure out. Most of my solutions came from social observances. My main observances were that girls liked guys with muscles, tall guys, athletic guys, and guys with confidence.

My problem: I wanted girls to notice me, and they didn't. I was the friend that they could talk to about other guys, but not the guy that they wanted to date.

Why weren't they noticing me? I was short and skinny, had acne and low self-confidence, and I was not athletic.

What did I have going for me? I had good personality and I was smart, but only because I worked hard and persistently.

What could I change? My height? Nope. My acne? I had medicine that didn't work. So it was "in process." My athletic ability? My peers who played the popular sports already had a huge head start on me. I was skinny: Definitely. Since I couldn't grow taller, I knew that I could grow wider. And by gaining muscle, I would gain more self-confidence.

My solution:

1. Find experts to help me gain muscle.

2. Read books and magazines and educate myself on the subject.

3. Take action and start weight training.

Well, to keep a long story short, no pun intended, and after following my plan persistently and consistently, I ended up gaining 20 pounds of lean muscle. I went from 135 pounds to 155 pounds with 6 percent body fat. And, yes, I did get noticed by the girls!

As I went into college, I still kept this "alternative" way of thinking. I read and researched more about health and exercise, and I started reading every diet book I could get my hands on. I learned a lot in this time about nutrition, which lead me to even more questions . . . ones that even the so-called "experts" couldn't answer.

On one random day, I came home from college and noticed my grandmother's 15 different daily medications. She wasn't getting healthier from taking these; she was getting worse and started getting dizzy spells. Wow, looking at the forest instead of the tree, I had the realization that since everything was related, this was not a good idea. So I called the doctor. Of course, I never got a call back. I pleaded with my grandmother, but because I wasn't the "expert" and just young Charlie boy, she wouldn't listen and neither would my grandfather who died from cancer that resulted from years of smoking. So I watched helplessly as my grandparents deteriorated.

These two deaths shook me to my core. I was really close to my grandparents. And to this day I still believe their deaths were preventable.

After that, I took a good, hard look at the rest of my family. They were riddled with obesity, diabetes, cancer, high cholesterol, high blood pressure, depression, anxiety, metabolic syndrome and heart disease . . . just to name a few. I watched my closest family members die horrible deaths due to these lifestyle diseases. My mother had her stomach removed due to cancer, and multiple aunts had diabetes; one even died from it. Four of my other relatives also died from cancer.

Once these hard truths hit me in the face, I made a vow, right then and there that I would not end up like my family members and that I would teach those who would listen what I knew. I didn't want anyone to have to go through senseless suffering like I did. I then decided to make health and fitness my life's passion. I sought out "experts" in medicine and health care. It seemed that the only ones that could fully answer my questions on how to get healthier were alternative medicine practitioners. I wasn't interested in managing disease; I wanted to create health and transform lives. They taught me how traumas, negative thoughts, and toxins would destroy your health. How do you fix this? Just do the opposite and create wholeness, change your thought process, and combat toxins by eliminating the source while adding nutrients to your body that create purity. Look at things as a whole and not just parts. This would lead to better health, weight loss, and even energy gain. This isn't a bash on traditional medicine, because without it, people would die in emergency situations.

At that point, I knew what I needed to do. My journey led me to become a chiropractor who specialized in nutrition and wellness. I opened my practice and was instantly able to transform lives—not just for neck and back pain, but I also had the pleasure of teaching people how to be healthy and lose weight.

I kept reading diet books and experimenting on myself to see what worked. Eventually, I created my own weight-loss system that was proven over and over again to be effective. I've tested it many times on myself and my clients. And, yes, I have been fat. I went through a bout of depression and started not watching what I ate. I started to develop abdominal fat. I then decided to gain muscle again, which meant I had to eat even more food. Well, instead of doing it the right way, I just ate anything I wanted and ended up ballooning from 165 to 190 pounds. I felt disgusting and went back to following the principles in my own system.

After a few weeks, I easily dropped back down to 175. It was so easy that I wanted to complete the cycle and drop down to 165 pounds so I would be extremely "ripped" for a photo shoot. Back to the drawing board. I did my research, consulted some other experts, and came up with a plan. In five weeks, I dropped down to 158 pounds, and my body fat was less than 5 percent.

I completed the cycle. I went from skinny to muscular and then from fat to muscular. I've been on both ends of the spectrum: I know what it's like to be overweight, and I also know what it's like to be too skinny. I discovered what people on both ends of the spectrum feel like.

Today, I have been able to successfully help over 100,000 people worldwide with their health and weight loss. I love transforming lives, and I will strive to continue helping people for as long as I live.

MY 4 SECRETS TO OVERCOME ANY OBSTACLE IN LIFE

1. The law of adaptation: It's always hardest to start something the very first time. This is because there is a learning curve or a phase of adaptation in life. Realize that the only thing holding yourself back from taking that first step is you. My advice is take that leap of faith and understand that even though it is uncomfortable now, it will get easier! Realize that we, as humans have been created to adapt to any situation so no matter how bad something seems at first, it will always get better.

2. Do what you've always done and get what you've always gotten. Albert Einstein said it best: "The definition of insanity is doing the same things over and over again and expecting different results." If you find yourself in a rut, doing the same diet, the same exercises, picking the same type of guy or girl, or even having no money at the end of the month, take a moment and just stop. Stop and analyze the situation. Find where that rut is and do something different. If you have been restricting calories for weeks, take a day and gorge yourself with your favorite foods. This will help to kick-start your leptin levels, which will, in turn, kick-start your metabolism and break you through that weight-loss plateau!

3. Have persistent consistence. People get discouraged and fall off and cheat on their diet. Realize that it's OK. That is normal behavior. Get right back on track. Progress will be made and lost. It's persistent consistence that will help you to succeed. There is no failure, just feedback. Learn from it and keep going. Figure out ways to help you reach your goal. Remember, slow and steady wins the race, and the race we are running is a life-long marathon, not a sprint.

4. *You are not a victim of your genetics.* Your genes are nothing but a light switch that can be turned on and off. The fingers that flip those switches are factors in your environment/lifestyle. By learning what these are, you can literally change your health and your life. Look at the contestants from the biggest loser. Look at their families. By deciding to make a change and taking the right action, they have successfully lost, 60, 80, 100-plus pounds of fat!

3 SIMPLE DIET TIPS THAT CAN INSTANTLY CHANGE YOUR HEALTH AND WEIGHT

1. *Stop eating wheat/wheat-based products (including white flour).* White foods, such as white flour, pasta and wheat, in my opinion, are one of the primary reasons why 70 percent of the U.S. population is overweight. Here's why:

- Wheat has gluten, which is a nondigestible protein that can cause autoimmune diseases, such as celiac, irritable bowel syndrome, and rheumatoid arthritis.

- The blood sugar spike is so great from eating two slices of bread, that it causes you to be tired, hungry, instantly store fat, and have difficulty losing fat.

Good alternatives to wheat: brown rice and quinoa

2. *Stop eating soy.* Here's why:

- It disrupts thyroid function, which leads to weight gain and other health issues.

- It has phytic acid, which is called an anti-nutrient because it blocks the uptake of minerals, such as magnesium, calcium, iron and zinc.

- It can inhibit protein digestion and affect pancreatic function (think insulin issues).

- It can disrupt estrogen levels because soy contains estrogen-like chemicals that lead to hormone imbalance, weight gain, and fertility issues.

Good alternatives to soy: hemp protein, brown rice protein, and quinoa

3. Stop eating/drinking dairy. Here's why:

- Dairy is a mucous-creating food that is related to allergies. Creating mucous is the body's natural response to protect itself.

- Pasteurized and homogenized milk destroys all the nutrients and causes the body to react to milk protein as foreign invaders, resulting in immune disorders and inflammation throughout the body.

- Milk contains antibiotics and hormones that can mess up your hormone levels, leading to metabolic issues and weight gain.

Good alternatives to dairy: almond milk and coconut milk

A SIMPLE WEIGHT LOSS PLAN TO INSTANTLY DROP FAT

- *Fast Weight Loss:* Follow the three rules above 50 percent of the time.

- *Faster Weight Loss:* Follow the three rules above 75 percent of the time.

- *Turbo Weight Loss:* Follow the three rules above 95 percent of the time.

MY NO. 1 SINGLE EXERCISE TIP

Movement is life, and life is about movement. Therefore, move yourself each and every day. Find things that you enjoy doing that are active. It could be as simple as walking or more complex like doing a cross-fit workout. Just move! Remember: Persistent consistence.

WHAT HAS MADE ME SUCCESSFUL IN HEALTH AND WEIGHT LOSS?

I chose to not focus on my problems in life but to take responsibility, adapt and create a solution. Now don't get me wrong, I recognize issues and problems, but I don't let them determine my outcome or my outlook. I hope and pray that you'll take this information and use it to take action. I would love to hear your success story! These principles can be applied to all areas of life, including your relationships, finances, health, emotional and spiritual well being. Keep in mind that the best solutions are simple, but that doesn't mean they're easy. Add a little bit of action to your solution and see what happens! Good luck and God bless.

Dr. Charles

About Charles

Dr. Charles Livingston, aka "Dr. Charles," is a board certified chiropractic physician who has certifications in wellness, nutritional response testing and kill-mode training protocols.

Dr. Charles received his doctorate of chiropractic, graduating with honors, from the world-renowned Palmer College of Chiropractic. He has studied a variety of healing techniques and has spent thousands of hours researching nutrition, exercise and weight loss.

Dr. Charles is a best-selling author whose No. 1 weight-loss book, *Fat Loss Factor,* has taken the internet by storm in several countries around the world. He has successfully helped over 100,000 people worldwide.

His approach focuses on creating an optimal environment for the body to heal, boost metabolism and burn fat by using the best techniques, state-of-the-art research, and the top-of-the-line nutritional supplementation. His goal is to give clients a lifestyle change that is simple, ultra effective and allows them to still eat their favorite foods.

Dr. Charles is an avid writer who has written hundreds of articles. His latest book, *Cellulite Factor,* has helped thousands of women to get rid of cellulite naturally. To learn more about his number-one weight-loss program and his "1 Simple Tip to Lose Belly Fat," go to www.fatlossfactor.com.

CHAPTER 33

DON'T PLAY THE WALL STREET CASINO GAME—AND LOSE:
HOW TO GUARANTEE INCOME FOR LIFE

BY BARRY ROSENBLUM

"Buying stocks or bonds is gambling. You're betting on prices—you're betting on buying them from those who don't know how much they're worth and selling them to somebody who thinks they're worth more."
—John Bogle, founder and former CEO of Vanguard Group

Not so long ago, Americans were the envy of the world. But today, we're a nation economically upside down. Why?

Because they stole our future.

We all know who "they" are—Wall Street. The people who told you, for all those years, that your money would be safe with them, that it would grow, that if you played by the rules, you'd have all the money you needed when you needed it—for your children's education, for retirement, even that trip around the world you'd always dreamed of.

You went on a trip, all right. Wall Street took you for a ride.

You did everything they told you to do. You worked hard all your life,

303

budgeted, scrimped and saved so you could put money aside every month. You followed Wall Street's advice, put your money in stocks and stayed there for the long haul. You did your homework and followed their advice, watched the TV experts, paid for the newsletters so when you selected investments for your IRA or 401(k), you felt confident that your retirement would be comfortable, with money left for your heirs.

And what did you get for it?

For many of you, your retirement is gone, your savings decimated, your trust in the system violated. Forget helping your children and grandchildren through college and graduate school. Now you have to worry about where the money will come from if you or your spouse gets sick and needs a nursing home or home health care.

It wasn't supposed to be like this.

When you walk into a Vegas casino, you know you're taking a gamble. But no one ever told you Wall Street was no different than a one-armed bandit.

The "experts" always advise you to "invest for the long term." Well, let's look at what happened over the long run...

In January 1999, the S&P Index was at 1,229. In January 2009, 10 years later, it read 1,000. That's an *18 percent decline.*

But people continue to invest, because Wall Street creates a false sense of security. They make it look and sound so easy, like anyone can make money in the stock market—even after the stock market collapsed and the real estate market went into the dumper.

Well, I learned the hard way that what happened in 2008 wasn't the exception—it's the rule.

ADVENTURES IN THE STOCK MARKET

Soon after I graduated from NYU, a fraternity brother approached me with an enticing offer- "I'm working for a brokerage firm that sells new issues, and *you can't lose.*" So I scraped together all the money I could find and managed to come up with $10,000 to invest. Over the next year, my $10,000 investment grew to $35,000. I felt like a millionaire. So when that same friend offered to reinvest my $35,000 in what he called "high quality stocks," it sounded great.

Then the market crashed. And suddenly, my original investment of $10,000 was worth $5,000.

I concentrated on expanding my family business and was tremendously successful. So successful, a big company came along and offered to buy me out for $3.3 million in their stock. They put me on their payroll and I became a vice president of the company. My stock skyrocketed from $15 to $26 a share. I made over $2 million before we even closed the deal.

A little more than two weeks after the deal closed, a respected financial reporter came out with the story that the company I sold to was cooking the books. My stock went from $26 a share to $2 a share. I lost everything. I went from being a millionaire to not being able to feed my family.

Eventually, I recovered some of what I lost and began a new career as an insurance agent. Knowing I needed to invest my money, I asked a mentor I trusted to put together an investment program for me. This time, I concentrated on mutual funds. I was careful. We selected from among the very top fund managers in the business, hired three professional money managers, and I stayed informed and on top of the management as well.

But my portfolio still deteriorated.

The experts told me not to worry—I was in these funds for the "long run." But after 12 months, I was down 40 percent. I had enough and I bailed out.

At that point, I was officially done with Wall Street. I changed my personal investment strategy, and today, I can sleep at night knowing that my wife and I will have a comfortable quality of life no matter what happens on Wall Street.

You can't beat Wall Street—so why would you join them?

THE SAFE ALTERNATIVE TO WALL STREET

I chose another direction for the Rosenblum Financial Group. In fact, we call ourselves "The Safe Money People," because we are all about helping our clients enjoy guaranteed income for life.

Here's an example of two such clients: a married couple named Julie and Marvin. Marvin had owned a small business, which he sold and did what their friends did—invested the proceeds in the stock market, where they ended up losing a lot of their money. They came in to see me because they were concerned that, if they lived too long, they would run out of their remaining funds. Marvin said, "I don't even know if you want to work with us. We're not rich, but we can't afford to lose any more."

Nine years later, I called Julie one night. I knew Marvin was sick, and I wanted to know how he was doing. Julie said to me, "Barry, we feel so blessed to have caring friends like you. We are so grateful for what you've done for us; we have never had to worry about our money since we came to you." Julie is 90 and Marvin is 94 now; if they had stayed in the stock market, they would have gone broke. Instead, they have more than enough to live on and are giving a substantial amounts to a number of charities while they are alive.

These kinds of stories, of course, make us proud of what we can accomplish. But you are probably asking, how can we provide our clients with income that's *not* dependent on Wall Street?

We use our "insurance products."

Most of us insure:

- Our homes
- Our cars
- Our health
- Our lives
- Even our appliances by having a warranty

But most of us fail to insure our most valuable assets—our money, our investments and our retirement—everything we will pass on to our spouses, and possibly eventually to our children and grandchildren.

Annuity programs offer this kind of security. An annuity is a contract with an insurance company made over a specified period of time. There is a minimum guaranteed interest rate, assuring that the money will grow as long as it remains with the company. These programs are based on guarantees, certainty and financial security—not greed and empty promises.

So why don't most people know more about annuity programs? The reality is Wall Street and their allies in the financial industry have gone out of their way to convince Americans that insurance companies are an inferior place to invest.

However, the new annuities are not like your father's annuities. Back then, an insurance company was allowed to keep the money in the event of an early death. The new annuities have named beneficiaries so the money goes to your heirs. And once you set your investment goals, these new "Annuities on Steroids" are designed to get you to exactly where you want to be—because the insurance company contractually guarantees you that you will achieve your goals.

While there are many different kinds of annuities, the one I recommend is called a Hybrid Annuity. Regarding Hybrid Annuities, a recent study by Wharton Financial Institutions Center for Personal Finance, following EIA (Equity Index Annuities) returns from 1995, stated: "There is no asset class category that outperformed them. We were extremely surprised, really just amazed."

There are several advantages to using a Hybrid Annuity strategy. Here are the main ones:

- Guaranteed growth of income that may be used for future retirement income
- The ability to receive *increased income as a hedge against inflation*
- Actuarially capped upside market potential with *no* downside market risk
- No direct investment in the market. Account will mirror the S&P 500 as well as other indexes
- In many cases, an opening bonus that will actually *increase* your initial investment—as opposed to opening a brokerage account with your investment *minus* fees
- In many cases, an annual increase that grows your income
- A fixed income percentage that increases every year based on your age that will give you a lifetime guaranteed income
- In some cases, an "income doubler," meaning that if you cannot perform two activities of daily living, your income will *double* for five years (no underwriting required)

Of course, there are also some negatives of using a Hybrid Annuity, which your financial advisor will almost certainly bring to your attention:

- You do not receive 100 percent of the upside of the S&P 500; your growth is capped (but you are also protected from the downside of the market).

- There are surrender charges, although these tend to go down yearly until they disappear after a period of years. Just keep in mind that good planning requires liquidity; you should never put 100 percent of your money into any investment, no matter how safe.

- There is a small fee, often .95 percent, deducted from the cash value of your account (which does not affect your income account).

You may wonder what happens if the insurance company goes under. This scenario isn't likely. Insurance companies are in the business of guarantees, not risk and greed. They receive premiums from policyholders and invest those in bonds with the intention of keeping the money safe to pay future claims. They pay out billions in life insurance claims, enabling millions of families to survive financially. They also guarantee the pensions of millions of people, guaranteeing them an income for the rest of their lives.

Beyond this, insurance companies follow a whole different set of rules than Wall Street. Insurance companies provide policyholders with another layer of protection beyond the claims-paying ability of the insurance company, through what's called the National Organization of Life and Health Insurance Guaranty Associations (NOLHGA). NOLHGA protects policyholders in the event an insurance company can't pay their claims.

Of course, you've probably never heard of this. That's because agents are strictly prohibited, under very heavy penalties, from discussing NOLGHA to induce a sale.

THINGS YOU MAY HAVE HEARD...*THAT AREN'T TRUE*

Wall Street doesn't want the insurance companies to win your retirement dollars. So they have sponsored major disinformation campaigns about annuities.

What kind of disinformation? Specifically, these two specious statements:

1. **You can't get your money out of an annuity.** This is a totally irresponsible statement. You can't get your money out of an *immediate* annuity, which is similar to a pension plan where you cannot get a lump sum; you can only receive an income. With an immediate annuity and a pension plan, you can have a joint and survivor option, taking less income in order to give your spouse a lifetime of income.

   I cannot think of any Wall Street product that will guarantee you a lifetime of income. However, unlike an Immediate Annuity, an "Annuity on Steroids" provides both a lifetime of income *and* liquidity. Problem solved.

2. **There are surrender charges**. This is true. It is similar to how banks charge a fee or surrender charge if you cash in a CD early. This exists to protect the financial integrity of the insurance company, which is making a long-term investment to protect each policyholder. That means if the policyholder gets out of an annuity early, other policyholders will not be seriously affected. The surrender charge protects the insurance company in that event.

What they don't tell you is that annuities allow you a 10 percent free withdrawal every year. Also, if you die or enter a nursing home, there are no surrender fees.

IS AN ANNUITY RIGHT FOR YOU?

Ask yourself this: Are you a risk taker and a gambler?

Are you willing to live with the uncertainty that you'll come up a loser in the Wall Street casino?

Because no matter what the Wall Street return may be or how good it might look, Wall Street *cannot promise a guaranteed income for life.* And if they lose your money, which they often do, they won't give it back. I can personally tell you that they won't even say "I'm sorry."

On the other hand, are you someone who wants certainty and guarantees?

Would you like to put your income on automatic pilot so when markets go up, you go up with them, but when they go down, your account stays the same?

If so, it's time to transfer your Wall Street IRA account or company retirement plan to a program that will guarantee you an income you will never outlive.

This especially holds true as you age. The older you are, the more you need an annuity. Even if you are 80, the safety and security of a deferred annuity makes sense when compared to the volatility of Wall Street.

It's true that as you get older, your primary concern is having access to the money you need for medical expenses, home health care or a nursing home. But imagine if you had to liquidate your brokerage account in a 2008 market—and took a 40 percent hit. Compare that to an annuity that has a liquidation feature (without penalty) if you go into a nursing home. Or a new rider on some policies that doubles your income if something impedes your daily living.

Annuities are also important for estate planning. Since they are an insurance product, there are named beneficiaries; those beneficiaries receive tax advantages and are able to stretch out *their* income for the rest of their lives, saving serious tax dollars.

At the Rosenblum Financial Group, we are dedicated to providing a real alternative to the Wall Street casino. You can dare to succeed in your golden years—with a guaranteed lifetime of income through Hybrid Annuities.

And you can rest easy knowing you and your loved ones are taken care of for the rest of your lives. You'll sleep well at night knowing you own "sleep insurance."

About Barry

Barry Rosenblum is a Retirement Planning Specialist with 27 years of experience in the financial service field. What makes Barry different is that he is 100 percent focused on protecting the assets of Americans who are either planning for or living in retirement. He deeply appreciates the fact that when people no longer have earned income, they cannot afford to take risks.

Knowing that seniors face many challenges, Barry presents numerous educational workshops during the course of the year. His discussions are always relevant and easily understood. He firmly believes that applied knowledge is the power that will enable people to make wise financial choices to protect their assets.

His firm, Rosenblum Financial Group, is committed to providing programs that address the specific needs of his clients, such as having access to their money when the unexpected occurs, protecting it from the ups and downs of the stock market, saving money on taxes, bypassing probate and safe lifetime income planning strategies. Frequent communication and superior, ongoing service are some of the reasons that Barry receives such positive accolades from his clients.

Barry is a graduate of New York University with a degree in finance. He lives in Wellington, Florida, with his wife and business partner, Marilyn. They are both avid golfers and are fortunate to have five grandchildren in the area and one attending Goucher College.

CHAPTER 34

CLEARING THE BLOCKS THAT LIMIT YOUR SUCCESS

BY DEANN SCHEPPELE

Do you ever get frustrated with the path in which your life has taken? Do you know your potential far exceeds the level at which you are currently living, but you can't seem to figure out how to advance or make a change? Whether you're struggling in a relationship, with your health, or in your career and having a difficult time seeing the light at the end of it all, rest assured there is light, and in this chapter, I'm going to teach you how to find it.

In my late 30s early 40s, my life was taking on a new direction, one that I didn't necessarily plan or anticipate. I was at a point where I felt like I was just maintaining or in survival mode. Often the conversations I was exposed to were redundant, irrelevant and empty; my daily routine was predictable; and my career was stagnant. The economy went into a downward spiral, and people were filing bankruptcy, foreclosing on their homes and losing their jobs. There was an incredible amount of negative energy surrounding me. I began to realize that the majority of our society lives in fear. I knew I did not want to fall into those trenches. One day I heard God tell me to live my life in love, not fear. What a gift. This beautiful message forced me to re-evaluate the essence of my purpose and who I truly am and how I wanted to show up in this world. So I resigned from my career of more than 20 years and began a journey to find my life's purpose.

I've always known that I had the gift of achieving whatever my heart desired, but what I didn't realize is that through the years I began to place limits on what I thought I was capable of achieving. As I began to mature, I noticed that all the trials and tribulations from my youth, along with negative words that people had spoken over me, began to place limiting thoughts in my conscious and subconscious mind. These negative files, past events and comments leave imprints that alter what we believe we are able to achieve. These stories can affect our self-esteem and confidence and take away our greatest desires.

You see, our thoughts dictate our beliefs and actions, which, in turn, can create blocks that form false or negative stories in our conscious and subconscious minds. These files are undesirable past events, traumatic events or words that people have said to us or about us that we chose to believe. Those files plant seeds. They are engraved in the mitochondria of our cells. They become strongholds that block us from expressing ourselves and reaching our fullest potential in life, love, family, friends, relationships, success and health.

We fill our minds with the thoughts and beliefs that do not serve us. Words that others feel compelled to poison us with. Once I realized this I began my quest to unveil the secrets on how to delete these patterns and behaviors. I was determined to move to the next level, and I was determined to reveal what it was that was holding me back. What was stopping me from moving beyond my comfort zone or safe haven?

As far back as I can remember I have struggled with receiving. It was difficult for me to ask for help. It made me feel incompetent. When I did ask it seemed to backfire. So I would just go it alone most of the time. So you see, I set that intention or sent the message out to the universe that I didn't need help. I told myself that I could do it better myself. So the universe responded to my thoughts and delivered exactly what I asked for. I had this belief that no one will help me. I didn't need their help. If I take their help, I am a failure. Do you see how these fears can cause us to become blocked?

Wow! What a huge realization. I knew that if I were able to dig deep in my soul, the universe would show me where this story began. Then I would be able to change the story, remove the stronghold, and stop repeating the pattern that blocked me from succeeding in many areas of my life.

People closest to me saw me as independent, strong and determined. I was all those things, but deep inside there were times when I yearned for someone to ask me if I needed help. But because I sent the message of not needing help, guess what? I rarely received it, and when it was offered, I rarely accepted it.

Receiving is not always about acquiring material things. It's about opening yourself up to the universe and allowing the divine energy to flow through you so you can receive the unique gifts, talents, experiences, and knowledge that God and the universe have given you or set aside for you. Allowing yourself to know and feel that you are worthy of these gifts and to be open to accepting and using them is the greatest gift of all.

I embarked on a journey to find the secret to clear the blocks that were holding me captive. I've spent that last several years honing on my skills, studying under many incredible mentors, and soaking up as much information as I could all in an effort to transform my presence in this world. Deep in my soul, I knew I could create and manifest anything, but somewhere along the way I was "wounded." I wanted to heal these wounds and clear them in an effort to find pure love, happiness and success.

As we grow up all the things our parents, siblings, friends, teachers, classmates say or do can be instantly imprinted or embedded in the mitochondria of our cells. Some of these words or events are positive and some are negative. As humans, we tend to concentrate on the negative more than the positive aspects of life. Some people get pleasure out of other people's downfalls. That is why the local, national and global news media promote the negative stories. Sadly, that is what our society is attracted to so that is what our media promotes, because it is what gives them the ratings and what makes them the most money. You see it's not about the stories; it's about what people relate to or find pleasure in. Unfortunately, the majority of our planet vibrates at a level of negativity, need and lack. So I am going to teach you how to eliminate and destroy the negative thoughts and energy you are harboring.

As I stated earlier, I have studied under the best teachers and mentors and gained a wealth of knowledge, techniques and modalities that completely transformed my life! After practicing and teaching others about love, abundance, health and success, I developed a series of steps that will transmute and rid you of these limiting thoughts, beliefs, patterns, behaviors and old stories that are interfering with your true essence, your fullest potential, your soul's purpose. When you delete these old stories and files, that is when you will come into your highest self. I call these "The 7 Essential Steps to Live in Bliss vs. Fear."

THE 7 ESSENTIAL STEPS TO LIVE IN BLISS VS. FEAR

1. **Set your intention.** Every morning when you wake up, set your intention for the day. Mentally state what it is that you intend to get out of the day. This is so important because it creates the blueprint for each day and what you expect to experience. If you don't set your intentions, then you are vibrating in survival mode. It's like knowing you have to run a race, but you never put your running shoes on. How can you race, if you don't intend to take the necessary steps to get to the track?

2. **Connect to the light.** The light is our Creator, Source Energy, the Universe. It doesn't matter what your spiritual beliefs are or what your religion is or who you connect to. There is only one Creator. Religions call their Creator by different names, but they are all one. Our Creator is the light and the light is the Universe and the Universe is Energy. Imagine a light several hundred feet above your head. This light can be any color. It can be white, gold, purple or even multicolored. If you don't see a light, it's OK. As long as you imagine connecting to a light, you will be connected. So connect to whatever you are comfortable with. Set the intention of receiving truth from the Universe in your highest and greatest good.

3. **Ask and acknowledge.** There are many ways of discovering your negative beliefs. The most common way is through meditation and prayer. When you are quiet and go into your own energy, these beliefs will show up. It's important to be connected and set your intention before asking for anything. That way, you will receive in your highest good. As you meditate or pray, ask the Universe to show you what it is that's blocking you. Acknowledge the truth; trust what you hear. When we become quiet and just be with your inner self, we hear this voice inside tell us what we may not want to hear. This is one of the main reasons people do not meditate. They hear things they don't want to hear. This voice is nudging us to acknowledge the message so we can delete it. For example, if you hear your inner voice saying, "You will never be successful! You will never get married! You can't

do that! You're a failure!" These are false stories! Stories that we chose to believe when a friend, parent, relative, teacher or whomever made a comment to you, and for some crazy reason, you decided to believe it. In that moment you created a sabotaging imprint that limits your ability to achieve your greatest potential. It's what I call a soul fear.

4. **Mentally clear and delete the story or negative files.** Once you've discovered your limiting belief or beliefs, then you must delete them. Mentally ask the Universe to clear and delete the story or file at the cellular level of your mitochondria. This is as deep as it gets. Don't try to make this complicated. This is as easy as it seems. Simply ask for it to be deleted, and it will be gone. Continue to delete again, and again until you feel the shift. You might get emotional and that's OK. It just means you are releasing the negative energy that no longer serves you. You may feel the release in a certain part of your body or you may just feel lighter.

5. **Fill yourself back in with love.** Now that you deleted the old stories and patterns, you want to fill that "void" with love and light. For instance, using a positive statement in the form of a question will fill the void. For example, I say, "How is it possible and what would it take to reach my fullest potential in/with _____ (*fill in the blanks*) _____ and anything that is in the way of that happening I delete is now!" Be specific with your statements. General statements can work, but specific statements manifest specific results. When you ask in the form of a question you are allowing the Universe to work in your favor. You don't need to tell the Universe how it needs to happen or when it should happen. It already knows what is best for you. When you dictate how you think it should happen, then you are placing another limit on what you are asking the Universe to do. You've already asked for the Universe to work in your highest and greatest good, so just let the Universe figure out all the details. Here is a good way to understand this concept. You go to a restaurant and order from the menu. Once you've placed your order, you expect and know that your food will come to your table. You don't have to reorder your food every time a server walks by or refills your drink. You order it once, and you trust and know that the chef is preparing your meal, and it will be delivered to you when he's finished. This is the same concept we must have in our daily lives. Ask for what you desire, and trust that it will be delivered.

6. **Be aware.** Now that you've cleared these thoughts, patterns and behaviors that no longer serve you, be aware. By that I mean if something triggers those old stories. acknowledge them immediately. Then make the decision to hear it only for that moment. Do not file that negative story again and carry it for a day, a month, a year or more. Delete it instantly!!!

7. **Live in love.** Succeeding starts by loving yourself. Once you make that transformation, all other successes will align with your purpose. When you love yourself you begin to vibrate at a higher level, and that's when the Universe starts working in your favor. We all have the ability to do, be or create whatever we desire, but you have to clear the old junk, so you can fall in love with yourself. It all begins with LOVE!

This is a very powerful technique that I encourage you to practice throughout your day. It only takes a couple of minutes. You will be amazed at how your life will begin to transform. You are a magnet, so whatever message you send out is the message you will receive. Your thoughts are your reality, so if you think something is impossible, then it will become impossible for you. Replace that thought with all things are possible, and I have the gifts to make them happen! The key is to erase the old stories and believe you can reach your highest and greatest potential. Open yourself to receiving abundance and love! Just know that by doing the statements, you are clearing, and the Universe is working on your behalf for all things that will benefit you in your highest and greatest good.

We are all human and have negative thoughts from time to time, but when this happens, make a choice. Am I going to carry this for a minute, a day, a month or for years? I choose to carry it only for a brief moment. It took a lot of practice to be able to clear the negative energies immediately, instantaneously, before they manifested into a story that didn't serve me. Practice, practice, practice and create an energy that is magnetic. Live your life in love and bliss, not in fear.

About DeAnn

Intuitive Life Coach * Inspirational Leader * Spiritual Healer * Philanthropist

DeAnn is an intuitive life coach, spiritual healer and inspirational leader. She is a martial artist, and second-degree Reiki practitioner. She is passionate about her work and committed to empowering children, men and women by teaching them how to raise their vibration of love, passion and purpose! To learn more about DeAnn and get access to her meditations and clearings, visit her website at www.DeAnnScheppele.com.

CHAPTER 35

ENERGY DRINK MARKETING:
ADDING A JOLT OF ENERGY INTO YOUR MARKETING

BY GREG ROLLETT

Energy: It's something everyone wants more of—and from every aspect of their life.

We want more energy:

- When we roll out of bed in the morning.

- To get through the week.

- To give more time and attention to our children, friends and families.

- To motivate our employees, partners and co-workers.

- In our marketing campaigns so the energy in our bank account increases as well.

Since we all want it, everywhere we turn we are being sold energy. There's a Starbucks or a Dunkin Doughnuts on every corner. There are billions of bottles of 5-Hour Energy drinks being sold, and a multibillion-dollar industry battle being fought by energy drink companies like Red Bull, Monster, Rockstar and others.

All these products are designed to give your mind and body a much-needed boost, from the every day and the mundane, from the been-there, seen-that world that we all casually and lackadaisically stroll through. For many people, that morning "Joe" or that afternoon pick-me-up is the factor that gets them from surviving their day to feeling great and thriving.

Marketing is not much different. Every day you suffer through the mundane act of deciphering email after email, phone call after phone call, and sales pitch after sales pitch. They run together, clouding your day.

Nothing stands out, and you see marketing and advertising in a hazy fog—a constant grey in a vibrant and colorful world. Worse yet is the money being spent to send out all this lifeless marketing.

In order to make the profits and growth you desire in your business, you cannot afford for your marketing to just get lost in our busy lives and busier world. You need to give your marketing the Red Bull effect. Your marketing needs some wings.

Just how much energy should you add into your marketing? Most entrepreneurs do not need to become legendary pitch man Billy Mays overnight, nor should every interaction with a prospect or client seem like it's happening on a late night infomercial for the latest slicer, dicer and electric peeler. But you do need to ramp up the energy. So how do you do it?

STEP 1: YOU GET THE MARKET TO KNOW YOU

After Jennifer gets off work, picks up the baby from day care, starts dinner, eats dinner, walks the dog and gets the mail, she has very little time for anything. She has trouble keeping in touch with good friends and family and has only a few brief minutes to sort through everything on her kitchen table.

When she does find the few minutes to sift and sort, it becomes a very quick game. A game in which legendary copywriter Gary Halbert calls the A Pile and the B Pile. The A Pile are the letters that appear to be personal. They are from people and companies that we know or are familiar with. The B Pile contains letters that are obviously selling something—the ones that have a commercial intent or are from companies we have never heard of.

I want every piece of marketing you ever write to get into the A Pile. Otherwise, they end up in the trash, whether under the kitchen sink or through death by the dreaded email delete button.

You accomplish this by getting the market to know you. When someone knows you, and you send them something, they get a little jolt of energy—a small shot of Red Bull. The best way to do this is to remind your prospects and clients that you exist. And that you are an expert who can help them solve a problem they currently have.

In our business, we began this process by writing the book on the subject. *Celebrity Branding You!*® is our best-selling book that teaches experts and entrepreneurs how to become the go-to expert, dominate their field and eliminate the competition.

Then we send out monthly newsletters. Our newsletter is called the *Celebrity Expert Insider*. Every month, our clients and top prospects receive a copy of this newsletter in their mailbox. It comes in an oversized envelope, and on the outside, you will find our logo, details of the contents inside, and my picture, along with those of my partners Nick, Jack and Lindsay.

We send out frequent videos, articles, blog posts and other pieces of content as well. We do this both online and offline. Our clients and prospects know exactly who we are. It's evident when we get to an event and people in the crowd know us by name, even though we had never met in person.

This allows our offers to be heard, our messages to be read, and creates stored energy in the hands of those who are reading our materials as they are always eager to see what we have coming out next.

You can create this first piece of energy by manufacturing "celebrity" in your business and getting people familiar with you. This means getting media attention and associating yourself with people, places and things that others find familiar.

One of the services we offer to our expert clients is to be seen on ABC, NBC, CBS and FOX. These channels are familiar to nearly everyone on the planet. They know these stations, and they know that not everyone can just get on TV and talk about their business.

The energy this creates is familiarity through association. Even if they do not know you, they know these stations. That is one step to getting your message in the A Pile.

Now you need to use this "celebrity" in your marketing—from your envelopes to your websites and everywhere in between. Once you do this, you get to the second energy creator.

2. YOU GET THE MARKET TO LIKE YOU

Every day you engage in countless conversations. Most are just a quick greeting or salutation, some small talk or water cooler banter. Then there are the conversations that bring life into your day.

- Your sister calls to say she is getting married.

- Your son talks to you about his great day at school.

- A prospect tells you that your latest campaign has brought in some amazing new business.

These conversations are the definition of energy. They bring life to an otherwise ordinary day.

This is what happens when you infuse your personality into your messaging. When you add a little more "you" and a little less "company." Humans by nature are attracted to interaction with others. We want to like people, and we want people to like us. But you have to give them that opportunity. You have to give of yourself and tell your story in order for others to embrace it.

Some of the most memorable stories today come from comic book heroes. Think about the origin story of today's top superheroes:

- *Batman:* billionaire, parents murdered as a child, sought vengeance, became a vigilante

- *Spider-Man:* teenager living with his aunt and uncle is bitten by spider, turns into superhero

- *Iron Man:* billionaire, playboy and philanthropist creates iron suit to save his own life and now uses the technology to save the world

The stories go well beyond their powers. We know of their childhood upbringing, love interests, parents, weaknesses, strengths, passions and more.

Just like the superheroes, to get your market to like you, people need to know who you are as a person. You do this by telling your Core Story: the story of who you are and why you do what you do. And you repeat this story over and over again in your messaging.

When you give a presentation, you tell your Core Story. When you write a special report, you tell your Core Story. When you shoot a video, you tell a version of your Core Story. You want this story to become folklore in your market. The same way that you know a comic book hero's story, you want your market to know your story.

For instance, whenever I give a presentation or meet a group for the first time, they hear my origin story. They learn that I was a rapper in a rock band, went for broke and ended up broke. I then fell into internet marketing, made my first sale online and was hooked. There are longer and shorter versions of the story that can be told depending on the type of media and the time frame I have in which to tell it.

Then you keep adding to the story. These days I add stories about my son, Colten, and his adventures, along with my own as a new dad. I add stories of how I got back into shape through CrossFit and now compete locally.

All these points make me more relatable to my audience. Someone that was a musician is instantly drawn into the conversation, and we end up having a great time together reminiscing about our playing days. Those that do CrossFit come up to compare times on certain workouts and talk about movements they just learned to do. This connection creates energy—an energy that cannot be replaced without that emotional connection.

Now that your market knows who you are, and they are starting to like you, the third piece to creating unstoppable marketing energy is:

3. YOU GET YOUR MARKET TO TRUST YOU

Trust is difficult to obtain. It cannot happen overnight. It takes time and attention to detail. And today it is harder than ever because we have all been sold something and been taken advantage, which has broken our trust.

When trust is broken, it is very difficult to regain. Lucky for you, you are moving quickly on the path toward the creation of trust through steps 1 and 2 above.

Familiarity is the first step toward trust. The more we see something or someone, the more we trust them. If people know you, they are more likely to trust you. That is why you need to be consistent in sending out messages, communication and valuable information. It is why we send out newsletters every month and why we send out emails on certain days of the week and times of the day.

The second piece is letting someone into your life, getting them to like you, that creates trust. We're more likely to trust someone who is transparent and gives us a glimpse into their life if we are going to let them into ours.

There are certain factors that help to build trust in your market that you should begin creating today. One is a book. To be seen as a trusted expert, you need to write a book that will help those in your market.

Another is being seen in trusted media sources, as we mentioned above. You need to be seen in major media outlets, like television as magazines, as well as in media specific to your marketplace.

A third is associating yourself with those who have the respect of the market. In finance, for example, that means associating yourself with a Steve Forbes, Warren Buffet or Suzie Orman. In health, it would be associating with a Dr. Oz or someone on that level. This allows you to borrow the trust that they have built with their audience.

You can also build trust through the results you supply for your clients and customers. These come in the form of testimonials and case studies.

If you are in a health and fitness space, you should document and gets results from your clients. How much weight have they lost? Do they have before-and-after pictures you can use? Do you have a testimonial for each type of situation?

- The mom who wants to lose her baby weight?

- The overweight corporate executive who only has 30 minutes a day?

- The stay-at-home mom who wants to keep up with the Joneses?

- The athlete looking to compete locally?

These are great ways to build trust with your audience.

When you have their trust, you have their energy. You are taking the energy that they are expending on thinking about the problem and moving it to getting the solution. That is powerful energy and last much longer than a 5-Hour shot that many people consume on a daily basis.

It's more like changing their diet completely to get rid of the processed marketing and changing it to the natural, clean marketing that will make a real impact on their life. That is energy they can bank on. And it's energy that will allow you to grow your business, impact more people, and keep the electricity flowing into your bank account.

About Greg

Greg Rollett, the ProductPro, is a best-selling author and online marketing expert who works with authors, experts, entertainers, entrepreneurs and business owners from all over the world to help them share their knowledge and change the lives and businesses of others. After creating a successful string of his own educational products, Greg began helping others in the production and marketing of their own products.

Greg is a front-runner in utilizing the power of social media, direct response marketing and customer education to drive new leads and convert those leads into long-standing customers and advocates.

Previous clients include Coca-Cola, Miller Lite, Warner Bros and Cash Money Records, as well as hundreds of entrepreneurs and small-business owners. Greg's work has been featured on FOX News, ABC, and the Daily Buzz. Greg has written for Mashable, the Huffington Post, AOL, AMEX's Open Forum and more.

Greg loves to challenge the current business environments that constrain people to working 12-hour days during the best portions of their lives. By teaching them to leverage technology and the power of information, Greg loves helping others create freedom businesses that allow them to generate income, make the world a better place and live a radically ambitious lifestyle in the process.

A former touring musician, Greg is highly sought after as a speaker, having appeared on stages with former Florida Gov. Charlie Crist, best-selling authors Chris Brogan and Nick Nanton, as well as at events such as Affiliate Summit.

If you would like to learn more about Greg and how he can help your business, please contact him directly at: greg@productprosystems.com or by calling his office at: (877) 897-4611.

You can also download a free report on how to create your own educational products at: www.productprosystems.com.

CHAPTER 36

BE POSITIVE, BE SUCCESSFUL

BY LUIS VICENTE GARCÍA

The attitude one has toward life will determine how successful we will be, since in order to succeed we need to have a positive attitude. We have to try hard at all we do, and we always need to do it with a positive attitude. Life itself is not a continuous line of events; it is rather, as I see it, a kind of up-and-down line, with its mountains and valleys; it's upward and downward trends. It is very easy to be positive when you are going up, but what truly is required—of each of us—is a really positive attitude when we are going down, when our own personal situation is not as smooth or as good as we thought it would be.

Not everyone is in the same stage in their life. The younger generation is beginning a process of study, growth and adaptation, and will have to start defining their future. Adults are learning from experience while changing to the reality of life itself, for which we need patience and perseverance. And those who are elderly need to understand and adapt to their new and changing needs. But regardless of which of these stages we are in, we all have before us one of the biggest challenges we will encounter in our lives: to grow, prosper, and develop always to our fullest potential, reaching a life of happiness and success. This actually sounds very simple, but to tell you the truth, this is only achieved with hard work, patience and continuous training, along with a positive attitude toward life. If we understand the changing processes we go through in life, then the important part of achieving success in the future is directly related to our attitude. As John Maxwell mentioned, *"Your Attitude Is the Profit of Your Future."*

What is *attitude*? It might be something related to the mood we all have, or an expression that relates to how we like or dislike people and events, and it may have different definitions for different people. I have tried to mix some different definitions and have come up with one that indicates that attitude is a *hypothetical state in which a person interprets what has happened and how he or she will face what will happen next*. Attitude could be positive or negative and will determine how a person will react to certain events and how it will affect our decision-making process. Attitude was defined by Carl Gustav Jung (Swiss psychologist) in 1921, as *"the disposition of the mind to react in a predetermined manner,"*[1] meaning that we would interpret events with the values and beliefs that each of us has learned and used throughout our lives.

Attitude is a complex issue that requires deep studies and a more detailed explanation of what I will try to do in these few pages. However, I want to point out that we need to guide our attitude toward what we want to achieve and attain throughout our lives, and then realize that our own personal attitude is what will help us to obtain the success we could achieve in our future. Success should not only be related to professional or financial activities, but we should also focus success as a way of life, in our relationships, in the way we treat others, or in the way we maintain our health, our body and our minds, but most important, understand that we are the ones who will define the predisposition toward what is or will be happening to us. We will define our attitude and our success, and it is important to understand how they are both interconnected and how they will be an integral part of our future.

As human beings we can always decide for ourselves what attitude to take. This automatically gets transmitted, consciously or unconsciously, to those around us. All that happens to us and around us will generate a positive or negative reaction. We are the ones who decide how to react, so think that in most cases we will all be better if we react positively. Therefore, always try to think of these two words: *positive attitude*.

Attitude is a very important issue in an era as complex as the one we live in now, as our attitude will inspire and determine how we are going

---

1 Jung, Carl Gustav (1875-1961). Psychological Types. *Collected Works.*
  Princeton University Press (1971).

to face what lies ahead of us. And let me tell you that we should not be in a passive state, or have a "we'll see what happens" reaction. On the contrary, it is with a determined and decisive attitude that whatever we are going to face is taken care of in a positive manner, and that we will take the necessary actions to address, or at least to try to initiate and begin to take steps in the right direction. The dictionary of the Royal Spanish Academy tells us the definition of the word "attitude" in the following context[2]:

a) *Human body posture, especially when determined by the movements of the mind, or express something effectively;*

b) *Mood expressed somehow.*

Putting all of the above together, we could define Attitude as *the mental state that guides and defines our disposition to act, based on our own previous experiences, which will generate a predisposition to the situations that we will encounter.* Our previous experiences will define what we think may happen when considering future actions. As Jim Rohn said, *"It is not what happens but the experience we get from what happens to us."* It is then with all these occurrences and events, our growth and contact we have with people, that we will shape our attitude, and mold and impact the way we behave.

It's easy to decide to have a positive attitude, but it is also very easy to decide to have a negative attitude. Like everything in life, things are easy to do, but also are easy not to do. It is our decision; only ours. If we decide to have a positive attitude, there is no guarantee that our world will change, but it is for certain that our relationships will change, at home, at work, with our friends, and in all that we do. Therefore, a positive attitude will produce a positive reaction that may even propel a chain of positivism. Simple phrases, such as a "have a nice day," or "you did an excellent job" (and actually meaning it), will generate positive reactions and even surprises from others. As Zig Ziglar once said: *"It is your attitude, and not your aptitude, that determines your altitude."*

Some years ago I attended the seminar "Unleash the Power Within"; a very intense four-day event, full of energy, and personal growth strategies. I called home one night, and my youngest son answered the phone.

He was only 8 at the time, and he asked me, "Daddy, what did you do

2 Diccionario de la Real Academia Española. http://lema.rae.es/dpd/

today?" I must admit it caught me a little off-guard, and as I was telling him that I was in a motivational seminar, it occurred to me that you can explain what motivation is with these simple words: *Motivation is what you carry inside of you that makes you wake up every morning ready to have a happy day.* And this is so simple and true, as happiness is something that we all have inside ourselves and the motivation for it is what we have to work and prepare for. So our motivation and our happiness also depend on our positive attitude.

We live in very complex times, with obstacles in our personal lives, our businesses, and our communities. And the only way to overcome this is to have inside us a great force with strong motivation and a positive attitude. We can define motivation as anything that makes us be energized from within, and which drives us to achieve what we want. And if we move with the correct attitude, we are motivated, we have new ideas and new goals that help us define new purposes for what we would like to achieve. It is with dedication, internal motivation, patience and self-improvement that we can achieve all that we are set out to achieve, and at the end, this is how we can succeed.

At the entrance of a seminar years ago I was greeted by a really friendly Lady with a very happy face. I was tired, tense, and had flown for many hours to get there. When she asked me, "Are you all right?" of course, I said, yes, to which she replied, "then tell it to your face." Actually we think that we are happy and content, but until our body and our personal attitude does not reflect how we feel, we have not reached the level of motivation we need to undertake and achieve our goals. Our attitude always reflects how we are and feel. So let us keep and maintain a positive attitude!

Life is a continuing process, and to be successful, we should always be positively motivated. We have to create the habits that lead us to do things the right way, and these habits should come naturally, not forced. As Tony Robbins said, *"Set a standard for yourself, but keep raising your standards."* We all have dreams to pursue. We have often heard the phrase, "It does not matter where you come from . . . what matters is where you are going." To understand this better, our past should be left behind while learning its experiences, and what is really important is what lies ahead of us; it means that our children, relationships, careers, and our future will benefit if we approach them with the correct and positive attitude and success. Scholars in the field of human behavior have maintained that 'If we have negative thoughts, we will generate negative actions"; and on the contrary, "if we have positive ideas, we'll generate positive actions." And the sum of all these positive ideas and actions will take us closer to what we want.

We all need to be change agents at this particular time, and we need to teach ourselves, family members and our teams the importance of three main tools: 1) positive attitude, 2) visualization tools, and 3) an awareness development program in order to encourage and motivate the people we can influence on a daily basis. We are able to generate this effect by being positive and by having positive thoughts and ideas that will generate positive actions.

Having a positive attitude begins in our own mind. Actions come from how we train our thoughts and our attitude, and when coupled with our actions, will determine who we are. The main issues then will be personal development, having a sense of belonging, knowing what you want, having the best possible job, enjoying a comfortable home, and having quality time with your family. Consider what is important to you, make your own list, define your priorities and act on them. To be successful, we need to act in a competitive world, and we must flourish in every part of our life stages to show what we are capable of, continuously improving ourselves. We must learn to use the tools that we have been provided with to nourish our body and our mind, reinforce our own continuous learning, and develop a positive attitude to be really successful.

One of the biggest challenges I experienced when I went from the manufacturing industry to the service industry was to understand that errors were seen differently. While in a factory errors are viewed as failures, in the service industry they are seen as areas of improvement. So we must ask ourselves, "How I can improve myself, my health, my finances, my education, or the amount and quality of time we spend with our family?" I mean we can all be better than what we are today; it's just a matter of having the right attitude. Change will only happen if we want it, if we try; again, it is a matter of attitude. You would have to say, *my attitude, my motivation, my way of being, and knowing what you want is the basis of my life's philosophy.* But also we need to understand that it is not something that will happen right away, as changing oneself is something that will happen over time, in months or years. Change takes time to be effective.

And in the end, success is to realize that we can improve continuously, being positive and optimistic. I think the journey in our life is not a destination but rather a process of getting there, taking the right steps and following the right path. It is the gradual evolution of ourselves and realizing that over time we might leave our own footprints on other people. In a recent article I published on my blog http://motivandoelfuturo.blogspot.com, I referred to both Brian Tracy and Jim Rohn, who have indicated that decisions are easy to make, but they are also easy to not make; that most things are easy to do, but they are also easy not to do. And this is so true that we need to understand it and then positively reinforce our attitude and our personality.

As Earl Nightingale said, *"Success is the progressive realization of a worthy idea."* Think of an idea, take action, take the steps to carry it out, plan everything necessary to make it happen, take the time to implement it, and then do it well. This long process of preparation, to take our idea or our project forward and make it operational (be it in our jobs or in our personal lives), is what will determine our success. To be successful requires hard work and big effort; it is a "progressive" process that will lead the way into what we want to achieve. In other words, to be successful, we need to understand all the little things we need to improve in a continuous and orderly manner, and make them better all the time. Taking this new approach will put us in a better situation than the one we are in today. And it should be related to our way of thinking; again, if we generate positive ideas, we will generate positive actions, which will, in turn, take us to be closer to what we want to achieve.

Success might have a different definition to each of us, and for most, it will include improving our attitude, our motivation, the philosophy of our lives, and our way of thinking. These words form a set of important factors that defines us as doers and performers, as people who generate ideas, and above all, as people who take action. And on the subject of ideas and success, positive attitude will always be fundamental, since our attitude on the experiences we have and the choices we make is what will define our actions, especially in a positive and optimist way. For me then, the sum of all these parts is what defines success. I hope for you too. So be positive, have a great attitude, and be successful in your lives.

About Luis

Luis Vicente Garcia is President and CEO of MEF Consulting Group, and a FocalPoint Business Coach in Caracas, Venezuela. He is also a best-selling author in the book *Ultimate Success Guide,* featuring Brian Tracy. He was chosen as one of the world's leading experts to give his expertise in how leaders need to develop in uncertain circumstances. He also published a book on franchising titled *Motivando al Futuro Franquiciado* in 2011. He has been married for 21 years and has two sons.

With a BA in economics from Georgetown University, an MBA from The American University, a graduate degree in service enterprise management from Universidad Metropolitana in Caracas, Venezuela—and graduate studies in management, strategy and leadership, among other studies —he is a firm believer in continuing education. He has worked in corporate finance most of his professional life, both in the manufacturing and service industries, and in a variety of companies, from well-established enterprises to publicly traded companies, from start-ups to family-owned businesses. This has allowed him to fully understand and appreciate the importance of *core values* that people and businesses need to succeed. In 2013, Luis started his new personal and business coaching practice, having acquired the FocalPoint Business Coaching franchise for Venezuela, while helping people and organizations move to new levels of success.

Luis Vicente has devoted many years to the study of how motivation and attitude affect regular, day-to-day people and their activities. He started writing articles about finance and franchising in the late 1990s and later about motivation, attitude and leadership. In 2010, these articles developed into a Spanish-language blog covering motivation and personal growth topics, called *Motivando El Futuro* (http://motivandoelfuturo.blogspot.com). He also frequently speaks on such topics as success, leadership, achievement and motivation.

He believes in providing all people with the right tools and opportunities to learn, in motivating and coaching them to perform better, while at the same time being a promoter of continuous training, personal growth and professional improvement. A team builder, a motivator and a confidence generator, always with a positive attitude toward life, Luis Vicente believes in being a leader for the people and organization he works with.

Contact: lgarcia@focalpointcoaching.com, www.luisvicentegarcia.com

CHAPTER 37

MATHEMATICAL FORMULA FOR SUCCESS:
A=R & NA=NR

BY LYNN LEACH

Ever notice how so many people have such great ideas, but never do anything with them? Do you have friends who have wonderful dreams and aspirations, but they never seem to accomplish them? How about you? Are there things you would like to change or create? Are you aware that all great programs, books, movies, etc., all began as a small idea? What makes the difference in someone succeeding in accomplishing great things or just always dreaming of something but never really accomplishing anything?

I am a network marketer. I look around and see so many people who want to change their financial circumstances but get stuck in how to go about it. They dream about it. Some even go so far as to begin to prepare to do something, but then are stuck in limbo. I've noticed six reasons for this:

1. **They let negativity creep in, either from their own mind, or from constant negative remarks and attitudes from the people they surround themselves with.** This can be such a dream killer. It can crush any idea they may have. It can stop them in their tracks.

Negativity can hold a person back, retard them in growth and keep them from accomplishing anything they may dream of.

2. **They lack self-confidence in themselves, their talents or skills and their knowledge and abilities.** They fail to understand that every person has both strong and weak areas but that they can determine what their weakest link in their skill set is and then work to improve in that area.

3. **They become overwhelmed in the enormity of what they want to accomplish.** How do you eat an elephant? One bite at a time. How do you accomplish an enormous endeavor? One step at a time.

4. **They may get hung up on the details and become paralyzed.** This is a danger zone for anyone who is a detail-oriented person. They may have the tendency to want perfection and not be able to move past certain tasks because they feel that the work is never good enough. The other issue is that they are so wrapped up in the details that they must read every word of every page of every document, even to the point of getting the magnifying glass out for all the fine print. They must look at every web page and have all the information on everything, but what happens is they get so bogged down with all these details that it really paralyzes them. They get stopped in their tracks before they even get on the launch pad.

5. **They may begin to prepare to initiate a project but then get stuck in a never-ending cycle of "Getting ready to get ready."** This happens when they get hung up on preparation. "I have to do this before I can do that." Or "I must have all my ducks in a row before I can begin anything." Another pitfall is always putting it off till another day. This is all linked to procrastination. And when this happens…you never get started on anything.

6. **They simply lack the discipline to move an idea into material physicality.** And this is the biggie! There are three things that will guarantee success:
DISCIPLINE!
DISCIPLINE!!
And more DISCIPLINE!!!

Discipline will make or break a person. It is the determining factor in character that will result in success or failure. Discipline is everything. Disciplined people are the leaders. They are the ones who can get things accomplished. They will always come out on top. The opposite of being disciplined is being lazy. That speaks for itself. The lazy person will not work, will not take action and, of course, will not accomplish anything. A person's work ethic is extremely important, and is, in fact, part of their character. A bad work ethic shows a lack of discipline and will squash all dreams, hopes, desires or ambitions a person may have.

Here is what I know to be truth:

A = R and NA = NR. This formula is the new math for success. And it is very important math. Action equals Results and No Action equals No Results. It's a matter of discipline and commitment. *You must be disciplined* to commit to take action—I prefer *daily action*. Action will move you forward. You cannot accomplish anything unless you are willing to take action.

Think about this: Boys Scouts of America, Girl Scouts of America, Habitat 4 Humanity, 4 H Clubs and any other worthwhile organization that may come to your mind. These are all great organizations that have helped many people. They started as a small idea or concept in one person's mind. They shared it with others and took *action* to birth the project. They were disciplined and committed to taking action and moving forward in such a way as to lay down strong foundations for these projects. The same is true of any person who has written a book, or wrote a song, or put a movie together. It is true of scientists who make great discoveries. It can be true for you too! All you need to do is understand how to move yourself in the direction of taking action to bring it forth. You can do it! You can birth ideas that come to you if you are willing to be disciplined enough to commit to taking daily action in moving toward the goal. You can form that nonprofit organization to help a certain segment of the population. You can write that book or song. You can start that brick-and-mortar business. You can set up a home-based business. You can build a huge network marketing downline. You can accomplish anything you set your mind to. All you need to do is get a blueprint to follow. There are some things you can do to guarantee your success in any endeavor you may want to undertake.

Here are eight factors that will guide you in *taking action*:

1. **Have the right mind-set.** Remove all negativity from your environment. Believe with every fiber of your being that you can accomplish anything you set your mind to. I do believe it is important to set your intention and to also have daily affirmations. If the people you surround yourself with are negative, remove yourself from the environment. Close your mind to the negativity. Have the confidence in yourself that you can learn any skill you need to succeed. Talent you are born with, but skills are acquired. Just know that you can break down the project into manageable pieces so you do not overwhelm yourself. It will be important to keep balance in your life by keeping your priorities straight so you do not feel pressure and stress during the foundational stages. And also know that you can work out all the details in a simple way so that you can begin to move into daily *action* that will move you to the end result. Purpose in your heart that you will be disciplined and that you will commit to planning in such a simple way that you will be able to accomplish great things.

2. **Identify the concept, the desire of your heart—what you want to accomplish with this project.** Go crazy with this. See the end result. Be very descriptive in what you really want this project to become. Paint a vibrant picture in your mind's eye of exactly how it would be.

3. **Visualization is an important aspect that many people overlook or decide is just a silly notion and elect to skip.** A Vision Board, sometimes called a Goal Poster or a Dream Board, can be a very powerful tool for you. This is a biblical concept, or one of God's cosmic laws that can really make all the difference for you. What you think about, you bring about. If you put a board together and place it in your bedroom so that it is the first thing you see in the morning and the last thing you see at night before going to sleep, then you will have your thoughts on the goal at all times. I even write my goals out and tape them to the mirror in the bathroom, the refrigerator, the visor in my car, on my day planner and on my computer monitor. The goals are then in constant view and continually on my mind. Keeping your goals constantly in front of you will keep your mind on the goals. When your mind is on the goal, you will be motivated to take constant action toward moving in the direction of the goal. Please do not neglect this step.

4. **Set your goals with time frames: short range, mid-range and long range.** Please remember that desires of the heart and goals are different. Goals always have a time frame. This breaks things down into manageable pieces so you do not become overwhelmed. Short-range goals would be what you would want to accomplish in the next 6 to 12 months. Mid-range goals would be things you would want to accomplish over the next two to three years, and long-range goals would be what you would like to accomplish in 5 to 10 years.

5. **Understand the importance of *time management*.** This is where so many people fall down, because they do not manage their time wisely. Use a weekly time sheet and block all commitments out. Make sure you put time in for *everything*, including travel times back and forth from work or school, family time, time with your significant other, housework, laundry, cooking, personal time, meditation, and all the other things that demand your attention. Color code everything so you can see if it reflects the priorities you have set up for your life. Whatever is left is the time you will have for your project. Block it out and color code it. Now you know exactly *when* you will be able to devote time to work on this new creation.

6. **Plan your work and work your plan.** Now that you know exactly when you will be working on your project, you need to map out what it is you will need to be doing. Write a list of everything you need to do and then schedule those items onto the weekly time sheets. This planning stage should be all encompassing…but not take up so much time that you are continually stuck in the planning stage. Make an outline. Organize your thoughts in the beginning. If you can get all of your thoughts down in the beginning, it will make it easier for you to design an easy plan to follow.

7. **Use a daily list of all of the things you need to accomplish that day.** Make it out the night before so that the next day you do not waste time on having to think about what you need to be doing. A few minutes of planning before you go to bed will make your days run smoother. When you get up in the morning, you will know exactly what you have to do. You will not waste precious time trying to remember everything you have to do, and your day will be more productive.

8. Daily discipline is the key. You must be disciplined to take action and this requires commitment. If you have followed the steps, you will not need to think so hard about every step you need to take on a continual basis. Everything will be mapped out for you and now it is just a matter of character. And the question is, do you have the character it takes to be disciplined enough to commit to daily action and do what is necessary to bring about the desire of your heart—the picture you have painted in your mind's eye—the actual intention you set in the beginning. If you never take action . . . it will never materialize. But if you take the action ... *great* things will be accomplished. Here's to *your success*!!!

About Lynn

Lynn has been married to her husband, Norman, for 42 years, and they have three sons and six granddaughters.

She has been involved in direct sales/network marketing for 45 years. She also has 13 years of experience in restaurant management. Her 44 years of ministry include serving on the board of directors in leadership positions for eight large organizations and also three national secular nonprofit organizations. She served as pastor of Mars Hill Baptist Church and was a gospel clown and had a puppet ministry. She now uses network marketing as a ministry to help families, ministers and missionaries and as a fundraiser to help nonprofit organizations and churches.

Marketing and teaching are two of Lynn's strengths, and she has developed her own training program to help people understand how to build their home businesses. She is the author of *Calling All Leads: The 10 Minute Interview*, which is the first book in her "Mentor With Lynn Series." It is available on Kindle. She is also a co-author of *New Rules for Success* with John Spencer Ellis.

Because she understands what a toxic world we live in, she has embraced the Q philosophy of maintaining our life essentials—air, water and nutrition. She was the first to achieve the rank of Premier, the highest position in Q International Inc.

Lynn is passionate about natural healing—on all levels: physical, emotional, relational, spiritual and financial. She owns Common Scents Health Research & Wellness Centers and is an aroma therapist and massage therapist. She specializes in essential oil science concentrating on emotional release, all natural pain management and all-natural first aide.

You can reach Lynn at pastorlynn@comcast.net or (724) 292-8481. Her training website is www.mentorwithlynn.com and her corporate site with Q International is www.qinternational.com/lynn.